Rights in Transit

Rights in Transit

PUBLIC TRANSPORTATION AND THE
RIGHT TO THE CITY IN CALIFORNIA'S EAST BAY

KAFUI ABLODE ATTOH

THE UNIVERSITY OF GEORGIA PRESS
Athens

© 2019 by the University of Georgia Press
Athens, Georgia 30602
www.ugapress.org
All rights reserved
Designed by
Set in 10/12.5 Minion Pro by Graphic Composition, Inc., Bogart, Georgia

Most University of Georgia Press titles are
available from popular e-book vendors.

Printed digitally

Library of Congress Cataloging-in-Publication Data

Names: Attoh, Kafui Ablode, 1983– author.
Title: Rights in transit : public transportation and the right to the city in California's East
  Bay / Kafui Ablode Attoh.
Description: Athens : University of Georgia Press, [2018] | Series: Geographies of justice
  and social transformation | Includes bibliographical references and index.
Identifiers: LCCN 2018011926| ISBN 9780820354217 (hardback : alk. paper) | ISBN
  9780820354200 (pbk. : alk. paper) | ISBN 9780820354224 (ebook)
Subjects: LCSH: Urban transportation policy—Citizen participation—California—East
  Bay. | People with disabilities—Transportation—California—East Bay. | Transportation
  and state—California—East Bay. | Citizenship—California—East Bay. | Municipal
  services—California—East Bay.
Classification: LCC HE310.E27 A88 2018 | DDC 388.409794/6—dc23 LC record available at
  https://lccn.loc.gov/2018011926

To
Angela DeFelice
and
My parents, Sandra Greene and Kodjopa Attoh

CONTENTS

FIGURES

PREFACE

This book is about rights and public transportation in California's East Bay—the conurbation just east of San Francisco of which the cities of Oakland, Berkeley, Richmond, and Hayward are all a part. Although the book is set in the East Bay, in many ways the questions that enliven it were first developed over two thousand miles away in Syracuse, New York. Fresh from Saint Paul, Minnesota, I arrived in Syracuse in 2006 as a new student in the university's geography department. At the time, public transit had become something of a live issue in Syracuse. Indeed, during my first semester, a local group had staged a protest demanding more clarity on the proposed relocation of the city's central bus hub. There were governance concerns as well. For the previous two years the city had failed to fill two of its three allotted seats on the county-level transit advisory board—a legislative body in charge of setting fares, changing routes, and allocating state and federal monies. With transit in the news, and with my adviser's encouragement, I decided to spend the next year riding local buses and learning about the system. Two years later, I defended a thesis based on what I had discovered. Despite a handful of quasi-insightful moments, in many ways the thesis was something of a flop. Indeed, during the defense, the central problem made itself all but apparent. Namely, in my zeal to say something new and clever about neoliberal urban governance or some other forgettable theoretical notion, I had omitted the very questions that most readers seemed curious about. What did public transportation actually mean for people? What was at stake in the various struggles that seemed to have erupted in the city—whether over the location of the bus hub or potential service cuts? Moreover, what exactly did I mean on the last four pages by a right to the city? What did rights have to do with anything?

In 2010 and well into the PhD program, I was hired as a research assistant on a project based in Oakland, California. The assistantship was a fortuitous one. In the East Bay, struggles over public transportation seemed to be bubbling up everywhere. A local law firm was in the midst of a civil rights lawsuit alleging racial discrimination in the provision of transportation funding. The Federal Transportation Administration (FTA) had just blocked funding to a new transit extension to the Oakland Airport after local activist groups had raised concerns over the lack of an adequate equity analysis. Bus drivers for AC Transit

(Alameda and Contra Costa Transit District) were in the midst of a prolonged labor dispute, and there were murmurs of a possible strike. Of course, compared to Syracuse, transit in the East Bay was a wholly more complex affair. Rather than just one transit authority, in the East Bay there were three. Not only was there AC Transit—the region's major provider of local and cross-bay transit service—but there was also BART (Bay Area Rapid Transit) and CCCTA (Central Contra Costa Transit Authority). Over the course of two years I conducted dozens of interviews with individuals, planners, and transit workers all variably connected to the region's transportation justice movement. I also spent a considerable amount of time in both the labor archives at San Francisco State University (SFSU) and in the private collection of local transit historian Ron Hook. In writing up this research—first as a dissertation and now as a book—in many ways I have simply returned to the same questions posed in Syracuse. These are questions on what transit means for people, on what is at stake when transit disappears, and on transit's role in securing more just and more democratic cities. More clearly still, these are fundamentally questions on rights: both how we talk about them and, more importantly, how we *ought* to.

If the questions that enliven what follows were first posed in upstate New York, the motivation to actually finish this book is no less indebted to the same place. In something of a twist of fate, the bulk of this book was written only three hours southeast of Syracuse in the city of Poughkeepsie, New York—a small municipality roughly ninety miles north of New York City. I moved to Poughkeepsie in 2013 after getting a job at the City University of New York (CUNY). Despite a rather long commute to work, for the last five years I've greatly enjoyed living in Poughkeepsie. It's a fairly walkable city, and I can bike to most everything. With that said, however, I do have some complaints, and these, curiously enough, are with Poughkeepsie's bus service. Despite being affordable ($1.75) and fairly convenient, the service scores low on reliability. Indeed, if one rides the bus frequently enough, one begins to notice that transit service in Poughkeepsie has an almost jazz-like quality—drivers freely improvise with both routes and scheduling. A left turn becomes a right turn on a whim, 3:45 p.m. blends into 4:15 p.m., and there are days when some routes simply stop running altogether—often without warning or notice. Free Jazz! I mention all this because while a good deal of this book's "drama" takes place in California and while the questions that undergird it first emerged in Syracuse, in many ways, this book owes just as much to my experience in Poughkeepsie. Two simple stories will illustrate my point.

Sometime in the fall of 2014, I decided to do what I had done for much of the year—walk to the corner of Fulton and Raymond Avenue and wait for the "Shopper's Special." The "Shopper's Special" bus is rarely ever on time, but in this instance something was clearly amiss. After waiting nearly twenty minutes I decided to call the system's dispatcher. I was with three other people, two of whom had been waiting longer than I. They too were eager to figure out what had happened. The dispatcher informed me that the "Shopper's Special" had been canceled, and the reason was simple enough: "the bus was broken." It was, to quote, "currently in the shop." As to when the bus would be fixed, the dispatcher couldn't say. I was annoyed. I was annoyed by the lack of notification, by the "put-upon" tone of the dispatcher, and I was annoyed by what seemed the bewildering absence of just one replacement bus. Beyond this, however, I was annoyed because almost everyone I talked to—including those who had been waiting with me at the bus stop—seemed wholly unsurprised. Poughkeepsie residents were only one broken bus away from being stranded, and nobody seemed to think anything of it.

The second story is from the spring of 2016. Indeed, it happened several weeks after I submitted the first draft of this book to the press. I was on a bus to the library when I overheard a conversation between three passengers. All three were sitting toward the front of the bus. Two of them were older women, and one was a youngish man who was clearly visually impaired. The conversation was wide ranging, but it hinged on the ongoing question of whether to merge Poughkeepsie's transit system with Dutchess County's LOOP system. Advocates of the plan had touted it as a cost-saving measure. All three passengers were skeptical. Would the merger mean more service or less service? Would it mean new buses with better seats or more of the same? As one of the women stated, her advice to anyone moving to Poughkeepsie was simple: get a car. The youngish man offered his own take: transit in Poughkeepsie wasn't great, but imagine if there was no bus service at all. People like him would be trapped at home and wholly dependent on others. The conversation went on and on like this. At some point, however, and my memory fades here, the bus driver—who evidently was also listening—interrupted the conversation with a comment. You folks, he said, "should go to the city council meetings and bring these questions with you." It would be good, he noted, for the council to "hear from riders for a change." In response, one of the two women laughed. City council meetings were held at 6:30 p.m. The last city buses left at roughly the same time. Even if one could make it to the meeting, getting home would be tricky.

Writing a book is obviously hard. While in the middle of rewriting this or that chapter, or tracking down some arcane footnote, it can be rather difficult to see "the forest for the trees" or to recall the broader conversation of which you are seeking to be a part. Of course, in addition to my eagerness to share the stories of bus riders and transit activists in the East Bay, or my enthusiasm for finally offering an answer to the questions that arose in Syracuse, my own experience in Poughkeepsie has been no less important in pushing me toward completion. If anything, it has been a reminder that for people in cities across the country the two anecdotes above are simply par for the course. That a bus breaks down without a replacement is hardly remarkable. That a city council hearing on transit starts after the last bus has left the station barely raises an eyebrow. Such events are annoying, but they rarely elicit moral outrage. One goal of this book, of course, is to suggest that some degree of moral outrage is indeed due. For any number of people, public transportation means the difference between a life lived in isolation and one lived with dignity and with rights. Public transportation, for these individuals, is nothing short of a promise. That promise says: "if your car breaks down, or if you are too old, too young, or too poor to drive, or if you simply want to lower your carbon footprint, you will still be able to get around." As this book argues, fights for better public transportation ought to be fought on precisely these terms. Of course, the more significant goal of this book is to convince those already outraged by the state of our public transportation systems—particularly those working under the banner of transportation justice—that there remains a desperate need not only to think about transit in rights terms, but to think critically about the types of rights at issue.

ACKNOWLEDGMENTS

In the process of writing this book I was fortunate enough to have an untold number of people in my corner. Perhaps the most significant among them was Don Mitchell. Apart from being a tremendous adviser and friend, Don has remained a singular force in shaping my growth as a writer, teacher, and thinker. His influence, suffice it to say, appears throughout. Whatever flaws are apparent in the following pages, there would be countless more if not for the work of Mick Gusinde-Duffy at the University of Georgia Press. Mick not only showed considerable patience with me, an anxious newcomer to the book-writing process, but he also offered encouraging words precisely when I needed them most. I am extremely grateful to both him and Nik Heynen for throwing their support behind this book. In the review stages of this manuscript I was lucky enough to get critiques from two anonymous reviewers. Despite a rather rough first draft, these reviewers saw value in the project, and their critiques played a central role in improving the book's argument. The introductory chapter of this book benefited considerably from the careful eyes of Joaquin Villanueva, Katie Wells, Joe Nevins, Jack Norton, Sandra Greene, and Hector Agredano. Dianne Ferris offered editorial comments on all four chapters and greatly improved their readability. Of course, many of the ideas developed in the following pages were first hatched in conversations with a wide assortment of friends, including Jacob Shell, Declan Cullen, Chris Grove, Eli Moore, Jamie T. Kelly, Sam Stein, Steve McFarland, Penny Lewis, Howard Lune, Spencer Resnick, Lynn Staeheli, and Eric Goldwyn. For the last four years I have had the honor of teaching at the Joseph S. Murphy Institute for Worker Education and Labor Studies. Over the course of that time, I have worked alongside an incredibly distinguished faculty and staff who have been deeply invested in my success. On this front, I owe a debt of gratitude to Michael Fortner, Penny Lewis, Stephanie Luce, Ruth Milkman, Josh Freeman, John Mollenkopf, Mimi Abromovitz, Juan Battle, Frances Fox Piven, Steve Brier, Ed Ott, Eve Baron, Maureen Lamar, Irene Garcia Martes, June Cumberpatch, Samina Shahidi, Padraig O'Donoghue, Rochelle Pinder-Cuffee, Michael Rymer, Rebecca Lurie, Nelly Benavides, Walter Romney, Zenzile Greene, Kelly Burgos, Dave Unger, Greg Mantsios, Veronica Ordaz, Sarah Hughes, Karen Judd, and Paula Finn. At the School of Professional Studies—of which Murphy is a part—both John Mogulescu and George Otte have been extremely generous and supportive and have made every effort to make me feel welcome at SPS. I continue to be grateful for that. In 2014, I participated in CUNY's Faculty Fellowship Publication Program. Over the course of a semester I was able to develop both a book proposal and two sample chapters. In this, I am indebted to the help of Stephen Steinberg, Jahi Johnson, Emily Thumpson-Molina, Devin Molina, Seth Offenbach, Melissa Borja, and Susanna Rosenbaum. In 2016 and well past the proposal stage, I was selected as a fellow at CUNY's Center for Place, Culture and Politics. Over the course of a year, I was able to workshop parts of this book with a talented assortment of graduate students and faculty from across CUNY. I am especially grateful to Ruthie Wilson Gilmore, Peter Hitchcock, David Harvey, and Mary Taylor, who convened our weekly seminars. In writing this book, I also enjoyed the support of the Mellon Mays Graduate Initiative Program of the Social Science Research Council (SSRC). In this, I am grateful to the Mellon coordinators Cally Waite and Debbie Chang. For editorial assistance in the later stages, I am grateful to both Jon Davies and Jane Curran. For assistance during the research process itself, I am especially indebted to Catherine Powell at the SFSU labor archive and the transit expertise of Ron Hook. No less central to the research process were those informants affiliated with Urban Habitat, the Alliance for AC Transit, and the Amalgamated Transit Union Local 192. I hope I have done justice to their voices. Of course, in the last three years, there have been any number of people whose support has had little to do with the text itself and more to do with simply keeping me sane. Along these lines, I would like to thank Susan Grove, Peter Rachleff, Freda Fair, Aaron Johnson Ortiz, Dario Sulzman, Wes Hannah, Bryn Roshong, Joe and Becky Fullam, Eli Moore and Claudia Jimenez, Linda Haselman, Jim Merrell, Rob Block, Maria Mendonca, Denise Nepveux, and the entire DeFelice clan. Of course, perhaps the most significant form of support has come from my own family. This includes my brother, Kwaku Attoh; my grandparents, Sara and Robert Greene; my aunts, Sharon McWilliams and Sylvia Claybrooks; my uncle Mel; and my cousins, Lori, Lisa, Keri, and Marcus. I owe a special thanks to my mom, Sandra Greene. As a distinguished faculty member and an author herself, my mom has been a steady source of encouragement, constructive feedback, and inspiration. Both personally and professionally, this book would have been impossible to write without her in my corner. Lastly, I owe an incredible amount of gratitude to my partner and best friend, Angela DeFelice. Perhaps more than anyone, Angela has had a front-row seat to the ups and downs of writing, to the bouts of self-doubt, and to the moments of irrational exuberance that come with completing a book-length project. Throughout, she has been there at my side encouraging me and pushing me forward. "Te dig."

Rights in Transit

For Rights

What is the use of discussing a man's abstract right to food or to medicine? The question is upon the method of procuring and administering them. In that deliberation I shall always advise to call in the aid of the farmer and the physician rather than the professor of metaphysics.

—Edmund Burke, *Reflections on the Revolution in France*, 1790

Where ends are agreed, the only questions left are those of means, and these are not political but technical, that is to say, capable of being settled by experts or machines like arguments between engineers or doctors. That is why those who put their faith in some immense world transforming phenomenon, like the final triumph of reason or the proletariat revolution, must believe that all political and moral problems can be turned into technological ones.

—Isaiah Berlin, *Four Essays on Freedom*, 1969

In 2010, transit riders in California's East Bay found themselves facing longer waits, slower commutes, and an uncertain future. Over the course of a year, the Alameda–Contra Costa Transit District (AC Transit) had discontinued four lines, made major adjustments to fifty others, and reduced overall service by 15 percent.[1] By most accounts, AC Transit's problems had begun a year earlier. In February 2009, in a bid to close its own budget deficit, the California State Legislature had raided $532 million in subsidies from the State Transit Assistance (STA) program—a program established in 1980 to provide operating support to the state's transit systems.[2] Compounding the loss of STA funds, AC Transit also entered 2010 facing the same challenge besetting transit agencies across the country—a weak economy and thus a reduction in tax revenue.[3] By late September 2010, having slashed service twice already, AC Transit was—once again—forced to do the unthinkable. Namely, for the third time in one year, the agency's board of directors prepared to vote on yet another round of service cuts. These would be even more extreme. On the chopping block: thirty-four of fifty-one weekend bus lines and two-thirds of all evening service.[4]

On the day of the vote, the AC Transit boardroom in downtown Oakland was "standing room only." Toward the rear, disgruntled bus riders stood cheek by jowl with security guards, nervous staffers, and a slew of reporters from local news outlets. Transit operators were there as well—many still wearing their grey work uniforms. Their union—the Amalgamated Transit Union Local 192 (ATU 192)—was in the midst of negotiating a new contract. In July, those negotiations had taken a turn for the worse when management had imposed a "cost-saving" work rule change without driver consultation. The response from drivers: a week-long "sickout."[5] Now, three months later, tensions remained, and there were even whispers of a possible strike vote. If the anxiety of more service cuts was not enough, the labor situation was just as worrisome.

After a brief presentation on the proposed cuts, the board of directors opened the floor to public comment. What followed was a predictably rage-filled two hours of personal testimonies and expletive-laced recriminations. Speakers included local transit activists, ATU 192 members, and representatives from social service agencies. The evening's most candid speakers were, of course, transit riders themselves. These included riders such as Ralph Walker, Michelle Russi, and Celia-Faye Russell. For each, the message to the board was simple: transit is our lifeline. After suffering a stroke earlier in the year, transit made it possible for Walker to receive the therapy he needed in West Oakland. Transit afforded disabled riders like Russi the ability to visit friends and attend meetings. For riders like Russell—precariously balancing a job, two kids, and college course work—transit service meant the difference between merely "getting by" and completely falling apart. Of all the remarks of the evening, however, perhaps the most memorable came from a bus rider named Karen Smulevitz. For Smulevitz, public transit was more than a lifeline. Public transit was also a right. Indeed, for her, it was a right of unique significance. Of all "the civil rights that exist," she argued, "whether it is food security, housing, healthcare or education, the right of transportation is the most integral to each."[6] Smulevitz's point was a clarifying one. The board's proposal to cut service not only violated people's "right to transportation"; it also violated the various other rights that transportation made possible—the right to get to a doctor's office, to keep one's job, or to go to school.

Taking inspiration from Karen Smulevitz, and using California's East Bay as a case study, this book is about rights, the "right to transportation" and the "right to the city." In many ways, this book is written for those who are already sympathetic to the Karen Smulevitzes of the world and who are thus already inclined to defend public transportation service as something approaching a fundamental right. Among this group, however, this book presumes that there are also those for whom questions invariably remain. What exactly do we mean by a right? How should we think about that right? And how does that right square with the rights of others—such as those of transit operators or taxpayers, for example? To the extent that this book addresses these questions directly, in almost every case it begins and ends with some version of the same answer: it argues that when public transportation service is threatened, it not only makes it harder for East Bay riders to accomplish the very basic tasks of getting to work or school, but it also fundamentally threatens—borrowing from the French Marxist philosopher Henri Lefebvre—their "right to the city." In starting here, this book marks a deliberate attempt to move beyond the liberal notion of civil rights that currently dominates debates on transportation injustices and to move toward viewing struggles over urban public transportation for what they are: struggles over "who should have the benefit of the city and what kind of city it should be."[7]

Initial Objections

In an effort to advance this argument about rights and public transportation, let me begin by addressing what I anticipate to be at least two immediate objections. The first of these objections is simply to "rights talk" in general. For those who have long bemoaned the outsized role that rights play in political discourse, this book will provoke almost immediate pushback. A right to public transit? Rubbish! A right to the city? Nonsense! Questions involving public transportation require pragmatism; the language of rights, by contrast, moves in precisely the opposite direction. Rather than prudence, it screams "more buses or the guillotine!" If this is the first objection, there is also a second yet deeper objection that comes from the radical left and is concerned less with rights talk in general than with its political utility—or lack thereof. Where the goal is to advance social justice, rights, these critics argue, are simply too indeterminate and too individualistic to be useful. While both these objections deserve a comment, it is the first more general one that ought to be the most familiar. In fact, this more general objection finds its antecedents in none other than Edmund Burke. For Burke, writing in reaction to the "pretended rights" of the French Revolution, the excesses of rights talk were painfully clear.[8] In place of reasoned debate and deliberation, the declaration of the "rights of man" had given way to something wholly different—the violence of a "swinish multitude" and a wholesale rejection of the customs and traditions that had long sustained society. As Burke noted, against the "new rights" of the revolution "no argument is binding," and "anything withheld from their full demand is so much of fraud and injustice."[9] In place of prudence and pragmatism, the so-called rights of man marked the victory of just the opposite—a descent into chaos.

In 1991, the political philosopher Mary Ann Glendon returned to many of these same criticisms. Writing a decade after the "rights revolution" of the

Warren Court, Glendon argued that political debate in the United States had been overrun by rights-based appeals. For Glendon, the problem was not simply that rights were intemperate or impractical, but that the eagerness with which people were wont to proclaim their right to this or that too often belied any discussion of responsibility, let alone duties or costs. For Glendon, the consequences for political debate were apparent. The "absoluteness of rights talk," she argued, had promoted "unrealistic expectations," heightened "social conflict," and "inhibited dialogue that might lead to accommodation, consensus," or common ground.[10] In place of compromise, rights talk made all political debate zero sum and winner-take-all. Indeed, rights came at the expense of democracy itself. In their implicit appeal to a higher court, rights too often meant shifting deliberation and debate to the cloistered office of some appointed judge.

Objections to rights talk are not, of course, limited to moral philosophers. In fact, the world of public transportation is rife with its own Burkes and Glendons. In 2010, I interviewed an AC Transit board member for whom rights talk was to be avoided at all costs.

> The idea of framing something in terms of a right is extremely complex. . . . How do we exercise that right? How do we legislate it? Say we want to recognize it. You [try and] write the law — it isn't easy. . . . The ones we're used to now, everyone understands and nobody challenges, but . . . when you start inventing new ones. . . . It's hard to talk about things in terms of rights. I would almost rather just say: let's just try and get a better transit system for everyone.[11]

For the board member quoted above, as it is for many people, the problem with rights is not so much their tone, nor proliferation, but rather the hoary issue of implementation. How will this or that right be legislated? How will it be enforced? Where will the money come from? What will it look like in *real* practical terms? Against such concerns, the questions inevitably arise: Why talk in terms of rights at all? Why not simply avoid them altogether? Of course, part of the goal of this book is to suggest just the opposite: that the impulse to dismiss rights talk, and especially in the name of pragmatism, is precisely the wrong one. Part of this belief is simply a reaction to the type of pragmatism that is so often trotted out. Note that Mary Ann Glendon or the above AC Transit board member are not appealing to some clearly articulated theory of pragmatism — à la Dewey or social contract theory. Rather they are simply trying to shut down the debate — whether because they fear losing the debate or because they disagree with the debate's entire premise. The board member's quote is a perfect example of this. Even for those unfamiliar with issues of transit, the idea of avoiding rights talk so as to simply get "a better transit system for everyone" is laughable — not only because it assumes that what constitutes a "better transit system" is self-evident, but also because it naively assumes that securing such a system can be achieved while the messy world of people's "rights" can simply be avoided. As this book will make clear, even a cursory glance at the East Bay reveals how impossible this is. Rights appear in the remarks of riders like Karen Smulevitz. They creep into contract negotiations between ATU 192 members and management. Rights intrude in lawsuits launched by minority and disabled riders, and they meddle in even the smallest disputes over where to place a bus stop, where to add a curb cut, or what constitutes a "Title VI" bus route—that is, a route deserving special civil rights protection. Barring the enactment of some illiberal speech code, the simplest argument against dismissing rights talk is thus apparent—it is simply part of how we speak. It is both how we express our politics and how we express moral concern. Whether we like it or not, any *practical* attempt to shape transit will come up against this fact. There is, of course, another yet more compelling reason *for* rights talk, and this reason is fairly simple. Rights remind us that the provision of public transportation hinges as much on moral questions as it does on technical ones. And to quote Isaiah Berlin in the epigraph, these are hardly questions that we can afford to leave to "experts or machines" alone. What is the place of public transportation in a democracy? Should there be a "moral minimum" to its allocation? If so, what ought it to be? If not, then what do we owe those in society for whom transit is the only option? Even accepting the difficulty of "talking in terms of rights"—to quote the board member above—to defend rights talk is to presume that these questions are worth tackling and that we lose something when we dismiss them.

As noted earlier, there is an even deeper objection to the language of rights. This objection, which often comes from the radical left, largely hinges on the question of political utility. In the effort to advance social justice or to advance some more specific progressive aim—such as better public transit, for example—these critics argue that any political strategy reliant on rights is destined to come up short. Perhaps most representative of this position is the legal scholar Mark Tushnet. For Tushnet, the problem with rights-based appeals was easy to glean. Rights, Tushnet argued, were simply too "indeterminate" to be useful.[12] Where the First Amendment right to free speech might protect the union picketer protesting her employer, it also protected that same employer against campaign finance laws. Indeed, the First Amendment might allow that very same employer, in the name of free speech, to contribute to the coffers of an anti-union candidate. Where the left works to expand the rights of the former, they also inadvertently expand those of the latter. For Tushnet, the problem with rights was not simply that they were too open, or that they allowed "opposing parties to use the same language to express their positions," but that rights—especially in their legal interpretation—were essentially individualistic.[13] Where leftists sought to advance the general welfare through "positive rights" and through state intervention, much of legal culture championed the reverse. More precisely, it championed the individualism of negative rights. These were the rights, as Karl Marx once observed, of both the "isolated monad, withdrawn into himself," and of the "egoistic man . . . separated from other men and from the community."[14] They were the rights, in short, "to be left alone." In this context, Tushnet argued, even when progressives managed to win in the courts, their victories were often short lived. Tushnet's critique went yet deeper. As he argued, the very openness of rights made them risky political tools and poor instruments for structuring anything approaching a rational argument about "what ought to be done."[15] For every Karen Smulevitz demanding a right to transportation, there was a taxpayer wielding an equally convincing counter-right against footing the bill. In such instances, speaking in terms of rights simply led to incoherence.

Tushnet was hardly the first to make this point. Over a century earlier, Marx had said much the same thing. For Marx, the problem with rights was that they obscured the real forces directing history. In his examination of the "working day" in the first volume of *Capital*, Marx offers a notable point:

> The capitalist maintains his right as a purchaser when he tries to make the working day as long as possible, and, where possible, to make two working days out of one. On the other hand . . . the worker maintains his right as a seller when he wishes to reduce the working day to a particular normal length. There is here therefore an antinomy, of right against right, both equally bearing the seal of the law of exchange. Between equal rights, force decides. Hence, in the history of capitalist production, the establishment of a norm for the working day presents itself as a struggle over the limits of that day, a struggle between collective capital, i.e. the class of capitalists, and collective labour, i.e. the working class.[16]

For Marx, the idea of appealing to some "pompous catalog" of bourgeois rights made little sense.[17] When balancing the interests of collective labor and collective capital, the problem, Marx insisted, was not one of rights but one of force — namely, the force of the latter over the former. Rights were not only beside the point; they obscured the real problem — capitalist exploitation.

Many on the radical left who object to the language of rights — and especially Marxists — do so for just these reasons. Rights, they argue, are simply too open, too indeterminate, and too individualistic to be useful. To these critiques, this book offers a counter. For those interested in improving public transportation in our cities, this book presumes that rights — however imperfect — still remain essential. Indeed, to paraphrase the geographer Don Mitchell, rights remain one of the few tools open to progressives to enact the changes they deem necessary.[18] To make this point, the above quip from Marx is a useful starting place. Where Marx observed that "between equal rights force decides," this book adds an addendum: it argues that rights are themselves a force — or, more accurately, they are an invaluable tool in organizing and directing force.[19] In debates over public transportation, rights *appear* to compel transit agencies to think twice before placing a bus stop. Through police power, they induce transit planners to forego cutting service without public review. They perform during strikes as the cudgel of aggrieved transit workers, and they descend from the gavels of judges to stand in the way of development. It is not by accident that riders like Karen Smulevitz appeal to the language of rights. They do so *because* rights—however imperfect—have long proven an essential tool in advancing social change—in either direction.

Rights Themselves

Moving beyond the above objections, a question remains: What, exactly, is meant by a right? In most political debate, and with few exceptions, a right is simply a "moral minimum." To quote the writer Charles Fried, "Rights are categorical moral entities such that the violation of a right is always wrong."[20] A right dictates the "least that every person can demand and the least that every person, every government, and every corporation must be made to do."[21] To assert a right is not only to mark out "the lower limits of tolerable human conduct, individual and institutional," but also to reject institutional arrangements that threaten to make a dignified life impossible.[22] Such arrangements, of course, are rife. Where the bulk of the law must reflect "the majority's view of the common good," rights—as scholars such as Ronald Dworkin have argued—are important for a very simple reason: they represent "the majority's promise to minorities that their dignity and equality will be respected," even when it is not politically expedient.[23] For others, of course, the danger is less majoritarian tyranny than it is tyranny of a different sort—namely, the tyranny of the unregulated workplace, or of the market itself. Here, too, rights, as moral minimums, are important. Where a right is understood in this more general sense, this book's opening claim—that rights ought to matter for how we understand public transportation—is hardly a controversial one. For most people, of course, the question is not whether rights matter in the abstract, but rather *which* rights matter and what *types* of rights deserve to be taken seriously. Indeed, this question is at the heart of most political conflicts.

When the United States condemns the Cuban government for denying the free speech rights of their citizens, Cuba invariably points to the United States' embarrassingly high rates of infant mortality, its denial of universal health care, and the extraordinary percentage of U.S. citizens who are homeless.[24] In this instance the question is not whether rights matter in any general sense, but whether "socioeconomic rights" to health care or housing are as important as people's "civil or political rights" to free assembly or to free speech. On one hand, and to continue with this example, for scholars such as Robert Nozick and other libertarians the answer is clear. Not only are socioeconomic rights less important, but they suffer the same problem inherent with all "positive rights."

Namely they require making claims on material resources that are scarce and exhaustible and that may already be owned by other individuals.

Unsurprisingly, for Nozick and many others, the only entitlements that count as rights are "negative rights." These are rights to noninterference and noncoercion and against state oppression and tyranny. Unlike a positive right to housing or to health care—which require that we consider the "inherent scarcity of resources"—negative rights require only that people are left alone.[25] The demands they make on the state and others are modest if not negligible. Of course, this view has had its critics. As many have observed, there is a tendency to forget the degree to which even negative rights—be they to free speech or private property—"still require more from the government than that it simply stay its hand."[26] Such rights must, after all, be enforced, and enforcement—whether through police power or the courts—means expending resources that may also be scarce. No less notable is the tendency to forget arguments such as those of Isaiah Berlin—namely, that negative rights alone often mean little to those lacking the most basic material needs. Is it not cruel, Berlin once asked, to "offer political rights and safeguards against intervention by the state to men who are half-naked, illiterate, underfed, and diseased?"[27] Such individuals need food and shelter before anything else. Indeed, their *liberty* requires it. Whether our politics are more in line with the Nozicks of the world or whether we are more inclined toward the welfare liberalism of, say, Isaiah Berlin or Jeremy Waldron, the broad lesson on rights remains the same. Namely, part of taking rights seriously not only means recognizing them as fundamentally moral claims, but acknowledging that there are different types of rights and that those differences matter. A commitment to negative rights may not square with a so-called socioeconomic right to housing. Similarly, appeals to group rights may come at the expense of individual rights or traditional civil rights. The types of rights we champion and the types of rights we disregard not only reflect our own political and moral commitments but the notions of justice and morality that undergird those commitments. In scholarly debates over public transportation, in many ways, the question of what rights rise to the top or what rights deserve attention has already been answered.

CIVIL RIGHTS

For the past fifty years the question of rights within scholarship on urban transportation has largely been one of civil rights. This has meant measuring transportation policies against our society's alleged commitment to equity, fairness, and, above all, racial justice. In the United States, as many will note, the history of public transportation has often shown evidence of just the opposite. For much of the twentieth century, racial discrimination and the provision of public transportation went hand in hand. Indeed, between 1896 and the late 1950s racial discrimination in public transportation enjoyed explicit legal sanction—namely, under the legal doctrine of "separate but equal."[28] As is well known, fights against racial discrimination in public transportation played a key role in the civil rights movement. Both the Montgomery bus boycott of 1955 and the Freedom Riders campaign of 1961 remain potent symbols of the movement's fundamental demand for racial equity.[29] In the last three decades, the notion of public transportation as a civil rights issue has reemerged, particularly in the form of new questions around transportation equity and environmental justice. For those who have been drawn to these new questions, the starting point has often been the same. As Robert Bullard has noted, "transportation continues to be divided along racial lines," and communities of color continue to be subject to policies that violate their civil rights.[30] These policies include everything from funding schemes that subsidize new transportation infrastructure in white communities at the expense of minority ones to transportation policies that disproportionately expose minorities to diesel exhaust and other environmental hazards. While the overt discrimination that spawned the Montgomery bus boycott may be gone, the reality, as Bullard and others have argued, in many ways remains unchanged; our national transportation system continues to deny "many black Americans and other people of color the benefits, freedoms and opportunities, and rewards offered to white Americans."[31] For Bullard, as well as for many others, fights against transportation injustice not only remain synonymous with rejecting transportation racism but with the "longue durée" of the civil rights movement—both the struggles in the Jim Crow South and the racial struggles against illegal dumping that jump-started the environmental justice movement of the 1980s.[32] In their 2007 book, *The Right to Transportation: Moving to Equity*, authors Thomas Sanchez, Marc Brenman, Jacinta Ma, and Richard Stolz build on Bullard's effort to highlight the role of federal and state transportation policies in reproducing racial and socioeconomic inequalities. As they argue, these inequalities often extend into other areas such as age, national origin, English proficiency, disability, and gender.[33] Federal and state transportation policies can be no less the source of exclusionary outcomes in these areas as well. Similar to Bullard's argument, however, the issue of rights and "the right to transportation"—to draw from the title of their book—remains, for them, largely one of civil rights and state-backed discrimination.

For as much as civil rights and racial equity continue to form the core of transportation justice debates, there have also been those who have sought to advance a yet broader agenda. In their work *A New Social Equity Agenda for Sustainable Transportation*, Todd Litman and Marc Brenman make an explicit attempt to move beyond what they see as the limits of a civil rights frame. As they argue, while the transportation system of Montgomery, Alabama, remains riven by inequity, today's inequity breaks along far different lines:

In terms of transportation, most Montgomery, Alabama, African American residents who can drive and afford an automobile are probably better off now because they have more mobility and do not face daily discrimination. However residents of all races who either cannot drive or would prefer to use alternative modes are probably worse off because their communities are less walkable, bus service has declined and development patterns are more sprawled. Transport system discrimination has changed: it results less from race or ethnicity and more from disability and poverty.[34]

While this measure of racial progress may be overly optimistic, Litman and Brenman's more general observation remains an important one: to the extent that discrimination continues to define federal and state transportation policy, the losers are just as likely to be racial minorities as they are to be the elderly, poor, disabled, or any other group who "cannot drive or would prefer to use alternative modes."[35] For these groups, of course, part of the problem is simply one of funding. In the United States only 20 percent of all surface transportation funds are dedicated to public transportation. The rest are slated for roads and highways.[36] Not only is federal and state funding biased against alternative transportation modes—whether public transportation or cycling—but that bias often extends to the ways that local metropolitan planning organizations (MPOs) evaluate the impact of transportation investment. Where MPOs often rely on "vehicle miles traveled" (VMT) or increased average speed to gauge the success of a given transportation investment, they invariably direct funds toward highways and away from the very transportation modes that are both the most affordable and the most likely to serve the poor—public transportation.[37] In this context, Litman and Brenman argue, what is needed is a social equity agenda that goes beyond questions of transportation racism to "consider a broader range of impacts, recognizes the problems of automobile dependency and the benefits of a more diverse transportation system."[38] For Litman and Brenman, the stakes of the status quo are clear: a transportation system with little modal diversity, where nondrivers face limited options, and where the socially disadvantaged continue to face a choice between the sometimes impoverishing costs associated with car ownership and, on the other hand, waiting for a bus that may never come.[39]

In his recent book *Street Fight: The Politics of Mobility in San Francisco*, Jason Henderson takes up some of these same themes. Using San Francisco as a case study, Henderson argues that debates over transportation policy often break along three ideological lines—a conservative defense of automobility, a neoliberal celebration of private alternatives to public transit, and a progressive commitment to livability and to defending public transportation.[40] For Henderson, like Litman and Brenman, questions of civil rights are secondary to simply reducing automobile dependency. This means promoting policies focused on what Jane Jacobs once deemed "automobile attrition"—policies that "steadily decrease the number of persons using private automobiles in a city" and that decrease both "the need for cars" and their convenience.[41] For Henderson, the costs of ceding the ideological terrain to conservatives or neoliberals is quite high: increased greenhouse gas emissions and cities that continue to be defined by congestion, sprawl, and noise pollution.

In relation to the work of scholars such as Robert Bullard and Thomas Sanchez, this book's message is fairly straightforward. It says: where transportation justice and equity are limited to questions of civil rights, transportation justice advocates not only lose sight of other rights—from those of labor to those that emerge from tort cases—but they also narrow their own notions of justice and equity. Transportation equity simply becomes racial equity, and transportation injustice simply becomes the injustice of intentional or disparate impact discrimination. As such, the injustices inherent to the political economy itself fall from view. In relation to the work of Todd Litman and Jason Henderson, this book offers a slightly different response. It argues that while issues of modal diversity, increased sprawl, and environmental sustainability are deeply important, the stakes involved in urban transportation policy also extend yet further. They extend to issues of urban democracy, of who is part of the public, and who—by dint of poor transit—is alienated from it. These are invariably the issues at the heart of the increasingly popular notion of "the right to the city." As this book shows, struggles over transportation in California's East Bay—whether in the courts or in the union halls—have hinged as much on civil rights, modal diversity, or sprawl as they have on the questions implicit in the demand for this more radical right.[42]

THE RIGHT TO THE CITY

As an idea, the right to the city comes out of the work of the French Marxist philosopher Henri Lefebvre.[43] Lefebvre defined the right to the city in rather broad terms. In his own words, it was "a right to urban life, to renewed centrality, to places of encounter and exchange," as well as a "cry and demand" for a more just city.[44] The context in which Lefebvre coined the slogan is both important and clarifying. As in much of the Western world, the end of World War II had ushered in a period of rapid change in France. The postwar years were ones, as the cultural critic Kristen Ross notes, in which French society was transformed "from a rural, empire oriented, Catholic country into a fully industrialized, decolonized and urban one."[45] Between 1955 and 1975, France's urban population increased by almost 15 percent.[46] Over roughly the same period (1945–1975), a rapidly expanding economy not only ushered in a newly affluent working class—with access to cars and washing machines—but it also laid the groundwork for the wholesale reworking of the urban fabric.[47] This included new highways like the Boulevard Peripherique as well as new large-scale housing developments—everything from the suburban "new towns" to massive public housing estates that would dot the urban periphery.[48] For many, the urban renewal of the postwar period marked tremendous progress. As Robert Price notes, while in 1954 "over one third of households lacked running water and only 17.5% had a bathroom or shower," by 1975, at least 70 percent of the population had access to both.[49] For others, such progress had come with a cost. Writing in the postscript to his book *Urban France*, the author Ian Scargill captures this paradox well:

> France has been transformed within the space of little more than thirty years from a semi-rural to an urban society. The effects of this transformation are everywhere apparent as historic city centres have been engulfed in a suburban tide of housing, factories, superstores and expressways. . . . . The rapid growth of French cities over the last thirty years has created problems as well as solving them. Houses and services have been provided *en masse* but at the expense of character and of those very qualities of urbanity which the city is meant to symbolize.[50]

For Henri Lefebvre, the "character" of the new French city was a profoundly disturbing one.[51] The working-class communities that had once given life to the city center had been "decentralized to lifeless dormitory suburbs."[52] While new highways and expressways had shortened the length of the commute, they had come at the expense of the city's organic unity. The city was more segregated, more fragmented, and more defined by separation. That separation was not only between the workplace and home, but also between and within social classes. A new affluent middle class had retreated into their "new electric kitchens"—removing themselves from both the public and politics itself.[53] In place of the "old quartier"—defined by a deeply politicized working class—there was now only the "new town," characterized by just the opposite: radical alienation. Rather than "the idiocy of rural life"—to quote Marx and Engels, who used *idiocy* in the classical sense as a synonym for "isolating"—the city of the new France marked the birth of a peculiarly urban idiocy, one marked by the same "privatized isolation" and the same political apathy that had lent rural life its stagnant quality.[54] The modern factory worker of the "new town," it seemed, was little different from the rural weaver who, to quote Engels, "lived only for their petty, private interests . . . and who otherwise remained sunk in apathetic indifference to the universal interests of mankind."[55] In this context, the right to the city, for Lefebvre, meant something quite radical and quite specific. It meant rescuing the city as place of meaning, of social encounter, of interaction, of working-class solidarity, and of political consciousness.[56] Moreover, it meant both defending the city as a site of radical politics and rejecting its newly alienating qualities.

Beyond a critique of France's new urban landscape, Lefebvre's conception of the right to the city was also a product of his own curious brand of Marxism. By the 1960s, his was a Marxism that rejected the dogmatisms of the French Communist Party and that had taken up a unique set of philosophical questions. These were on the contours of capitalist alienation, on the meaning of class consciousness, and, most importantly, on the nature of urbanization. As Neil Smith argued, Lefebvre's work charted new territory in the study of cities. Not only did it mark a break from the constraints of traditional urban sociology—typified by Ernest Burgess and Robert Park of the Chicago School—but it also marked a break from those within the Marxist tradition whose interests rarely extended beyond the class politics of the industrial factory.[57] For Lefebvre, of course, it was a mistake to ignore capitalism's role in shaping the modern city, and it was no less a mistake to ignore the role of the city as a site of radical anticapitalist struggle. While Lefebvre's Marxism was clearly nondogmatic, his commitment to class struggle and the importance of a class politics never waned.[58] For Lefebvre, what mattered, and what the new French city so clearly proved, is that the class struggle necessarily went beyond the factory—it extended outward into the streets, into the daily life of the city, and into the very process of urbanization. In sum, the city had become the factory, and thus the terrain of class struggle had become yet broader.[59]

In the last three decades the concept of the right to the city has enjoyed something of a renaissance. Part of that renaissance is invariably tied to what is now an inescapable reality—for the first time in human history, more than half of the world's population now resides in a city. Not only are more people living in urban areas, but the pace of urbanization has—in many parts of the world—shown no sign of slowing.[60] Thus, for many people, Lefebvre's right to the city remains important for a simple reason: cities continue to be defined by exclusion, alienation, and injustice. In the cities of the developed world, many of those injustices should be familiar. They are related to gentrification, displacement, homelessness, lack of affordable housing, and a generalized sense that cities are abandoning their poorest residents in pursuit of global capital. In the developing world, and where the pace of urbanization has been the most rapid, the problems are even more acute: substandard housing, poor sanitation, lack of land tenure, slum clearances, and a wholesale absence of secure employment. Given these circumstances, scholars, grassroots organizations, and international nonprofits have all found in Lefebvre's right to the city a useful framework. In 2001, and after decades of grassroots activism, Brazil's legislature enacted the "City Statute," or Federal Law number 10.257.[61] Inspired by Lefebvre's conception of the right to the city, the City Statute strengthened the federal constitution's commitment to an already progressive set of principles. These included principles for advancing the social function of urban property, the democratization of municipal governance, and the regularization of informal settlements.[62] At both the municipal and international level, there continue to be efforts along similar lines. At the municipal level, this has been apparent in such cities as

Mexico City and Montreal. Internationally, UNESCO and a number of grassroots organizations have, since 2004, tried to establish a "World Charter for the Right to the City." While this charter includes many of the rights already established in the UN Declaration of Human Rights, it also lists an additional set aimed directly at the injustices associated with urban development: the human right to "land, sanitation, public transportation and basic infrastructure."[63]

Of course, for many scholars and activists the right to the city is useful not because it is a juridical or legalistic claim, but because it offers a broad and compelling way for directing radical political action.[64] This has certainly been the view of scholars like Peter Marcuse and David Harvey. For Marcuse, rather than a legal claim, the right to the city is best understood as a moral claim aimed at mobilizing "one side in the conflict over who should have the benefit of the city and what kind of city it should be."[65] David Harvey's notion of the right to the city runs in a parallel direction.[66] For Harvey, as with Marcuse, the right to the city is less a juridical claim than a way of organizing a more meaningful politics—namely, one that recognizes the injustices of capitalist urbanization. As Harvey writes: "Only when it is understood that those who build and sustain urban life have primary claim to that which they have produced, and that one of their claims is to the unalienated right to make the city more after their hearts' desires, will we arrive at a politics of the urban that will make sense."[67]

This book presumes that many of the same questions that compelled Lefebvre, and that continue to inspire scholars and activists worldwide, are questions that ought to play a central role in how we think about public transportation. These are questions about what constitutes a more democratic city, what is required to combat the alienation and the isolation of urban life, and what it means to defend the city as a site of radical politics.[68]

In starting and ending with a right to the city, this book also marks an explicit break with the notion of rights that continues to drive much of the work on transportation equity. In almost all respects, that notion remains a quintessentially liberal one. In a society where the bulk of the law must reflect "the majority's view of the common good," rights, in this conception, must represent "the majority's promise to minorities that their dignity and equality will be respected," even when public opinion dictates otherwise.[69] Within this tradition, we find not only classic liberties like the right to free speech but also the civil rights appeals that so dominate debates on transportation justice and transportation equity. For many of those drawn to the idea of a right to the city, the reality of the modern world demands rights of a different order. As ought to be clear, in cities across the globe—whether in the developing or the developed world—the laws governing urban life are often less a product of the "majority's view of the common good" than they are a product of other forces—from the vagaries of real estate capital to the pressures that all cities face in attracting investment. When slums are cleared for a new development, or when long-time

Of course, whether we start with the above analysis of BART, or the protests directed at the OAC in 2010, we inevitably reach the same conclusion. Indeed, it is the conclusion reached by R. D. Marx Greene in 1917. Namely, in places like the Bay Area, part of engaging debates on urban public transportation invariably requires engaging a set of larger questions on the power of urban elites, on the impact of interurban competition, and on the inherent class politics of urban development. Perhaps more clearly still, it means asking this: Who are cities for? Are they for the Celia-Faye Russells of the world or for the global investor for whom projects like the OAC are clearly the target? Are they for bus riders like Karen Smulevitz or, as the history of both BART and the Key System seem to suggest, are the interests of cities simply the interests of downtown property holders or industrialists like Francis "Borax" Smith? In assessing the nature of urban public transportation these questions have, of course, hardly gone away. Indeed, they have been at the heart of a set of recent controversies in the East Bay over the emergence of Google buses—the private shuttles used to cart elite tech workers from Oakland and San Francisco to the tech campuses of Yahoo, Google, and Facebook. Despite early complaints focused on their illegal use of municipal parking spaces, the vast majority of the criticisms launched at such shuttles—and that have resulted in protests and vandalism of the buses themselves—have come in response to their impact on the city more broadly. To the degree that such buses have made it easier for affluent tech workers to live and purchase property in San Francisco and the East Bay, they have driven up rents and further facilitated the ongoing gentrification of the region. Indeed a report released in 2014 found that between 2011 and 2013 "69% of no-fault evictions in San Francisco" were within four blocks of a Google bus stop.[89] With an influx of affluent tech workers, property owners were responding as one might expect—raising rents and trading in old tenants for new wealthier ones. As with the debates over the OAC or Whitt's critique of BART, for those protesting the influx of Google buses, the real target of their frustration was not the shuttles but what they represented—the ongoing transformation of the city into a playground for the rich and in which the poor, to quote Lefebvre, lacked any right to the city at all.

As noted earlier, the central contention of this book is not simply that rights are important for how we think about public transportation, but that there are different types of rights claims and that those differences matter. When we champion traditional liberal civil rights our concerns are generally with the dangers of majoritarian tyranny, discrimination against minority groups, and threats to individual freedom.[90] When, on the other hand, we champion so-called socioeconomic rights—be they a right to basic housing, or to food, or even to transportation—we do so precisely because we believe that providing liberty or freedom to individuals who are hungry, or sick, or naked is, to quote Isaiah Berlin, "to mock their condition."[91] Such individuals need shelter and basic services for those freedoms to have any meaning. To start with a right to the city, of course, is to foreground a different set of concerns. These concerns are less with individual freedom or the lack of basic services than they are with the political economy itself and the role of capitalist urbanization in producing cities defined by alienation, isolation, and exclusion of the economically disadvantaged. Indeed, they are excluded from the very socioeconomic rights that many liberals most care about—rights to housing and to food. To start with the right to the city is to start from the assumption that even securing these basic socioeconomic rights requires that we challenge the political economy itself. Given this book's broader argument about rights and public transit, Lefebvre's right to city is thus significant in at least two ways. The first way, and perhaps the least consequential, is that it allows the book to make sense of a set of transportation struggles that may at the outset seem disparate and distinct. These are struggles that erupt in court rooms, labor halls, and the streets themselves. To turn to Lefebvre is to see the links between these struggles and to place them centrally within a larger debate on who cities are for and what types of social relation ought to predominate in them. The second and the perhaps more important way that the idea of the right to the city is significant for this book is that it foregrounds a set of concerns that rarely figure in contemporary debates on transportation justice or transportation equity. These are concerns with the alienation and isolation of urban life, the political economy of cities, and the tyranny of urban policies that function to both exclude the poor—many of whom ride public buses—and to betray the democratic promise of cities themselves. As this book shows, for any number of people in the East Bay these concerns are real and deserve attention. More importantly—and given the above history of local transit—they are concerns that require us to think critically about what kinds of rights are necessary and thus what kinds of rights deserve championing.

Organization of the Book

In the following chapters, this book approaches struggles over the provision of public transportation in the East Bay from four primary vantage points: the courts (chapter 1), the local transportation justice movement (chapter 2), transit labor (chapter 3), and transit planners (chapter 4). Each chapter is organized around a question. The first chapter, on the courts, starts with a fairly simple question: Where do the legal duties of transit agencies begin and the rights of transit riders' end? As becomes clear, this is hardly a simple question and depends a great deal on the rights the courts are asked to recognize. Chapter 2 begins with a different question: What is meant by transportation justice in the East Bay? What type of political project is it? Indeed, what type of rights does it

champion? Chapter 3 takes up the perennial "labor question": How do we reconcile the rights of transit workers with those of the people they carry—who
are often much poorer and less secure? The last chapter asks about alternatives:
What are the transit alternatives that have been floated in the East Bay, and what
type of politics or ideology is required to see these alternatives through?

Although each of these chapters engages a different area of public transportation policy—from the law to labor relations—each chapter ultimately returns to
a set of three related arguments. The first is simply that rights matter. And while
there will certainly be those who prefer to ignore rights in order to focus on the
practical task of just getting "a better transit system for everyone," such wishful
appeals, as this book makes clear, are just that—dangerously wishful. Rights are
part of how we speak, they are how we engage in politics, and they are one of the
few ways that we express moral concern. Any *practical* attempt to shape public
transit in more just ways will involve confronting this reality—whether we like
it or not. Secondly, this book argues that the *types* of rights we champion matter.
As scholars such as Jeremy Waldron have long noted, there are different types of
rights claims—from civil rights to collective rights—and those differences are
important. Not only are they a reflection of our political commitments, and our
notions of justice, but they reflect the types of questions we are willing to ask.[92]
Indeed, the types of rights we champion are often an indication of the outer limits of what we believe justice requires. Lastly, this book argues that when posed
with the questions "What do we mean by a right to public transportation?" and
"What type of right is at issue?" those who share a progressive vision for urban
public transportation would do well to invoke transportation's role in securing
not only our civil rights but also our right to the city.

CHAPTER 1

Torts, Transit, and the "Majestic Equality" of the Law

The law, in its *majestic equality*, forbids the rich as well as the poor to sleep under bridges, to beg in the streets, and to steal bread.
    —Anatole France, *The Red Lily*, 1894

Your honor, you are about to enter, with your glossary, a seemingly complex, jargon filled world of transit planning, and you are going to have to learn a new language of funding sources and regional transportation. However, this case, at bottom, is actually simple. As evidenced by the existent factual stipulations, there are many facts that are not in dispute. MTC agrees that AC Transit is in dire need of operating funds. MTC agrees that it does not fund all of AC Transit's operating needs. MTC agrees that AC Transit's ridership is overwhelmingly composed of members of the plaintiff class. . . . MTC agrees that it allocates billions of dollars to rail expansion while bus systems in the Bay Area are experiencing a reduction in service levels. While they may not agree with this characterization, what this comes down to is favoring one component of the region's transportation system over another.
    —Bill Lann Lee, Opening Statement in *Darensburg v. MTC*, October 1 2008

In his book *Democracy in America*, Alexis de Tocqueville observed that there was "hardly a political question in the United States which does not sooner or later become a judicial one."[1] This chapter suggests that a similar insight might be said to apply to urban mass transit. As with most areas of public policy, urban transit has hardly been immune from the influence of the courts or from judicial review. When transit officials stake out new routes, when they threaten to cut service, or even when they deign to add a new bus stop, not only must they confront the scrutiny of the public, but they must also, invariably, confront the possibility of a summons, or of legal action. To the degree that this chapter focuses on the court's impact on transit, it also returns, yet again, to the skeptics of rights talk with whom the book began. To recall, for such skeptics—like the AC Transit board member quoted earlier—rights were a waste of time. Indeed, they were a distraction. Far more important than rights was the practical task of simply getting a "better transit system for everyone."[2] The focus ought to be on "improving what we've got." Of course, as we argued, such demands, however understandable, often rest on a rather flimsy premise—namely, that avoiding rights is actually possible, and that securing a "better transit system" can be accomplished without dirtying one's hands in hoary disputes over moral minimums or entitlements. Nowhere is this appeal to pragmatism or this disregard for rights more clearly dispelled than when transit agencies like AC Transit come face-to-face—as they are prone to do—with an enterprising lawyer or an aggrieved transit patron who believes that their rights have been thrown under the figurative bus.

This chapter begins with a question: In the East Bay, where do the legal duties of transit agencies begin, and where do the corresponding rights of the transit-riding public end? To this question, the chapter turns its attention to three court cases: *Bonanno v. CCCTA*, *Lopez v. SCRTD*, and *Darensburg et al. v. Metropolitan Transportation Commission*. While the first two are tort cases—that is, they deal with questions of liability and tortious behavior—the last case is a civil rights case and thus hinges on questions of equal protection under the law. As becomes clear in discussion of these cases—especially the tort cases—legal disputes over the rights of riders play a fundamental role in shaping what transit looks like. Legal disputes dictate everything from where transit agencies site bus stops to how drivers interact with patrons. In debating the future of transit, rights are hardly distractions; indeed, they are inescapable. The following cases also serve to make yet another point—and this is most evident in the Darensburg case. To the extent that the courts take a necessarily narrow view of what transit means for people or of its role in cities, they are often simply responding to the narrowness of the alleged rights at issue.

Torts and Transit

Tort cases are ubiquitous. They are the cases that deal in personal injury, product safety, and assigning fault in accidents. As noted by legal scholar William Prosser, torts are best defined as civil wrongs.[3] Tort laws, by extension, refer to the rules governing what constitutes a wrong and how to assign responsibility when a wrong is identified. Public transit agencies, like many government agencies, are often subject to tort challenge. In fact, these challenges can be quite daunting. A 1994 report by the Transit Cooperative Research Program (TCRP) noted that tort liability payments, on average, accounted for 5.67 percent of total fare revenue. At one agency, this number was nearly 23 percent.[4] As the following examples suggest, the implications of tort rulings extend beyond fiduciary concerns to impinge on what the transit map actually looks like.

In 2010, an AC Transit senior planner responded to a question regarding the challenges of transit planning in the East Bay by making note of a curious case, and the even more curious court ruling that followed. The case was *Darlene Bonanno v. Central Contra Costa Transit Authority* (CCCTA). In 2003, the California Supreme Court held the CCCTA liable for injuries sustained by Darlene Bonanno while she approached a bus stop. Per the decision, transit companies were now liable for accidents in which the company was directly involved (i.e., a bus hitting a pedestrian), as well as for accidents "caused" by the very location of a bus stop.[5] According to the planner, the ruling fundamentally shaped the nature of transit planning in California.[6] The details of the case are notable and worth rehearsing.

On November 16, 1993, while en route to a bus stop at the intersection of DeNormadie and Pacheco Boulevard in the East Bay city of Martinez, Darlene Bonanno was struck by a car. After initially lapsing into a coma, she later regained consciousness and underwent surgery on her foot. In 1994, Bonanno sued the CCCTA, Contra Costa County, Jeremy McClain, the negligent driver, and Kaiser Hospital, where she had been treated. By 1999 all defendants but the CCCTA had settled, and Bonanno was left to try her case against the CCCTA alone. Bonanno's theory of liability against the CCCTA was an interesting one. It relied on California State Government Code sections 830 and 835—sections that identify what types of tort actions against public agencies can proceed. Government Code section 835 mandates that public agencies can be held liable for injuries caused by a dangerous condition of public property. Government Code 830 further defines a "dangerous condition" as a condition of property "that creates a substantial risk of injury when such property or adjacent property is used with due care and in a manner in which it is reasonably foreseeable that it will be used."[7] The question before the court was whether the location of the bus stop at DeNormandie and Pacheco constituted a dangerous condition of public property.[8]

The plaintiff's burden of proof was substantial. The plaintiff was asked to prove that (1) the bus stop in question posed a persistent risk; (2) that Bonanno's use of the bus stop was reasonable and in accordance with how a bus stop might be used by others; and (3) that the CCCTA had knowledge of the potential risks posed by the location of the bus stop. The plaintiff's counsel rested its argument on historical facts as well as testimony. Pacheco Boulevard, the plaintiff noted, had always been a busy street. As early as 1980, local residents had complained about the dangers of crossing it. In 1986, Kimberly Chittock, a local resident, was struck by a car at the intersection of Pacheco and DeNormandie while jogging to catch a bus. Chittock both lodged a complaint and filed a suit against the CCCTA. Although Chittock reached a settlement with the CCCTA, the bus stop at the intersection remained in the same place. During the Chittock trial, traffic engineer Thomas Shultz testified that the CCCTA should move the bus stop from Pacheco and DeNormandie to a safer intersection.[9]

The CCCTA's defense focused less on challenging the plaintiff's assertion of the intersection's danger—which was obvious—and more on asserting the agency's powerlessness in preventing accidents like those that befell Bonanno. It would be one thing if the bus stop sign or the bus shelter itself collapsed and injured Bonanno, but Bonanno was injured by a car driven by a negligent driver on a property several meters from the bus stop. Since the CCCTA neither owned nor controlled the sidewalk, nor the shoulder adjacent to the bus stop, the CCCTA argued that it was erroneous to suggest that the agency be held liable under Government Code sections 830 or 835. Where these codes held that public agencies could be held liable for injuries occasioned by a dangerous condition of public property, the CCCTA argued that the location of a bus stop failed to meet that criterion. Even if the CCCTA wished to remedy the situation by moving the bus stop, it would still require the consent and authorization of Contra Costa County—a wholly separate entity.[10]

The court found this defense lacking. The court ultimately ruled that the location and maintenance of the bus stop on Pacheco and DeNormandie constituted a dangerous condition of public property. Following the Chittock incident, the intrinsic danger of the intersection was well known, yet CCCTA had done nothing about it. In 2003, and after several appeals, the California Supreme Court found the CCCTA liable for Darlene Bonanno's injuries. The court ordered the agency to pay Bonanno $1.6 million. The Supreme Court's decision was not without its critics, two of whom sat on the court itself. Judge Marvin Baxter and Judge Janice Brown's dissenting opinions were strongly worded. For Baxter, the view that "location" could amount to a dangerous condition of public property was an "inapposite theory of liability." Owners of property, he added, "should not be made to ensure the safety of all persons who encounter nearby traffic-related hazards in reaching their property."[11] To make his point, Judge Baxter offered the following hypothetical:

> A public entity owns a building with two spaces for rent, located directly adjacent to a crosswalk on a busy street. One of the building's renters is subject to a two year lease; the other rents on a month-to-month basis. Like the situation here, there are no traffic lights or stop signs at the crosswalk, and the building's location therefore presents a dangerous condition. . . . Under the majority's rule, the public entity owner would escape liability because it could not feasibly move the building. The month-to-month renter likely would be subject to liability because terminating the tenancy and relocating appears to be feasible. The two-year lessee might or might not be subject to liability, depending upon a jury's assessment of feasibility. Thus even though all three defendants appear equally at fault in terms of attracting visitors to the same dangerous location they will not be held similarly accountable.[12]

Judge Baxter argued that the majority's opinion reflected a logical fallacy. Moreover, Baxter also raised a set of more practical worries. By significantly broadening the concept of what constituted a dangerous condition, the court's ruling promised to deplete the already scarce resources available to public entities. Baxter noted that under the rule of joint and severable liability, agencies like CCCTA and AC Transit might now be on the hook for 100 percent of the economic damage incurred in tort litigation—as well as whatever the percentage of culpability would be for noneconomic damages.[13] In her dissent, Judge Janice Brown reiterated many of the same concerns. Like Judge Baxter, Brown argued that the concept of a dangerous condition ought to be limited to the "purely physical condition" of the property itself—not its location or geographic context.[14] Bonanno's injuries, Brown asserted, were caused solely by the negligent driver. Judge Brown's dissent also raised some of the more practical concerns first broached by Baxter. Bonanno's award of $1,606,130, Brown noted, was not an insignificant sum—and especially for a public agency like CCCTA. The court's decision, Brown noted, would also necessarily function to compel transit agencies across California to conduct costly traffic studies. Both the potential litigation and the cost of avoiding litigation promised to come at an enormous cost to taxpayers and bus riders. While the ruling in *Bonanno v. CCCTA* had expanded the duties of transit agencies to their riders, the consequences of that expansion did not necessarily benefit the average transit rider.[15]

The central conflict in *Bonanno v. CCCTA* was over how to define a dangerous condition of public property—and whether a dangerous condition referred to the faulty condition of the property itself, or whether it instead could constitute the property's location. Of course, the court's decision in favor of Bonanno offers a partial answer to the question with which the chapter began—namely, of where the rights and duties of riders begin and end. In *Bonanno v. CCCTA*, the court's answer was quite clear: the duties and liabilities of transit agencies are not limited to the agency's property, but instead they extend to adjacent properties as well. For Baxter and Brown, who both dissented, this quite literal expansion of duties came at an excessive cost. For transit planners, the costs were not simply financial. As one senior planner related, the costs were to service itself: "So let's say there is a senior citizen that asks for a bus stop in the hills, and we . . . look at it and . . . there is no safe place to get [the senior citizen] off the bus and no safe place for [the senior citizen] to cross the street so we can't [provide the service]."[16] For local transit planners in the East Bay, *Bonanno v. CCCTA* raised a number of new logistical concerns. These were as much over service geography as they were over the future of litigation. Are transit agencies now liable when they place a bus stop in an area known for high levels of crime? Or without lighting? Or in areas of the East Bay where safe passage to a bus stop might only be assured through costly capital improvements to the street itself?

Lopez v. Southern California Rapid Transit District

The San Francisco State University Labor Archive plays host to a collection of papers from the Amalgamated Transit Union Local 192—the union representing the drivers and mechanics at AC Transit. The collection contains everything from strike materials and old transit schedules to doodle-scrawled napkins. Among the reams of material, I stumbled upon a unique clipping from an obscure law journal making reference to a 1985 lawsuit tried before California's Supreme Court, *Lopez v. the Southern California Rapid Transit District*. The union's interest in this lawsuit is easy to determine. As with *Bonanno v. CCCTA*, *Lopez v. the Southern California Rapid Transit District* hinged on the supposedly tortious act of a public transit agency. In the Lopez case, the court was asked to decide whether a public bus company had the duty to protect passengers aboard its buses from assaults from other passengers. In answering in the affirmative, the court held that transit agencies indeed had a duty to protect passengers from such assaults. The peculiarities of the case, as with *Bonanno v. CCCTA*, are worth exploring.

After sustaining injuries on a bus operated by the Southern California Rapid Transit District (SCRTD), Carmen and Carla Lopez, Yolanda and Jose de Dios Lopez, and Zenaida Arce brought suit against the SCRTD seeking damages. While the plaintiffs were on the bus, a group of juveniles began harassing passengers, and a violent argument ensued. The bus driver, though notified of the altercation, took no precautionary steps to address the conflict. What began as an argument escalated into a violent conflict at which time the plaintiffs were injured. Given that the particular route on which the plaintiffs were traveling had a well-recognized history of violent conflicts, the plaintiffs claimed that the SCRTD "negligently operated, owned, maintained, supervised, entrusted, inspected, controlled, and drove the bus so as to allow passengers involved in a violent argument to engage in a violent physical fight."[17] More specifically, the plaintiffs argued that the actions of the SCRTD violated California's Civil Code section 2100, a law stating that "a carrier of persons for reward must use the utmost care and diligence for their safe carriage, must provide everything necessary for that purpose, and must exercise to that end a reasonable degree of skill."[18]

In its defense, the SCRTD cited California Government Code sections 845, 820.2, and 815.2—all of which grant public agencies some degree of immunity from liability. Section 845, for example, asserts that public agencies in California cannot be held liable for failing to "provide police protection service."[19] Similarly, sections 815.2 and 820.2 assert that public agencies in California cannot be held liable for injuries sustained due to an act of omission—that is, doing nothing to stop a fight.[20] The general principle undergirding such laws is a simple one: namely, that a public agency should not be held accountable for failing to protect members of the public from third parties. [21] From the perspective of the Lopez counsel, the legal particularities of the transit industry itself created an actionable liability.

Ultimately, the Supreme Court of California agreed that the SCRTD driver was not duty bound to call the police. The court did suggest, however, that the SCRTD could have certainly taken an alternative action that may have gone some way to prevent the injuries sustained by Lopez. Most importantly, the court argued that Government Code section 2100 was explicit in its demand that common carriers show the utmost care in transporting passengers. Such care, the court ruled, included taking action to stop a fight. The court based this decision on its finding that bus transit itself presumed a "special relationship" between passengers and drivers, and that such a "special relationship" compelled transit agencies to protect members of the public from third-party assaults. [22]

Legal scholars define a "special relationship" as one in which a public or private entity voluntarily assumes a protective role and induces reliance on it. [23] Such special relationships are quite common. These include the relationship between an innkeeper and his or her boarders, between a police officer and a prisoner in custody, between a landholder and his or her guests, or the relationship between a psychiatrist and his or her patients. While public agencies generally have no duty to protect members of the public from third-party assaults— as this duty would be quite burdensome and costly—this does not hold where courts find that a special relationship exists. In the Lopez case, the Supreme Court not only ruled that the SCRTD had violated California Civil Code section 2100, but it sustained this ruling after finding a special relationship between passengers and drivers. In defining the relationship between passengers and drivers as "special," the Supreme Court's majority opinion reiterated the opinion of the appellate court in suggesting that the bus itself might be described as a moving "steel cocoon." In defining the special relationship, the Supreme Court noted:

> Bus passengers are "sealed in a moving steel cocoon." Large numbers of strangers are forced into very close physical contact with one another under conditions that are often crowded, noisy and overheated. At the same time, the means of entering and exiting the bus are limited and under the exclusive control of the driver. Thus the passengers have no control over who is admitted on the bus and, if trouble arises, are wholly dependent upon the bus driver to summon help or provide a means of escape. These characteristics of buses are, at the very least, conducive to outbreaks of violence between passengers and at the same time significantly limit the means by which passengers can protect themselves from assaults by fellow passengers. We believe the characteristics of public transportation along with the duty of utmost care and diligence imposed by Civil Code section 2100, provide a more ample basis for designating a special relationship between common carriers and their passengers. [24]

In the same way that a police department—according to the special relationship doctrine—might be liable for injuries sustained by a prisoner while in their custody, the court's ruling asserted that transit agencies are liable for the safe passage of their riders and are liable if they get injured even by a third party. Passengers, by the court's definition, are literally captives of the vehicles they enter. While such a metaphor may seem strange, it partially explains why the Lopez case mattered to the ATU Local 192 and AC Transit—whose drivers were now akin to prison guards. Fights on AC Transit buses were common, and so the court's ruling was particularly notable. The case also stands in odd relief to the case of Bonanno. Whereas in the Lopez case the court suggested that the space of the bus itself gave rise to a new set of duties, in the Bonanno case the courts ruled that these duties ostensibly continue to extend beyond the bus itself and into adjacent properties. The very distinction upon which the courts decided *Lopez v. SCRTD*—the entrapment of passengers in a steel cocoon—only adds complexity to the already complicated map of liability evidenced in *Bonanno v. CCCTA*.

Darensburg v. Metropolitan Transportation Commission

Moving away from the law of torts, personal injury, liability, and negligence, the following case takes up a different area of law by turning to questions of civil rights and the rights of minority riders to equal treatment under the law. We start with a 2005 class action lawsuit filed against the regional Metropolitan Transportation Commission on behalf of AC Transit's minority bus riders. First, a bit of background on the commission.

Created by the California State Legislature in 1970, the Metropolitan Transportation Commission (MTC) is the designated metropolitan planning organization (MPO) for the nine-county Bay Area. Its remit extends from the East Bay counties of Alameda and Contra Costa to the counties of Sonoma, Napa, San Mateo, Solano, San Francisco, Santa Clara, and Marin. As with all MPOs, the MTC functions to funnel both federal and state money to a range of different transportation projects and initiatives across the region. These include everything from the retrofitting of bridges and the repaving of roads to capital and operating support for public mass transit.[25] In order for the MTC to receive federal funds—which account for a large proportion of the MTC's highway and mass transit budget—the agency is tasked with updating a regional transportation plan (RTP) every four years. This plan outlines and justifies the selection of various transportation projects in the region for funding and implementation. In formulating the RTP, the MTC takes the long view and bases its budget on a twenty-five-year projection of demographic, economic, and land use change within the nine counties. Crafting the RTP can be a contentious process and often involves years of debate between various stakeholders in the region. In recent years, and as evidenced in the following case, these debates have not only been over the general level of transit funding but also whether certain transit projects—and by proxy, certain transit riders—are more important than others.

In 2005, Sylvia Darensburg of Oakland, California, along with two other minority AC Transit riders, filed a class action lawsuit against the MTC.[26] Facilitated by the public interest law firm Public Advocates, the suit accused the MTC of violating both Title VI of the 1964 Federal Civil Rights Act and California's Government Code section 11135—a state law barring public agencies from discriminating on the basis of race, color, or national origin.[27] The suit alleged that in 1998, 2001, and 2005, the MTC engaged in policies that both violated Sylvia Darensburg's civil rights and injured the entire class of individuals that Darensburg represented—namely, AC Transit's minority bus riders. The specific contention of the plaintiffs was quite simple: that the MTC consistently made funding decisions that "adversely affect AC Transit's largely minority riders, in comparison to the more affluent and white riders of the other larger carriers in the Bay Area."[28] In 2008, the U.S. District Court for Northern California agreed to try the case on the grounds of disparate impact discrimination under California Government Code § 11135.[29] The trial focused on a number of quite technical questions—questions of legal standing, of the private right of action, and of disparate impact discrimination itself. The trial also raised a set of broader and deeper questions—questions of rights, of corresponding duties, and of the idea of transit justice.

From the very beginning, the Darensburg case became something of a cause célèbre among transit justice activists in the East Bay. In some ways, the image of Sylvia Darensburg herself lent itself to that very purpose. In 2005, Sylvia Darensburg lived in East Oakland. She was a mother of three teenage boys and was a part-time student. Darensburg relied on AC Transit for both work and school, and like many AC Transit riders, she struggled to cope with fare hikes and service reductions. Not only were fare hikes stretching her budget thin, but reduced transit service was limiting her ability to keep and maintain jobs. Slow buses and transit delays meant that Darensburg occasionally arrived late to work and was docked pay. With cuts to evening services, Darensburg was also finding it almost impossible to attend the night classes she needed to advance her career and climb out of poverty. Of course, in many ways, the challenges Darensburg faced were far from unique. Indeed, this was what made her case so compelling. As a woman, as an African American, and as a transit-dependent rider, Sylvia Darensburg embodied the very class of riders in the nine-county Bay Area for whom transit was increasingly unreliable, costly, and inefficient. At the heart of the lawsuit was the claim that the challenges Darensburg faced were rooted in policies endorsed by the MTC. These were policies that functioned to subsidize white rail commuters at the expense of AC Transit's minority bus riders.

The idea that AC Transit's minority riders might have a strong civil rights case against the MTC surfaced long before the Darensburg suit. As early as 1997, Kevin Siegel—a law student at Berkeley's Bolt Law School—made exactly that case. Fresh off the success of the Los Angeles Bus Riders Union's suit against the Los Angeles MTA, Kevin Siegel's essay "Discrimination in the Funding of Mass Transit Systems" suggested that a similar suit could be successful in the Bay Area. According to Siegel, one way to make a prima facie case of disparate impact discrimination was to look at the MTC's allocation of both capital and operating subsidies, normalized by rider and transit system. Basing their calculations on the constrained capital plans for BART and AC Transit from 1996 to 2005, Siegel and transit planner Thomas Rubin went on to argue that MTC subsidized BART passengers at a rate of 71 percent more than AC Transit riders ($4.98 for BART riders and $2.91 for AC Transit patrons). Siegel also suggested that riders could challenge the allocation of certain uncommitted and committed streams, whether those funds came from vehicle registration surcharges, or whether they came from the county sales taxes.[30]

In some ways, the exact origins of the Darensburg case remain something of a mystery. We do not know, for example, if it was Darensburg herself who initiated contact with Public Advocates, or whether it was the other way around. Similarly, we do not know whether it was one incident in particular or several that prompted Darensburg to take legal action. What is not disputed, however, is that throughout the trial, the image of Sylvia Darensburg loomed quite large. As the East Bay's own Rosa Parks, not only did Darensburg seem to embody an older tradition of civil rights activism, but she also seemed to embody an emergent movement in the East Bay focused on transportation justice, one that was eager to use the courts to advance its goals.[31]

For observers at the national level, the Darensburg suit may have seemed old hat. Ten years prior, in fact, the New York Urban League and the NYC Straphanger's Campaign had brought a similar suit against the New York Metropolitan Transportation Authority (MTA). In their suit, the New York Urban League challenged the MTA's decision to raise fares disproportionately on inner-city subway and bus riders, while seeking a far more modest fare hike for commuters riding Metronorth, a suburban rail service.[32] In New York, inner-city subway and bus services largely catered to low income and minority patrons. Metro-North service, on the other hand, catered to a more white and affluent clientele. While a general increase in fares might have been necessary,[33] the agency's decision to impose a relatively greater fare hike on inner-city bus and subway users seemed patently unfair. In light of this, the New York Urban League and the Straphanger's Campaign accused the NYMTA of violating Title VI of the 1964 Civil Rights Act and of enacting a policy that, if not discriminatory on its face, certainly had a disparate impact on minority bus and subway riders.

In 1994, a year earlier, the Los Angeles Bus Riders Union (BRU) had brought a similar class action lawsuit against the Los Angeles MTA. The issue was largely the same. In 1994, the Los Angeles MTA budgeted $123 million to expand the Pasadena Blue Line—a commuter rail line serving the largely suburban and relatively affluent area of Pasadena. The hope was that the expansion would attract new patrons and divert commuters from the city's already congested highways. Of course, transit advocacy groups such as the BRU were not opposed to expanding transit ridership. For the BRU, however, the MTA's decision to simultaneously reduce local bus service and raise local bus fares reeked of a blatant and cynical effort to transfer resources from poor people of color to the largely white and affluent residents of Pasadena.[34] Critics of the project found further justification, after it was revealed that the $123 million estimate for the construction of the Blue Line was almost exactly the amount of money accrued through the cost savings associated with the bus service reductions ($126 million). After winning a restraining order, the BRU also won a consent decree from the MTA stipulating a plan to reduce overcrowding, improve bus service, and expand the bus fleet by 15 percent.[35]

In many ways the 2005 Darensburg suit emerged in the context of an already established transportation justice movement. At the national level, this involved such organizations as the Transit Equity Network (TEN), Reconnecting America, and Smart Growth America. At the local level this involved such East Bay groups as Urban Habitat, the Alliance for AC Transit, Building Opportunities for Self-Sufficiency (BOSS), Communities for a Better Environment (CBE), and the Bay Area Transportation and Land Use Coalition (BATLUC).[36] Of course, support for the Darensburg suit also extended beyond the transportation justice community. In late 2005, in a letter to then MTC chairman Jon Rubin, both state assemblywoman Loni Hancock and federal House member Barbara Lee offered their firm support to Darensburg and what she represented.[37] East Bay transit riders, they argued in the letter, not only "deserved to be treated equitably" but also deserved both an "equitable subsidy of public dollars" and "equal access to a vital transit service."[38] Along with lawyers from Public Advocates, Darensburg's counsel team also included Bill Lann Lee, who had been the lead lawyer in the successful Los Angeles BRU suit against the Los Angeles MTA in 1995. He had also served as the assistant attorney general for civil rights under Bill Clinton. Despite a great deal of community support and an experienced legal counsel, judges at both the federal district court level and at the appellate court level ultimately ruled in favor of the MTC.[39] The arguments upon which these decisions were based bear closer examination.

Argumentation

The Darensburg suit went to trial on October 1, 2008. The presiding judge was Elizabeth Laporte, and the suit was tried in the United States District Court for the Northern District of California. As is customary in cases involving disparate impact discrimination, the trial followed a rather straightforward formula. Plaintiffs were asked to prove that the occurrence of certain outwardly neutral practices had a significantly adverse and disproportionate impact on minorities. If such an impact was proven, defendants were then required to demonstrate a substantial justification for undertaking the policies in dispute. Lastly, if defendants met this burden—often by designating such policies in terms of a "business necessity"—plaintiffs were then required to show that there existed an alternative practice that was both less racially disproportionate and equally effective.[40]

Over the course of the trial, the Darensburg council focused on three ostensibly neutral MTC practices that it believed disparately affected AC Transit's minority riders: the MTC's allocation of "uncommitted funds"; the MTC's allocation of "committed funds"; and the MTC's adoption of Resolution 3434: the Regional Transit Expansion Program (RTEP). The plaintiffs argued that in all three cases, the MTC used its discretion to allocate money to projects benefiting the predominantly white riders of BART and Caltrain, while doing nothing to stem service reductions and fare hikes at AC Transit.

With respect to "uncommitted funds," the Darensburg counsel focused on the MTC's use and allocation of federal funds provided by the Federal Highway Administration (FHWA). These funds included those authorized by the Surface Transportation Program (STP), the Congestion Mitigation and Air Quality Program (CMAQ), and the Transportation Enhancement Activity Program (TEA).[41] The plaintiffs argued that in each case, the MTC had made the decision to "artificially restrict the availability" of such funds and to ignore the obvious capital and operational needs of AC Transit.[42] The plaintiffs noted that in 2004/2005, the MTC received a "windfall" from both the CMAQ and STP programs. While the MTC directed a considerable amount of these additional funds to BART and Caltrain projects, none of these funds were allocated to AC Transit.[43] Similarly, the plaintiffs noted that in 2006, the MTC had taken the extraordinary step of allocating STP funds to BART in the form of preventative maintenance. This was a rather unusual practice, but it allowed BART to address a shortfall in its capital rehabilitation budget. Drawing on these examples, the plaintiffs argued that the MTC was behaving in ways that not only ignored the needs of AC Transit riders but also clearly gave preference to operators like BART and Caltrain and, by proxy, clearly gave a preference to the more affluent and white riders who patronized those systems.[44]

With respect to "committed funds," the plaintiffs focused on two areas: the MTC's allocation of FTA formula grants and the MTC's allocation of funds under the State Transportation Improvement Program (STIP).[45] While the MTC allocated FTA formula funds on the basis of a scoring system, the MTC's allocation of STIP funds was a more complicated process. In particular, the MTC was only able to allocate STIP funds after compiling and submitting a list of its priority projects to the California Transportation Commission (CTC).[46] During the trial, the plaintiffs took issue with both the scoring process by which the MTC directed federal formula money, as well as the way the MTC selected projects to receive STIP funding.[47] In both cases, the plaintiffs argued that the MTC gave preference to capital projects and rail expansions, while neglecting the operational needs of AC Transit.

Lastly, the plaintiffs took issue with the MTC's adoption of Resolution 3434: the Regional Transit Expansion Program (RTEP).[48] The MTC adopted Resolution 3434 in 2001. At its simplest, Resolution 3434 was a list of high-priority rail and express bus projects to be included in the larger RTP. Of all their arguments, the plaintiff's case against Resolution 3434 was perhaps the strongest and the most straightforward. The plaintiffs argued that the overrepresentation of rail projects in Resolution 3434 functioned to have a disparate impact on AC Transit's largely minority riders. In making this point, the plaintiffs highlighted the distinctive racial character of Bay Area transit. In the Bay Area, bus transit largely catered to minority riders. Rail passengers, by comparison, were more likely to be white.[49] By dint of this fact, the overrepresentation of rail projects in Resolution 3434 necessarily benefited white riders more than riders of color.[50] The plaintiffs went on to cite a number of instances in which Resolution 3434 had clearly excluded bus projects in favor of rail projects. In 2001, the plaintiffs noted, AC Transit had requested funds under Resolution 3434 for a Bus Rapid Transit project connecting Berkeley to San Leandro. They also requested funding for ten additional "bus only projects" along several transit corridors in the East Bay. Of the nearly $1 billion requested, AC Transit received only $200 million.[51] Ultimately, the 2001 RTP included five BART projects, two Caltrain projects, and only parts of two AC Transit/Bus Rapid Transit projects. This same disparity appeared in 2005. As Thomas Rubin testified, nearly 95 percent of all Resolution 3434 project funding in 2005 went to rail projects, while less than 5 percent went to bus projects.[52]

On March 27, 2009, the court submitted its verdict. Judge Laporte concluded that the plaintiffs had failed to prove disparate impact discrimination with respect to the MTC's allocation of committed and uncommitted funds. The court did, however, raise concerns with respect to the disparate impact implications of Resolution 3434. Judge Laporte confirmed that Resolution 3434 funds in 2005 resulted in greater support for rail projects and less support for bus projects. Moreover, given the racial breakdown of bus versus rail transit in the Bay Area, Judge Laporte agreed that Resolution 3434 necessarily had a disparate impact on minority bus riders in the East Bay. Despite this finding, the court also concluded that the MTC offered a compelling justification for this policy. This justification rested on the MTC's statutory need (i.e., "business necessity") to "balance competing interests and satisfy diverse and sometimes conflicting mandates."[53] Apart from its duty to AC Transit's minority riders, the MTC had other duties. Many of these duties, in fact, were defined by federal statute. Citing

Title 23 and Section 134 of the U.S. Federal Code on Highways, the court noted
that the MTC's priorities and duties were quite clear. These duties included:

(A) Supporting the economic vitality of the metropolitan area, especially by
enabling global competitiveness, productivity, and efficiency;
(B) Increase the safety for motorized and nonmotorized users;
(C) Increase the security of the transportation system for motorized and
nonmotorized users;
(D) Increase the accessibility and mobility of people and for freight;
(E) Protect and enhance the environment, promote energy conservation,
improve the quality of life, and promote consistency between transportation
improvements and State and local planned growth and economic
development patterns;
(F) Enhance the integration and connectivity of the transportation system,
across and between modes, for people and freight;
(G) Promote efficient system management and operation; and
(H) Emphasize the preservation of the existing transportation system.[54]

Given these duties, the MTC's adoption of Resolution 3434 made perfect
sense. As the MTC argued, expanding BART and Caltrain service was central to
meeting their statutory duty to enhance regional connectivity, increase global
competitiveness, and move people from single-occupancy vehicles into transit.
In a veiled reference to the proposed Oakland Airport Connector, Kimon Manolius—the MTC's lead defense attorney—noted that reliable rail access to the
region's airports was both in line with the goals of reducing congestion, cutting
down greenhouse gas emissions, and improving regional efficiency.[55] In siding
with the MTC, the court not only endorsed the "business necessity" of Resolution 3434 but also advanced the MTCs broader point: that the benefits of expanded rail service would certainly not be limited to white riders alone, but the
East Bay's minority riders would also stand to gain. As Kimon Manolius argued
in his closing statement, for a minority rider traveling from Oakland to Sonoma
County or from Berkeley to Warm Springs an expanded rail system would far
outweigh the benefits of simply more local buses.[56] As Manolius added, the idea
of singling out AC Transit for "special treatment" or as the "victim of injustice"
not only ran counter to the MTC's duties to regional connectivity and global
competitiveness, but it ran counter to the demands of minority riders who were
no less entitled to extended rail service.

In 2011, the Ninth Circuit Court of Appeals not only affirmed the lower
court's ruling against Darensburg, but it doubled down on this last point. As
Judge Barry Silverman argued in the opinion:

Although Plaintiffs' statistical evidence shows that minorities make a greater
percentage of the regional population of bus riders than rail riders, it does not

necessarily follow that an expansion plan that emphasizes rail projects over bus projects will harm minorities. Plaintiff's theory forecloses altogether the possibility that MTC could devise *any* rail-centered expansion that could benefit minority riders, while the evidence shows that Bay Area minorities already benefit substantially from rail service. . . . Not only does Plaintiffs statistical evidence fail to prove discrimination, but their circumstantial evidence does not support any inference that MTC's adoption on the Regional Transit Expansion Plan was motivated by racial bias.[57]

In a concurring opinion Judge John Noonan offered an even more tersely worded attack on the entire premise of the case. Not only had the plaintiffs ignored the MTC's broader duties to regional connectivity, or the possibility that rail expansion might benefit minority riders, but they had also ignored the reality of racial progress.

The court is asked to assume the identity and interests of various parts of the population characterized by the litigants in terms of categories created by the racial origins of the persons living here today. Using these categories—hopelessly outdated in the Bay Area—the litigation presents a controversy in which the court is asked to determine the fairness of future plans dependent on at least seven factors which the court would have to measure, combine and evaluate as a balanced or unbalanced combination. The twentieth century racial categories so confidently deployed no longer correspond to American life among the young. . . . What is true of the young is already characteristic of the Bay Area where social change has been fostered by liberal political attitudes, and a culture of tolerance. An individual bigot may be found, perhaps even pockets of racists. The notion of a Bay Area board bent on racist goals is a specter that only desperate litigation could entertain.[58]

In the years that have followed, there have been any number of responses to the Darensburg ruling. Within the transportation justice community, the most common response has been to refute Judge Noonan's view that racism in transportation policy requires explicit "racial animus." As Aaron Golub, Richard Marcantonio, and Thomas Sanchez have noted, such a view fundamentally overlooks the legacy of past racial injustice. Using an "environmental racism framework" they argue that "a closer look at the historical record" of the East Bay reveals how ostensibly race-neutral policies—like those of the MTC—continue to reproduce and reinforce a racialized geography of exclusion. Where the legacies of white flight, redlining, and racial discrimination are at the root of the East Bay's contemporary racial disparities, "race neutral policies" like Resolution 3434 do little but reinforce inequity.[59] Writing in response to the Darensburg ruling, Alex Karner and Deb Niemeier argue much the same thing. In addition, however, they also suggest that given the "incredibly high bar" facing plaintiffs in Title VI jurisprudence, transportation justice advocates would do well to think beyond the courts.[60]

In 2010, AC Transit's Board of Directors faced its own mini–civil rights controversy. As noted earlier, 2010 was a horrible year for AC Transit. By the fall, the agency had already cut service twice, and more cuts were on their way.[61] On September 22, AC Transit's planning staff presented the governing board with yet another list of lines to be cut in December. These cuts were to be the deepest yet and promised to reduce service to levels not seen since 1996. Given the extent of such cuts, AC Transit's planning staff—as required by federal and local statute—conducted a preliminary Title VI analysis. Their analysis selected a number of routes to be cut, while also identifying a number of routes that were ostensibly deemed "untouchable." These latter routes included Route 26 operating in West Oakland, Route 76 in East Oakland, and Route 45 in North Richmond. Despite having relatively low ridership, these routes operated in areas with a high concentration of minorities and low instances of car ownership. AC Transit's staff proposed retaining these three lines to obviate a Title VI legal challenge. On September 22, AC Transit's staff presented this preliminary analysis to the board and to the public.[62] At the public board meeting, observers were treated to a heated exchange between Greg Harper—an elected board member, from the city of Emeryville—and the agency's equity analyst, Tina Spencer. Harper challenged the validity of the preliminary Title VI analysis and questioned aloud why the agency ought to spare poor performing lines like Route 26, while axing popular lines like Route 14. The exchange proceeded as follows:

HARPER: Staying on the subject of Title VI, I have some real problems with how Title VI was brought to bear in North County. [Title VI] is supposedly put there to save the 26 which has 652 riders [per weekend day]. [At the same time] we are cutting the 14 which has 2,000 riders and the 62 which has 2,000 riders and both routes go through very low income areas . . . I'm trying to figure out how this is working.

SPENCER: Well it's only a preliminary analysis . . . , it was based on the identification of a map. We basically looked at the map and matched it up with census tracts of low income and minority neighborhoods. We realized that in certain neighborhoods there were no alternatives at all. In West County, there . . . were potentially hundreds of blocks with no service and we knew that that would be a problem in the future when we did the full Title VI analysis. . . . We do realize that we are going to have to do more analysis when we get more data available to us. . . . We didn't say [however] that the 300 people who are on the bus in West County have more or less of a right to the bus than people on the 14, that was not what we looked at when we did this preliminary review.

HARPER: Well that is kind of how it looks like it came out. I mean, I think when you save a bus with 652 people on it and you are cutting buses with 2,000 people on it, you better damn well have a good explanation for why in the world that's happening.[63]

For Greg Harper, the Title VI analysis conducted by AC Transit staff was obviously flawed. In a system that was 78 percent minority, why, Harper asked, would riders of Route 26 have more of a right to their bus than low-income riders of Route 14?[64] Why was it fair to eliminate service for the 2,023 weekend riders on Route 62 only to save a line with 652 weekend riders? AC Transit's analysis, Harper seemed to suggest, also completely missed the fact that just over 34 percent of all AC Transit trips involved a transfer—and the plurality of those were either to or from another AC Transit vehicle.[65] Who wasn't to say—Harper might have asked—that those same West Oakland riders on Route 26 wouldn't find themselves without a Route 62 to which to transfer? The very idea of designating individual lines as "Title VI lines" belied a much simpler truth: the entire system ought to be considered Title VI.

While AC Transit ultimately postponed the December cuts, Greg Harper's broader concerns with the application of Title VI to AC Transit are notable because in some ways they highlight the rather narrow notion of equity upon which Title VI analyses can rest—whether applied at the level of a single carrier or at the regional scale. In the case of AC Transit that narrowness is obvious. While preserving Route 62 at the expense of Route 14 might immunize AC Transit from a Title VI claim, there are few people who would describe that action as advancing equity or justice—even in the narrowest of terms. Indeed, at the scale of an individual bus system, the application of Title VI analysis becomes even stranger when applied elsewhere. One can imagine applying a similar analysis to a transit system that is equal in all respects except one—the racial demographics of riders are reversed. Where the ridership is 78 percent white, the idea of protecting those routes with the highest percentage of minority riders would seem no less ludicrous.

In the case of Darensburg, the narrowness of the Title VI analyses advanced by the plaintiffs may be less obvious. The Darensburg case, of course, hinged on a rather simple question: Does the MTC's preference for rail transit in Resolution 3434 constitute racial discrimination? Where the district court found that Resolution 3434 was justifiable as a "business necessity,"—despite having a disparate impact on minority riders—the appellate court found little evidence of any racial discrimination at all, intentional or otherwise. To the extent that transportation justice advocates have attacked these rulings, they have largely limited their attack to countering the views of Judge Noonan—whether by pointing to the region's long history of racial inequity or by challenging the notion—advanced by Noonan himself—that we now live in a color-blind society. Of course, for those who followed the Darensburg case, the rulings obviously raised yet other issues worth challenging. These hinged less on the distinction between intentional and disparate impact discrimination or the region's legacy of racial exclusion and more on the purpose of transit itself. For the MTC that purpose remained fairly clear. As the district court revealed, the MTC's first statutory duty was to enhance "global competitiveness" and "economic vitality." When the MTC directs new investments into transportation, it measures the impact of such investments on those lines. One can, obviously, imagine any number of *other* ways to judge the value of transportation investments—whether in their capacity to pull people out of poverty, to increase the mobility of the transit dependent, or enhance racial integration. While Judge Noonan's tortured reading of race relations is certainly worth countering, so too is the equally tortured view of public transportation advanced by the MTC—a view that sees public transportation as simply a tool for enhancing the region's "global competitiveness."[66] Countering this latter view, of course, means going beyond the narrow tests associated with Title VI litigation. Indeed it means going beyond the traditional civil rights frame that continues to dominate debates on transportation justice. It, instead, means asking about a broader set of rights and how such rights might reframe how the MTC defines a "business necessity."

The Limits of Legal Rights

Wherever public transit is the subject of debate, one invariably encounters the observer for whom the very idea of rights or rights talk appears an unhelpful distraction. As this observer may argue, where the goal is to improve urban transit, the hoary language of rights "must simply be avoided." As the above cases suggest, reality can be uncooperative. This is particularly true when that reality involves the courts. To the extent that transit agencies must regularly face questions of liability and accusations of discrimination, rights and courtroom debates are inescapable. Indeed, as this chapter shows, the courts often play a central role in shaping what transit looks like. They dictate everything from where transit agencies place bus stops to the ability of these agencies to invest in new projects. For those interested in shaping transit policy or defending the dignity of transit patrons, the lesson is thus clear enough: the courts remain a central arena of both struggle and debate. Of course, what should be equally clear is that such debates are often limited by the very types of rights that the courts recognize. Where tort law creates legal entitlements and duties aimed at addressing the harms of negligent behavior, the primary debates are often rather narrow. They are over whether a bus is more akin to a "sealed steel cocoon" or a public park, whether a bus driver is akin to a prison guard, and whether the location of a bus stop can constitute a dangerous condition of public property. To the degree these debates deal with culpability and the cost of negligence, they are debates that deal with cost in the narrowest sense. These are the cost in damages accrued by the "individual monad, withdrawn into himself."[67] Part of the argument of this chapter and of this book more broadly is that the debates that arise in legal disputes over the civil rights of minority transit riders are no less narrow. Following the steps associated with Title VI compliance, these are debates on both the nature of discrimination—whether intentional or disparate impact—and on how to address transit policies that are found to be racially discriminatory. This focus on Title VI law is understandable. For transportation justice advocates eager to use the courts to secure a more just transportation system, Title VI remains, as Alex Karner and Deb Niemeier note, the only "related law that creates enforceable legal rights."[68] While Title VI law is useful, the above cases also suggest that where the focus is limited to Title VI—and thus to questions of racial discrimination alone—debates on transportation justice can appear quite narrow. Indeed, such debates seem to ignore the very questions that appear to matter most: namely, what is public transportation for, or more importantly, how do we reconcile a more just public transportation system with the broader political economy of cities and the drive for "global economic competitiveness"?

For those who wish—such as the board member quoted earlier—that we might avoid rights talk in favor of simply "getting a better transit system for everyone," the above cases indicate how quickly that logic breaks down. For every new bus stop, route adjustment, or service cut, we find rights talk. Rights appear in the form of Title VI regulations, tort claims, and budget allocations. Where judges must routinely delineate where the rights of riders begin and the duties of transit agencies end, judges play a central role in shaping what transit looks like. To ignore rights is to ignore this fact. For those interested in transforming transit, the lesson that emerges from the above cases, however, is also a cautious one. Indeed it is a lesson that finds no better expression than in the dictum from Anatole France: "the law, in its majestic equality, forbids the rich as well as the poor to sleep under bridges, to beg in the streets, and to steal bread."[69] As I understand it, France's point is twofold: first, the law and justice are not always coterminous, and, second, the law is only as just as the types of rights it has been forced to recognize. As the following chapter attempts to demonstrate, the fight for transportation justice in the East Bay has taken this lesson seriously and has not only engaged in any number of fights outside of the courts but has often done so by going beyond—even if implicitly—the language of civil rights, à la *Darensburg v. MTC.*

CHAPTER 2

Transportation Justice and the Alliance for AC Transit

The bourgeoisie has subjected the country to the rule of the towns. It has created enormous cities, has greatly increased the urban population as compared to the rural, and thus has rescued a considerable part of the population from the idiocy of rural life.

—Karl Marx and Friedrich Engels, *The Communist Manifesto*, 1848

On Tuesday, February 14, 2010, the Federal Transportation Administration (FTA) dropped a bombshell. After a brief investigation, the FTA announced that it had decided to pull $70 million in stimulus funds from the Bay Area Rapid Transit district's planned Oakland Airport Connector (OAC)—a 3.2-mile elevated train slated to connect Oakland's Airport to an existing BART rail station. The FTA's logic was clear—BART had failed to conduct an adequate "equity analysis" measuring the OAC's impact on minority and low-income communities.[1] As the FTA's Peter Rogoff noted, in the absence of such an analysis, BART stood in violation of Title VI of the 1964 Civil Rights Act.[2] The FTA's decision was the first of its kind and was telling in a number of ways. At its broadest, the decision served to remind public agencies across the country that not only would stimulus projects have to be "shovel ready," but they would also have to be equitable.[3] In the East Bay, the FTA's decision was notable for yet another reason. Namely, it marked "a rare victory" in the fight and demand for "transportation justice."[4] In the East Bay, that fight and demand had, in many ways, already developed a strong following. Alongside such groups as Public Advocates, TransForm, Urban Habitat, and Genesis—which had spearheaded the initial civil rights complaint—the East Bay boasted an increasingly vocal community of activists for whom transportation justice was as much a slogan as it was a veritable political project. This chapter asks two simple questions: What, exactly, does transportation justice mean in the East Bay? What type of political project is it?

In the East Bay, the demand for transportation justice has taken a number of forms. In addition to FTA complaints, it has congealed in public protests, detailed policy papers, and the civil rights lawsuit *Darensburg v. MTC*. Of course, it has also appeared as a guiding principle for any number of local advocacy organizations—from groups like Urban Habitat to smaller outfits like the Alliance of Californians for Community Empowerment (ACCE) Bus Riders Union. In whatever form it has taken, the demand for transportation justice has almost always started by foregrounding the need for a more "just" and "equitable" allocation of transportation funds. In the East Bay, this has largely meant a Rawlsian commitment to what transportation scholar Todd Litman has deemed "vertical equity"—that is, a commitment to distributing transportation resources in ways "that favor economically or socially disadvantaged groups."[5]

The fight against the OAC was, in many ways, fought on precisely these terms. At an expected cost of $500 million, the problem with the OAC was not only that it skirted FTA Title VI rules, but that it directed transportation resources in ways that were wholly misaligned with even the most basic principles of social justice. Pitched at a moment when AC Transit's predominantly low-income and minority riders were facing yet another round of service cuts, BART's OAC aimed at improving transit service for the very types of people who needed it least: those wealthy enough to purchase a plane ticket.[6] Of course, for many transportation justice advocates, this was only part of the problem. In addition to shifting resources to the affluent, the OAC marked the ascendance of what seemed a dangerously narrow vision of both public transportation and public transportation's role in the city. Designed by an Austrian firm known for its ski lifts, the OAC was built as a so-called legacy project aimed at allowing Oakland to finally "catch up" to neighboring San Francisco, which had built a similar "airport connector" a decade prior.[7] Rather than improving transportation in any meaningful way, the OAC's primary function was as a marketing tool and as a way for the East Bay to improve its competitive position in the global hunt for investment capital. As this chapter argues, while the fight for transportation justice in the East Bay continues to be a fight aimed at both advancing a more equitable distribution of transportation funds and at defending the civil rights of the East Bay's minority riders—by both enforcing FTA Title VI rules and in pushing lawsuits like *Darensburg v. MTC*—it has also been a fight over the idea of the city itself and transportation's role in it. In making this argument, the chapter focuses on the rise of the Alliance for AC Transit—one of the first transportation justice groups in the East Bay—as well as the range of organizations in the East Bay that have developed since. The chapter ends by remarking on the vision of urban life and public transportation that has emerged, however implicitly, in their struggles for transportation justice. As with Lefebvre's utopian demand for a "right to the city," fights for equity in public transportation have also been fights against alienation, isolation, and what Marx and Engels should have called the "idiocy of urban life."

The activism against the OAC was hardly surprising. In many ways, it fit within a long tradition in the Bay Area of protesting new transportation investments. San Francisco had been ground zero in the anti-freeway revolts of the 1960s. In 1959, after four years of protests from residents in communities such as Glenn Park, Sunset, Telegraph Hill, and the Marina District, the San Francisco Board of Supervisors famously blocked seven of nine freeways scheduled for construction in the city. The decision marked a stunning defeat for the California highway lobby, and it spoke to the resolve of local organizers determined to protect their community's quality of life.[8] In the East Bay the story was similar. When construction on BART began in 1964, it met with almost immediate opposition from both minority groups in West Oakland and resident groups in Berkeley.[9] Indeed, protests from Berkeley residents successfully forced BART to redraw its plans for the city completely. Rather than running an elevated route through the city center, BART was forced to construct the rail below ground—at even higher costs to the agency.[10] In the late 1970s and early 1980s, Berkeley's Independent Living Movement focused a considerable amount of energy on making transportation more accessible to the disabled.[11] The fact that transportation has frequently been a political flashpoint for communities in the Bay Area should come as little surprise. Where new highways may open up new regions to development, they afflict others with blight and congestion. Where commuter rail projects like BART can promote regional integration, they can also make certain business districts redundant.[12] And, similarly, while certain bus designs may meet the needs of one population, they may restrict the mobility of others. The heated debates that so often arise around transit investments are thus rooted in justifiable concerns about who will benefit and who, in turn, will lose out. In the Bay Area, the idea of "transportation justice" has been a relatively recent addition to these debates. Nevertheless, there have been a growing number of organizations in the region for whom it has already become an important organizing principle. In the East Bay, one of the earliest of these groups was the Alliance for AC Transit and Bus Riders Union. Its story is an important one—and one that has thus far garnered scant attention.

The Alliance for AC Transit and Bus Riders Union

The Alliance for AC Transit and Bus Riders Union began in response to a crisis. In 1995, 40 percent of all transit agencies in the United States either cut service or raised fares. As is often the case, the crisis was political in origin. The Republican takeover of Congress in 1995 not only saw sweeping cuts to social services but also equally deep cuts in federal aid to local transit agencies. Between 1994 and 1996, federal operating aid dropped from $802 million to just over $350 million.[13] In 1998, all federal aid was phased out completely. For agencies like AC Transit, the loss of such aid was devastating. With $5.5 million less in federal operating aid at the end of 1995, AC Transit was forced both to raise fares and to cut service.[14]

In late 1995, a group of local activists from Oakland and Berkeley formed the Alliance for AC Transit. According to founding member John Katz, the Alliance began as an offshoot of a larger progressive coalition. That coalition—led by Alameda County supervisor Keith Carson—had formed to defend local social service providers against the perceived threats posed by the Republican takeover. The Alliance for AC Transit began as the transit subcommittee of that larger coalition. According to Katz, the Alliance emerged as a separate entity following the events of June 16, 1996, when a still nascent group of transit supporters organized a successful rally in downtown Oakland in protest of AC Transit's slated service cuts.[15] In addition to attracting several politicians, the rally also drew the attention of activists such as Charlie Betcher. Earlier in the year, Betcher had started to organize a local Bus Riders Union. Drawing inspiration from a similar organization in Los Angeles, Betcher aimed at organizing local bus riders to advocate for better service. As Katz recalled, the rally on June 16 served as the catalyst. Not only was it successful in drawing attention to the severity of service cuts, but it was successful in proving to all involved that there was "a constituency to try and keep bus service at a high level."[16]

By 1998, the Alliance for AC Transit had 115 members and the support of eleven affiliated organizations, including Albany/El Cerrito Access, AFSCME Local 3916, ATU Local 192, the Center for Independent Living, Energy Services Network, Gray Panthers, Regional Alliance for Transit, Sierra Club, and the United Seniors of Oakland and Alameda County.[17] By 1998, Charlie Betcher's Bus Riders Union had, in many ways, become something of a subcommittee of the Alliance. It operated as the more grassroots wing of the organization by focusing on the recruitment of low-income bus riders.[18] By 1998, the Alliance had also absorbed a group called "People on the Bus"—a group of largely upper-middle-class riders that had formed in 1992 in response to cuts to Transbay bus service.[19] The stated goals of the Alliance for AC Transit and Bus Riders Union were as follows:

1) To advocate for adequate funding for AC Transit's local, transbay, and paratransit services.
2) To educate the public and decision-makers about the need for public bus transit.
3) To advocate for the interest of AC Transit riders.
4) To develop a constituency supportive of AC Transit.[20]

Over the course of a decade, the Alliance spent a considerable amount of its energy on the first goal—namely, making sure AC Transit received its fair share of funding. Indeed, within a year of forming, one of the organization's first actions was to fire off a letter lambasting a draft of the MTC's Regional Transportation Plan. Citing the plan's overemphasis on highway projects, the Alliance accused the MTC of neglecting AC Transit's minority riders and of adopting policies that would lead to a Bay Area resembling Los Angeles "more [than] it resembled the Bay Area."[21] After a failed campaign in 1996 to support the passage of Ballot Measure JJ—a new parcel tax for AC Transit—in 1998, the Alliance was part of a winning coalition that successfully lobbied the Metropolitan Transportation Commission to redirect $375 million from highway projects to local transit service ($51.5 million of which went directly to AC Transit).[22] In 2000, it played a key role in the passage of Measure B—a ballot measure that allocated $256 million of local sales tax revenue to AC Transit over twenty years.[23] Similarly, in 2002, the Alliance helped direct $7.4 million to AC Transit operations through their lobbying efforts around Measure AA—a $24 parcel tax on all real property in Alameda and Contra Costa Counties.[24]

Apart from securing money, the alliance also engaged in a number of initiatives that had decidedly more abstract goals. These initiatives focused on educating the public about transit, building a constituency supportive of local transit service, and defining the rights to which East Bay bus riders were entitled. As much as these initiatives were aimed at improving service, they were also aimed at developing a sense of community.

In 2001, the Alliance for AC Transit and Bus Riders Union published *Bus Riding 101: A Guide for Discerning Travelers*. This forty-two-page booklet was intended as a "how-to guide" for Bay Area residents intimidated by East Bay bus transit. With chapters on "Bus Identification," "Transfers," "Bicycles," and "Transbay Services," the booklet instructed "first time riders on how to avoid cross-cultural gaffes" and how to navigate a complex system of routes.[25] It even included a quiz at the end on "Bus Etiquette." For the Alliance, riding the bus was not only an "urban skill," but one that they had a duty to share. Along with *Bus Riding 101*, the Alliance also published a monthly newsletter, *Omnibus*. The *Omnibus* reported on the AC Transit board's latest actions and on upcoming ballot initiates or service changes. The *Omnibus* also included film reviews, individual rider profiles, and a section called "Bus Buzz," which published rider responses to questions ranging from where riders liked to sit on the bus to the impact of recent service cuts (Figure 1). The *Omnibus* had a number of goals. Apart from keeping members of the Alliance abreast of the latest policy developments, it also offered members a forum through which to engage each other as members of a community with a shared interest in better transit.

One of the Alliance's most notable campaigns was its fight to prevent the relocation of AC Transit's main transfer station out of downtown Oakland. Located at the corner of 14th and Broadway, and only one block from City Hall, the station was arguably situated at the very heart of the city center. In 1997,

Question: How have you been affected by the October 10, 1999 schedule and route changes on the bus lines you ride?		
Nura J. El Cerrito	Line 7	It takes forever to come or it drives right by. The space between when buses arrive is too long on weekdays. I don't ride it on weekends.
Joseph H. Oakland	Line 40	I haven't noticed much change but it needs to be improved. It should run more frequently, like once every ten minutes or so, because it's a basic line on a very busy thoroughfare.
Hilda K. Alameda	Line 51	Service could be better, but if it wasn't there I'd really be stuck. I try as much as possible to ride in safe areas and not too late at night so the schedule changes don't really affect me much.
Julia B. Albany	Lines 7 and 52	Once an hour on Sunday on the #7 is not often enough if you depend on it for work. Also when they claimed they were extending the 52, it was only the 52L. In fact they cut the regular 52 schedule so it doesn't go down Cedar at all after 5 or 6 p.m., and not at all on weekends.
Lillian D. Berkeley	Line 64	Coming from Shattuck and Kittredge the #64 is not running south on Shattuck anymore, but on the campus. So I have to wait for the #40 to go back to Dwight and Telegraph.
Peter S. Kensington	Lines 7 and 67	We like the security of knowing we can count on the #7 on weekends as well as weekdays. I'm happy to see the #67 come back on the weekends, and I like the fact that you can take a bicycle on it. If there's a route change, AC Transit makes a point of notifying people with posters and signs. I wish more people would ride AC. I've been riding it for 45 years and my son has for 18 years.

FIGURE 1. "Bus Buzz" column by Ruth C. Hadlock. Reprinted from *Omnibus* 3, no. 2 (1999), 4.

Oakland's downtown business community proposed that the city move the station to an off-street and slightly less central location. A new station, the business community argued, promised to both relieve congestion and to stem endemic loitering. Their proposal was built on a study released in February 1997 by the Broadway Corridor Committee—a committee of downtown property owners. In their report, they observed that AC Transit's transfer station not only contributed to "congested sidewalks" and the "perception of loitering and litter," but that such realities posed a serious threat to both attracting investment to the area and to capitalizing on the economic windfall of the tech industries in Silicon Valley.[26] The Alliance rejected these findings, as well as the report's conclusion to move the station. The report, the Alliance argued, was little more than a veiled attempt to push low-income bus riders and people of color out of the city center.[27] The Alliance emphatically believed that the station's current location was the most convenient, and it also believed in the importance of having transit and bus riders be a visible presence in downtown Oakland. Having the transfer station in the heart of the city, the Alliance suggested, made it clear that both transit and transit riders were, in fact, important to urban life.[28] Bowing to the Alliance's sustained pressure, in December 1998 the Oakland City Council voted 6–0 against moving the popular bus station. Over the next several years, the Alliance became a central partner in the eventual redesigning of the facility—ultimately achieving wider sidewalks and canopies for bus riders at the original location.[29] Around the same time, the Alliance emerged as a leading advocate in a campaign related to reinstating Oakland's long-neglected bus shelter program. As many noted, bus riders in Oakland were regularly forced to wait for buses in the rain. After sustained pressure from the Alliance, Oakland's bus shelter program was finally restored in 2003. In both the campaign for bus shelters and its campaign to keep a downtown bus station, the Alliance's argument was clear: not only did transit riders deserve a safe and dry place to wait for the bus, but they also had a right to be in the heart of the city.[30]

Although the Alliance for AC Transit and Bus Riders Union often worked through official channels, at other times its activism was more ad hoc. In 2000, for example, Steve Geller, a retired engineer and a longtime member of the Alliance, started a guerrilla signage campaign. In this campaign Geller spent months printing and photocopying transit schedules, encasing them in hard plastic and using zip-ties to attach them to bus stops throughout the East Bay. Bus riders, the argument went, were entitled to see up-to-date timetables and to know when the bus was set to arrive or when it was late (Figure 2). While AC Transit initially expressed disapproval—even threatening legal action—it was not too long until AC Transit began its own signage campaign, perhaps out of embarrassment.[31] In 2000, in another memorable example of this more ad hoc approach, Charlie Betcher—who had founded the Bus Riders Union in 1997—began a campaign for a Bus Riders Bill of Rights. The proposed charter included nine statutes:

1) The right to courteous, competent service at all times
2) The right to a clean, well-functioning bus
3) The right to buses that arrive and depart according to schedule
4) The right to be seated, or holding on to some fixed support, before the bus starts
5) The right to have the lift or kneeler lowered on request
6) The right to be picked up when waiting at a bus stop
7) The right to have current bus schedules for that line available on the bus
8) The right to hear audible announcements about main cross streets and transfer points
9) The right to have a procedure for filing complaints, compliments, or suggestions, that is simple, timely, and responsive.[32]

FIGURE 2. "Steve Geller's Guerrilla Signposting Campaign" by Allen Stross, in which Geller attaches a schedule to a Berkeley pole. Reprinted from *Omnibus* 4, no. 1 (2000), 1.

Endorsed by the United Seniors of Oakland and Alameda County, the Oakland City Council and the Berkeley Transportation Commission, Betcher's Bill of Rights aimed at both asserting and securing the dignity of East Bay transit riders. Rude treatment, bus delays, and unreadable schedules were not merely inconveniencing; they were also, according to Betcher, a violation of what transit riders were owed. While Betcher's Bill of Rights was neither endorsed by AC Transit nor the Metropolitan Transportation Commission, its symbolic import was notable—as was its appeal to rights—in reframing the fight for better bus transit as a fight for the dignity of riders.

Over the course of a decade, the Alliance encountered its fair share of challenges. Some of these challenges came from predictable sources, such as those associated with a rigid state tax structure and the lasting effects of Proposition 13, as well as the challenges associated with a constituency of supporters with meager resources and little free time. Other challenges, however, came from less predictable sources. These were often challenges from other progressive groups, many of whom had either divergent political goals or starkly different priorities. In 1998, for example, the Alliance for AC Transit and Bus Riders Union found itself at odds with the Sierra Club over Measure B. Although Measure B promised to put millions of dollars toward AC Transit's operating costs, the Sierra Club and other environmental groups opposed it, citing the billion or so dollars that the measure put toward "environmentally destructive highway projects."[33] Similarly, in 1999, the Alliance found itself in disagreement with a Berkeley City Council intent on forcing AC Transit to convert its diesel buses to compressed natural gas—a costly undertaking that would only exacerbate AC Transit's ongoing financial struggles.[34] In 1998, the Alliance even ran up against opposition to its bus shelter initiative when Oakland's City Council voted 5–3 against starting a program because it was in violation of the city's ban on outdoor advertising. In order to save the city money, the Alliance had pushed for a bus shelter program funded entirely by advertising revenue. The fight for better transit, in these instances, was not a fight against conservatives or libertarians but against other progressives.

Lastly, some of the Alliance's challenges were internal to the organization itself. As John Katz, the Alliance's first president, noted, one of those was a tension between the more grassroots work of organizing people—often around service cuts—and the separate work of effecting broader policy change.[35]

> One of the big struggles that we had, or tension we had, is making sure that people at the grassroots understood what the real source of the problem was and didn't start pushing their anger at AC Transit when AC Transit was just the deliverer of bad news . . . and that they should really aim higher: first at MTC, which was sort of the quasi villain, but the real problem was the state tax structure, state government and the federal government, not with agencies involved in delivering these cutbacks.[36]

In 2006, and perhaps for the reasons noted above, the Alliance for AC Transit and Bus Riders Union dissolved. As Katz noted, by 2006 much of the work that the Alliance had been doing was being done by other groups. More importantly, these groups were doing it better. This was especially true at the policy level. The legacy of the Alliance for AC Transit and the Bus Riders Union was, however, an important one. They were the lead advocates behind improving Oakland's principle transfer station at 14th and Broadway and were key proponents in restarting Oakland's bus shelter program. In 1998, they were part of a larger coalition of organizations that successfully lobbied to redirect $375 million from highways to transit. In both 2000 and 2002, they helped pass ballot initiatives providing direct financial support to AC Transit. Over the course of a decade, the Alliance played a key role in any number of local debates on transportation justice. For the Alliance, transportation justice meant not only securing transit funding but also organizing riders—through newsletters, meetings, and protests—to demand a range of rights: rights to courteous treatment, to timely service, to bus shelters, and to remain a visible part of downtown Oakland rather than be shunted off to the periphery—which business owners seemed to prefer.

Urban Habitat, TransForm, Genesis, and ACCE

After 2006, a range of groups emerged to take up the Alliance's work. These included such organizations as Urban Habitat, TransForm, Genesis, and the ACCE Bus Riders Union. Of all these groups, Urban Habitat was perhaps the most prominent. Founded in 1989 by activist and regional planner Carl Anthony, Urban Habitat began as an attempt to bridge the gap between fights for racial equity and those for environmental sustainability. Urban Habitat's focus on transportation justice began in earnest in 2003 when it emerged as the lead convener of the Transportation Justice Working Group (TJWG)—a forum for nonprofit, labor, civil, and faith-based groups in the East Bay committed to working for transit equity.[37] Since 2003, Urban Habitat's transportation justice work concentrated largely on the regional scale, focusing its efforts on reforming the Metropolitan Transportation Commission (MTC). For Urban Habitat, the MTC's role in perpetuating transit inequity was a significant one. As the designated metropolitan planning organization (MPO) for the nine-county Bay Area, the MTC was, since its inception in 1970, the lead authority in directing federal and state money toward local transportation projects. Every four years the agency was tasked with updating a regional transportation plan (RTP), which outlined the agency's funding priorities for the next twenty-five years. For Urban Habitat, the fight for transportation justice largely meant demanding that the RTP better reflect the needs of minority and low-income transit riders. In 2005, Urban Habitat publicized a study suggesting that a great deal of work was needed. As the report showed, the MTC's funding of mass transit was hardly equitable. The study found that while Caltrain and BART riders enjoyed subsidies of $13.79 and $6.14 per trip, respectively, AC Transit riders only received a subsidy of $2.78.[38] As Urban Habitat made clear, Caltrain—the carrier with the highest proportion of white riders—received the highest state subsidy per trip. Conversely, AC Transit—the carrier with the fewest white riders—received the lowest.[39] Apart from bolstering Urban Habitat's focus on the MTC, the study became a key feature in the 2005 civil rights lawsuit *Darensburg v. MTC*.

Like Urban Habitat, TransForm focused its attention on the question of regional transportation equity. TransForm was founded in 1997 and originally was called the Bay Area Transportation and Land Use Coalition (BATLUC). It gained prominence in 1998 after playing a lead role in the successful effort to redirect $375 million in highway funds to local transit. In slight contrast to Urban Habitat, TransForm's focus on issues of transit equity often emerged alongside an equal emphasis on questions of environmental sustainability. TransForm was a strong proponent of Bus Rapid Transit, Transit Oriented Development, smart growth initiatives, and environmentally sustainable housing. Despite this broad emphasis on sustainability and sustainable transportation, TransForm was also clearly committed to questions of equity as its role in drafting the initial Title VI complaint against the OAC made apparent.[40]

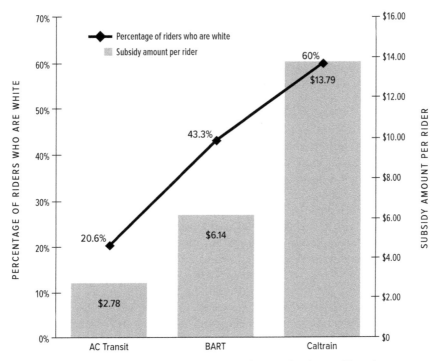

FIGURE 3. "Public Subsidies and Race of Riders." Based on graphic from Public Advocates reprinted with permission from *Race, Poverty and Environment* 12, no. 1 (2005), 22.

Before dissolving in 2006, the Alliance had focused a considerable amount of energy on grassroots organizing. In its absence, that task was taken up largely by Genesis and ACCE. Founded in 2007, Genesis was part of the larger Gamaliel Foundation—a nationwide network of faith-based organizations committed to progressive interventions in social policy. True to its Alinskyite roots, many of Genesis's members were recruited as members of church congregations. To quote directly from its stated mission, Genesis's primary goal was to unite and activate a "multiracial, income-diverse community to promote effective, equitable solutions to stubborn regional problems"[41] Starting in 2007, Genesis's efforts in the East Bay focused almost exclusively on issues of transportation justice. Its most notable campaign was for a "free student bus pass"—an initiative it began in 2010. The campaign started from a rather simple premise: students in the East Bay ought to be able to get to and from school without having to pay bus fare—as was common practice elsewhere. As Genesis's local chair, Rev. Scott Denman, argued in 2010, "If you're not providing a way for students to get to school, you're denying them the right to education itself."[42] Within the Transportation Justice Working Group, Genesis's importance was its grassroots connections. It was central in organizing public protests, starting letter-writing campaigns, and working with other members of the TJWG to direct attention to the plight of the region's transportation disadvantaged. It did all this by organizing riders themselves.[43]

As of 2011, the last group to adopt the mantle of transportation justice was the ACCE Bus Riders Union.[44] Forced to change its name from ACORN to ACCE after a deluge of bad press and a sustained right-wing smear campaign, the Alliance of Californians for Community Empowerment was officially formed in 2010 as an effort to advance progressive reforms in education, housing, and urban social policy more generally.[45] In the East Bay, ACCE focused its energies on organizing low-income and middle-income communities to win progressive tax, budget and policy reform.[46] In 2010, and as part of this larger strategy, ACCE spearheaded the formation of an East Bay–based Bus Riders Union. Like Charlie Betcher's Bus Riders Union, ACCE recruited its members by leafleting buses, attending rallies, and waiting at bus stops. In the face of the 2010 service cuts their demands focused on dampening the blow of such cuts by advocating the creation of a weekend "super pass" for frequent riders and the extension of "timed transfers" from two hours to four hours.[47]

In many ways, Urban Habitat, TransForm, Genesis, and ACCE simply represented a continuation of the work originally advanced by the Alliance for AC Transit. The Alliance's focus on helping AC Transit secure consistent funding, its focus on addressing the petty inconveniences of slow buses and costly transfers, and its inchoate efforts to organize bus riders to demand better treatment remained key elements for all four groups. There were also obvious differences. Compared to the Alliance, Urban Habitat and TransForm boasted a paid staff of professionals familiar with the ins and outs of transit planning, and Genesis and the ACCE Bus Riders Union were run by professional organizers with experience from other campaigns. Of course, for all their differences, each evinced a commitment to the idea of transportation justice. This not only meant a commitment to fairness in transit funding but often to transportation justice as a broader political project. The full nature of that project is worth discussing.

Beyond "Vertical Equity"

In some ways, transportation justice in the East Bay has been a classically Rawlsian project for what Todd Litman deems "vertical equity."[48] In his recent work *Evaluating Transportation Equity: Guidance for Incorporating Distributional Impacts in Transportation Planning*, Litman distinguishes this specific notion of equity from what he calls "horizontal equity." Where the latter is concerned with the "distribution of impacts between individuals and groups considered equal in ability and need," the former concerns itself with the "distribution of impacts between individuals and groups that differ"—whether by income, social class, physical ability, or race.[49] As Litman argues, for transportation planners committed to evaluating the equity impacts of any given planning decision, the distinction is an important one. Where planners focus on horizontal equity alone, transportation policies will be deemed equitable if they simply avoid "favoring one individual or group over another," or if it simply means that consumers ultimately pay their "fair share." Where these same planners focus on vertical equity, what counts as "equitable" will be radically different. Transportation policies will be "equitable if they favor economically and socially disadvantaged groups," and if such policies work against structural or historic injustices.[50] For groups like Urban Habitat, TransForm, Genesis, and even the Alliance for AC Transit, transportation justice has, in many ways, been aimed at securing equity on vertical terms. Whether the focus has been on promoting free student bus passes, on redirecting highway funds to mass transit, or restarting Oakland's defunct bus shelter program, the goal has largely remained the same—to direct transportation resources in ways that help society's least advantaged. Indeed, the fight against the OAC is yet another example. Where the choice was between investing money in a glorified "ski lift" or in using that money to shore up local bus service for the East Bay's transit dependent, the answer for such groups was clear: transportation justice meant fighting for the latter. There have, of course, been instances in which the fight for transportation justice in the East Bay has reflected a more simple commitment to horizontal equity. In this regard, the issue of public subsidies is a case in point. Where AC Transit riders only get a public subsidy of $2.78 per trip, while BART riders get a subsidy of $6.14, the issue is simply one of basic "egalitarian" fairness. In making sense of the East Bay's transportation justice movement, Litman's schema is useful only to a point. At its best it highlights the importance of approaching issues of equity with a clear sense of what we mean by it. At its worst, however, Litman's schema says little about the broader concerns that often drive fights for greater equity. For any number of people, these concerns are clear: they are concerns with what public transportation is for, its role in securing peoples' rights, and its importance in advancing a more democratic city. In this, of course, issues of distributional equity cannot be ignored.[51] Indeed, for people like John Katz, of the Alliance for AC Transit, questions of distribution remain at the heart of the matter: "It's almost always totally a questions of resources. . . . Basically tax the rich to get more people into buses. . . . I mean literally take money from people who have it and give it, not just to transit but to all needed public infrastructure [so that it's] viable, equitable, and sustainable."[52] For other people involved in the local transportation justice movement, "distributional equity" is only one part of it. Just as important is the ability to state why a more "viable, equitable, and sustainable" transportation system is important. This, in many ways, has been the tact taken by people such as Lindsay Imai of Urban Habitat. As she argued:

We see transportation as a civil right in that it provides access to opportunity—educational, health, economic and other sorts of opportunities. And because it has the potential to play an equalizing role, enabling historically disenfranchised communities to elevate and overcome long-standing discriminatory impacts of racism and classism. We see transportation as being a very basic building block of society, like education, like good healthcare.

. . . we see mobility as a kind of fundamental right, a human and a civil right. Good affordable, safe and reliable public transportation needs to be a part of what a society provides all people just like high quality free public education, high quality free healthcare. Urban Habitat isn't out there advocating for single-payer but it's part of our overall vision of a society that cares for all communities equally well and that ensures a true leveling field.[53]

While questions of vertical or horizontal equity were important for Imai, they were only important to the degree that they were part of a much larger political project. For Imai, that project was one that aimed at securing a society that "cares for all communities equally," that worked toward a common good, and that started from the presumption that public transportation was a human right and should be part of the menu of things that should be provided to all people. In many ways, this broad conception of transportation justice is not an uncommon one. Indeed, there are any number of groups outside of the East Bay that also share this conception.

Perhaps the most famous of these groups is the Los Angeles Bus Riders Union (BRU). Founded in 1992—as an outgrowth of the Los Angeles Labor/Community Strategy Center—the Los Angeles BRU gained national attention in 1994 after winning a landmark civil rights settlement against the Los Angeles Metropolitan Transportation Authority (MTA).[54] The victory not only stalled the MTA's plans to build a costly light rail line to the affluent area of Pasadena but also successfully redirected billions of dollars to local Los Angeles bus riders—riders who had been poised for yet another fare hike.[55] Since 1994, the BRU has achieved several additional victories, including a reduction in the cost of monthly bus passes, the replacement of 2,100 dilapidated buses, an expansion of the bus fleet by more than 300, and the city's first Bus Rapid Transit line.[56] According to BRU organizer Eric Mann, the demand for transportation justice in Los Angeles went beyond a demand for more buses; in fact, the BRU was an effort to put forward a new model of political organizing in order to "generate an urgently needed debate about an alternative vision for mass transportation and urban policy."[57] More polemically still, Mann saw the BRU as an essential antidote to "the bipartisan free market disaster" that was "destroying our cites."[58]

At the national level, groups like the Transit Equity Network (TEN) have put forward a conception of transportation justice that has been no less radical and no less ambitious. Originally conceived in 1997 under the auspices of the Center for Community Change, TEN has focused much of its efforts on demanding that federal transportation legislation include stronger civil rights and environmental protections. In 2003, as part of the lead-up to the reauthorization of the Transit Equity Act of the 21st Century (TEA 21), TEN was a key player in ensuring that the law gave attention to issues of transit dependency, public participation, and environmental justice.[59] Apart from lobbying for greater federal support for public transit, TEN's own founding documents suggest a commitment to a broader belief—namely, a belief that better public transit can go some way in "repairing America's inequalities" and in "restoring our collective commitment to public life."[60]

For East Bay groups like Urban Habitat, TransForm, and the Alliance for AC Transit, as well for organizations like the Los Angeles BRU and TEN, fights for transportation justice are rarely fights over transit alone. Indeed, they often function to invite a set of more robust debates over cities themselves. Scholar activists such as Rebecca Schein have championed this very quality. Following her experience with the "Free Transit Campaign" of the Greater Toronto Workers' Assembly, Schein was taken with the potentials inherent in basing a working-class movement around a fight for transportation justice. As she noted:

> What is exciting to me about the free transit campaign is that the expression of a radical anti-capitalist principle—the outright de-commodification of public goods and services—actually serves in this instance to invite rather than foreclose genuine political dialogue about values, tactics, and strategies. . . .
>
> Most Toronto residents would draw a blank if asked to "imagine a world without capitalism," but what Torontonian who has ever waited for a bus can't begin to imagine an alternative future for the city, built on the backbone of a fully public mass transit system? The invitation to imagine free transit is an invitation for transit riders to imagine themselves not simply as consumers of a commodity, but as members of a public entitled to participate in conversation about what kind of city they want to live in. Without devolving into abstract and alienating debates over the meaning of, say, socialism, the call for free transit invokes the things we value: vibrant neighbourhoods; clean air and water; participatory politics; equitable distribution of resources; public space where we are free to speak, gather, play, create, and organize.[61]

In the East Bay and beyond, fights for transportation justice have hinged on a similar set of beliefs. Advocates of transportation justice believe that "affordable, efficient, and environmentally sound mass transit is a human right."[62] They also believe that fighting for a more just distribution of transportation resources is an essential part of making that right a reality—whether that has meant rejecting projects like the OAC or fighting to derail a new metro link to Pasadena. More abstractly, fights for transportation justice have also rested on yet another belief—namely, that debates over transit are rarely just about transit. They are also debates—to paraphrase Schein—over the type of city people want to live in.

"You Are Not Shut Off from the Rest of the Community When You Ride the Bus"

Following Lindsay Imai, or Rebecca Schein, to the extent that the fight for transportation justice in the East Bay has been part of a larger political project—and
one that has been about far more than "vertical equity"—in some ways the contours of that project are easy to glean. Drawing on the evidence provided above,
that project is one aimed at securing a society that "cares for all communities
equally well" and that invites bus riders to imagine "the kind of city they want
to live in." Against initiatives like the OAC, it is a project aimed at prioritizing
the demands of the poor and transit dependent over those of global investors or,
alternatively, downtown businesses eager to improve Oakland's market position
vis-à-vis other cities. Of course, as the next section shows, this political project
can be framed in yet richer terms—and especially if we begin by asking what
public transportation actually means for bus riders themselves. In addition to a
project that "cares for all communities equally," or that seeks to expand democratic participation, to talk with any number of local bus riders is also to see the
fight for transportation justice as a fight for a less alienating city and against the
isolation of urban life. The comments of bus riders like Steve Geller—a rather
active member of the Alliance—speak directly to this.

> I must admit that I meet a lot of friends on the buses, a lot of people I know ride
> the buses, so it is a social thing. I don't know if I think of the bus as being a thing
> I go to for sociality only, it's a way of getting places, but effectively it turns out that
> there are a lot of social interactions that occur. I have noticed that fellow riders
> tend to be good to each other, when you are on the bus they know you are a fellow
> bus rider, they know you are in the same class. People will help you out a lot more.
> When anyone has a question, you can always depend on people who are back in
> their seats to pop up with various suggestions about what to do. I think that's good.
> I think [public transportation] encourages people to cooperate and get along and
> share something.[63]

For Geller, public transit was not simply about getting from point A to point B;
it was also about being part of a *public*, engaging with others, and "sharing
something." To use public transit was, for Geller, to come into contact with
other people and especially people of the "same class." Geller was not alone
in this view. Fran Haselsteiner, yet another transit activist affiliated with the
Alliance, said much the same thing: "I like riding the bus, I like the sense of
community, I like the whole thing. You are not shut off from the rest of the
community when you ride the bus."[64] In a focus group conducted with members of the East Bay Center for the Blind (EBCB) one participant—reflecting
on the prospect of additional service cuts to AC Transit—expressed this same
sentiment in yet a different way. For those without access to a private automobile, or a chauffeur service, public transportation, she argued, was simply the

only method for securing a life lived out in the open: "If you can't drive, or if people aren't at your beck and call . . . you are a prisoner of your house. If you aren't able to walk very far or to take buses or use paratransit, your rights are taken away—the right to move about the city. Your right to participate is being taken away. Because we can't drive, we can only go so far as we can walk, and some of us can walk less and less as we get older."[65] Perhaps yet more forcefully, for members of the EBCB, securing public transportation meant securing a set of rights. It meant securing the "right to participate" and the right not to be a prisoner of one's own home. More clearly still, it meant securing a right to be part of the public rather than isolated from it. For Chris Mullen, an employee at Berkeley's Center for Independent Living (CIL), public transportation was about independence. As the center's mobility manager, Mullen was tasked with teaching both disabled and elderly clients how to use public transportation to accomplish basic tasks. As Mullen noted, for many of his clients, public transportation meant the difference between "feeling limited" and taking "control over your life." Transit is "an instigator and pusher for people with disabilities who feel limited. For seniors it's like a reintroduction into taking control over your life. The senior I will be working with this afternoon worked the polls last week and so one of our first trips we took was to her polling place, and again, she had tears in her face."[66]

Where such comments enrich our view of public transportation, they also speak to a set of concerns that obviously go far beyond those that generally enliven debates on transportation justice—and particularly where justice is simply a synonym for "vertical equity." These are concerns with people's ability to participate in urban life, to get to the polls, and to live their lives out in the open. Moreover, they are concerns with the attendant isolation and alienation that befall individuals when public transportation disappears. For those familiar with the work of Henri Lefebvre such concerns, of course, may feel familiar. Writing amid the tumult of the late 1960s, Lefebvre gained fame for not only drawing attention to what he saw as the increasing isolation and alienation of urban life, but also for what he saw as the solution: a working-class demand for a "right to the city."[67] As noted earlier, Lefebvre coined this term in response to what he saw as the rapid transformation of French urban life. The prosperity of the postwar had given rise to a new city. This was a city of high rises, new suburban towns, and new highways. It was a city with more cars, more modern conveniences, but coincidently less social interaction. Most notably, it was a city in which the very communities that had once sustained the vibrancy of urban life increasingly found themselves excluded from it.[68] In this context, the right to the city, for Lefebvre, was as much a rallying cry for those seeking inclusion as it was an attempt to push an alternative vision of both whom and what cities were for. In some ways, Lefebvre's vision of that city was simply an extension of the view first articulated by Marx and Engels a hundred years prior. As they noted in the *Communist Manifesto*, cities were important precisely because they promised to "rescue a considerable part of the population from the idiocy of rural life."[69] As the Marxist historian Hal Draper argued, Marx and Engels used *idiocy* in its classical sense as a synonym for "privatized isolation."[70] In contrast to the isolating tendencies of the feudal countryside, cities offered just the opposite. More importantly, they offered, as Marx and Engels argued, the very types of social encounters necessary for political organizing. Whether on the street or on the factory floor, the city provided newly industrialized workers the rare opportunity to engage in collective struggle. In his book *The Condition of the Working Class in England*, Engels captured the paradox of the industrial city quite well: "If the centralisation of population stimulates and develops the property-holding class, it forces the development of the workers yet more rapidly. The workers begin to feel as a class, as a whole; they begin to perceive that, though feeble as individuals, they form a power united . . . the consciousness of oppression awakens, and the workers attain social and political importance."[71] For Lefebvre, the French city of the postwar evinced the limits of the above view. Urbanization and political radicalization had been decoupled. Not only was working-class militancy on the decline, but the very spaces once associated with that militancy were fast disappearing. Rather than awakening working-class consciousness, the city of the postwar was becoming more alienating, more isolating, and ever more idiotic. In this context, the importance of Lefebvre's right to the city suddenly becomes clear. The right to the city was a "right to centrality," a "right to be at the heart of urban life," and a right to places of "encounter and exchange."[72] In the face of both urban planners eager to kill the street and a "new bourgeois aristocracy" eager to colonize the central city, the right to the city was a right aimed at recovering the radical potential that Marx and Engels first ascribed to cities.[73] In sum, it was the right against the idiocy of *urban* life.

There is little to suggest that Steve Geller, Fran Haselsteiner, Chris Mullen, or members of the EBCB would be familiar with Lefebvre. There is even less to suggest that they would be familiar with the radical project of which he was a part. At the same time, to listen to their comments is to get a view of public transportation and its place in cities that speaks directly to that very project. When members of the EBCB bemoan losing their "right to participate" or when Steve Geller celebrates the bus as a space of "encounter and exchange" and one in which people tend to be "good to each other" because "they know you are in the same class," both are invoking sentiments that are quintessentially Lefebvrian.[74] To start with such comments is to see the fight for transportation justice and the fight to secure a right to the city as part of the same political project. That project is one aimed at rejecting the alienation and isolation of urban life, at reclaiming the city for those too often excluded from it, and at rescuing the radical potential of cities that is compromised by poor transit. Indeed beyond the above comments, the work of the Alliance for AC Transit itself offers further evidence of the link. In seeking to prevent the relocation of Oakland's central transfer station, the Alliance—in pure Lefebvrian fashion—not only sought to secure the rights of riders to be at the heart of urban life, but to rebuke the business interests eager to push them out. Where the comments of people like Steve Geller enrich our understanding of what transportation means for people, the work of Henri Lefebvre helps us make sense of those comments and enriches our view of what struggles for transportation justice can and should be about.

This chapter began with two simple questions: What, exactly, do we mean by transportation justice? And what type of political project is it? In some ways the answer to both questions is rather clear. In the East Bay, fights for transportation justice have been, at their broadest, fights for "vertical equity" and a fairer distribution of transportation resources. Rather than pushing money toward projects like the OAC or projects aimed at extending BART, fighting for transportation justice has meant fighting to redirect resources toward the poor and the transit dependent—and thus largely in the direction of AC Transit. It has also meant pushing for MPO reform, demanding that the RTP better reflect the needs of minority and low-income populations, and supporting ballot measures that will allow AC Transit to either maintain or expand its service. For many in the East Bay involved in the fight for transportation justice, of course, securing "vertical equity" is only part it. Fights for transportation justice have also been part of a far more ambitious political project. To quote Lindsay Imai, that project has been one aimed at advancing a vision of a society "that cares for all communities equally well." To use the language of Rebecca Schein, it has been one aimed at inviting transit riders to imagine the "kind of city they want to live in." This chapter concludes by noting that to start with the comments of bus riders like Steve Geller or members of the EBCB is to begin to put some flesh on what precisely that broader political project might entail. Beyond securing a more equitable distribution of resources, or securing Title VI compliance, or advancing MPO reform, to listen to bus riders is also to see a political project aimed at securing a city that is less alienating, less isolating, and less idiotic. In connecting with the central theme of this book, to the extent that this broader political project implicates rights, they are as much the rights discussed in chapter 1— the civil rights of *Darensburg v. MTC* or the rights engendered by tort law—as they are the rights associated with Lefebvre's postwar demand for a right to the city. These include the "right to participate," the right—despite the demands of business interests—to be at the heart of urban life, and the right to not be "shut off from the rest of the community." These are rights, in short, against the idiocy of urban life and the idiocy attendant when public transportation disappears.

CHAPTER 3

The Rights of Transit Labor

They call them work rules, we call them working conditions.

—**Tony Withington, International Representative, Amalgamated Transit Union, December 8, 2010**

We don't call each other drivers, we call each other operators—because any fool can drive a bus—but it takes skill, experience and diplomacy to be an operator.

—**Anthony Rodgers, Amalgamated Transit Union Local 192, November 19, 2010**

Contract negotiations between the Alameda–Contra Costa Transit District (AC Transit) and its unionized drivers have never been easy. In fact, the triennial process of hammering out the details of wages, benefits, and other working conditions has often proved to be downright onerous. Not since 1977, however, have members of the Amalgamated Transit Union Local 192 (ATU 192) resorted to a strike. The year 2010 threatened to be different. Running a deficit of $56 million, AC Transit was broke. State aid for transit had dried up, and service cuts earlier in the year had not yielded nearly the amount of savings the agency had hoped for. Moreover, by the end of May, contract negotiations between management and transit operators had stalled indefinitely. Perhaps it is unsurprising then that on June 30, 2010—and breaking with over thirty years of tradition—AC Transit management decided to abandon the process of collective bargaining altogether and simply impose a new contract on their workers unilaterally. In response, on Monday, July 19, roughly two hundred AC Transit bus operators called in sick.[1] An official strike it was not, but its effects on the riding public were largely the same: indefinite delays, missed connections, and overcrowded buses.[2]

From the outset, AC Transit's position was quite clear. As one AC Transit board member admitted rather bluntly, "The worst contract I can get [labor] the more service I can put on the street."[3] More surprising, however, were the responses from those one might otherwise expect to side with the union, namely

progressive transit activists like Steve Geller and Joyce Roy—each of whom
had strong ties to the East Bay's transportation justice movement. In pushing
for labor concessions, they stood with management.[4] For Steve Geller, Joyce
Roy, and surely many other transit riders left stranded at bus stops during the
summer of 2010, the problem was not so much the right of labor to collective
bargaining, or the right of transit workers to a decent wage; the problem was
that those entitlements seemed to run counter to the rights of Oakland's poor
and transportation disadvantaged to get to work, to attend school, and to access
the city in the only way available to them—through cheap and reliable transit.

> JOYCE ROY: I think it is true that drivers should be giving more into their
> retirement. They have also made it impossible for them to hire part-time
> drivers. And it means sometimes that drivers have a four-hour shift and four
> hours of nothing. I am sort of friends with many bus drivers but I don't bring
> much of this up because I think that the unions have to do more.[5]
>
> STEVE GELLER: The union needs to ease up a little bit on their demands if they
> want to have jobs. There was a big demonstration over in San Francisco in
> front of the federal building. It was put on by a lot of local unions primarily,
> and the big push there was to try and get some federal funding to subsidize
> the buses all around the country. . . . Their major interest was not so much
> the convenience of the bus riders but keeping their jobs, and that's what the
> union is about, and I guess I can't object to that, because that's what unions
> are for, but I must say that when the squeeze comes down, the people who are
> squeezed the most are the people that ride the buses.[6]

To the extent that this book has engaged rights—whether in legal terms or
as they have appeared in struggles for transportation justice—it has done so
largely by focusing on the experience of transit riders and the transit dependent.
But what of transit workers? What are we to make of their demands? How might
we understand their rights in relation to those of the people they carry? Over
the course of a century, East Bay transit workers have fought and struggled to
secure a range of entitlements aimed at improving working conditions. This
chapter starts with a simple proposition that such fights and struggles ought
to matter. Not only should they matter for advocates of transportation justice,
but also for those engaged in debates over a right to the city—debates in which
workers, unions, and labor in general have largely been absent.[7] In making this
claim, this chapter explores the history of the ATU 192 and the range of disputes and strikes that have marked the union's development since the turn of
the century. In this respect, this chapter is perhaps reminiscent of the work of
historians such as Josh Freeman, whose book *In Transit: The Transport Workers
Union in New York City, 1933–1966* is perhaps the most comprehensive history
of organized labor in transit.[8] In it, Freeman offers both an institutional history
of the union and a vivid picture of the social world of transit workers—one in

which communist sympathies, nationalist rhetoric, and religious duty were all inextricably connected. This chapter does not reach the same depths. Moreover, it places the history of the ATU Local 192 in a different frame. Less concerned with the social world of workers, this chapter focuses mainly on the efforts of East Bay transit workers—through strikes and negotiations—to secure a set of rights and protections of their own. More importantly, it asks what such efforts mean in the context of remarks such as those from activists Roy and Geller. As the comments of such activists suggest, the demands of transit workers can often seem at odds with those of the people they carry. Where finances are limited, the choice can often appear to be a zero-sum vote between worker pensions and the needs of the wider public to cheap transit. As will become clear—and by drawing on both the history of the ATU 192 and the words of individual drivers—this choice is a false one. It is false because it requires seeing workers as separate from the public, and because it ignores the central role that transit workers can play in creating a more just city.

The Carmen's First Contract

At 3:45 a.m. on May 29, 1906, and by a vote of 510 to 55, the conductors and motormen of Division 192 of the Amalgamated Order of Street Railway Employees of America voted to strike.[9] Reports from Grier Hall in downtown Oakland—where the vote was taken—told of a room "packed to overflowing with blue coats and numbered badges."[10] Having just finished their last runs, conductors and motormen who arrived late found themselves standing in the hallway and straining "their ears and eyes to keep posted."[11] President Mahon of the National Carmen's Union had traveled from Detroit for the vote. He was joined on stage by President William Ellison of Division 192 and President Cornelius of the Carmen's Union in San Francisco. Letters of support from other unions were read aloud, and President Cornelius—who had recently led the Carmen of San Francisco in a strike—encouraged those present to keep fighting: "Be firm and insist on your rights, and you will surely get them."[12] The vote had been several weeks in the making. In early May, members of Division 192 had, for the first time, submitted a written draft of a working agreement to the president of the Oakland Traction Company and its sibling company, the San Francisco-Oakland-San Jose Railroad (the Key Route). The proposed agreement included a demand for a flat hourly wage of $27^{1/2}$ cents, a closed shop, and recognition of the union.[13]

The response from the company was a flat denial.[14] According to Willis Kelley, the general manager at the time, "We have no promises, no concessions [and] no compromises to make." The company, he insisted, would not cede to a few men its right to "determine how it will conduct its business."[15] While the company had softened its position on the union over the previous four years, a written contract was something else altogether. Thus, by the end of May the two sides had reached an impasse. The company blamed the discord on the "machinations of a few disgruntled spirits and unscrupulous leaders."[16] Others believed the strike action to be instigated by competing traction companies, like United Railroad and Southern Pacific. The United Railroad company had previously tried to purchase the Oakland Traction Company but had failed. By encouraging a strike, some argued, United Railroad hoped to drive down the company's stock just enough so that it could buy a controlling interest.[17] Others pointed to the machinations of Southern Pacific. In the instance of a strike, no company would benefit more than the Southern Pacific Railroad, whose ferry service—in the last several years—had lost ground to the Key Route's twenty-minute ferry crossing to San Francisco.[18] Whether the crisis could be traced to a few "bad apples" or rather to the collusion of competing firms, such explanations said little about the nature of the union's demands—which were substantial. The foremost demand of Division 192 was of recognition. Division 192 had been incorporated by East Bay transit workers in 1901, under the American Association of Street Railway Employees.[19] The union's relationship with the company, since incorporation, had been both informal and relatively peaceful. Although the company had proven to be fairly responsive to union demands—raising wages when necessary—the carmen nevertheless lacked any form of recognizable working agreement or any official contract under which they might formally appeal grievance matters. The crisis of 1906 may have begun with a demand for a flat wage, but the sticking point for both the carmen and the company was not wages, but rather the demand for a fixed-term contract.

On April 4, 1906, after weeks of tension and two days of closed meetings with the union, the Oakland Traction Company signed a written agreement with Division 192. It would be the division's first contract. There was no wage increase, but the more substantial concession was approved: the recognition of the union and the approval of a one-year contract. President Mahon, who had traveled all the way from Detroit to preside over the negotiations, declared it a victory: "From now on the traction company will recognize our organization. . . . Recognition of the union, such as has been established by the local company, affords the men a far better means of protection than they ever had before."[20] The contract contained fifteen chief provisions:

1) Complete recognition of the union
2) Discharged employees have the right to appeal for a hearing before the board of directors of the corporation
3) If discharged employee is reinstated as a result of an appeal he is to be paid for the time lost for dismissal
4) Officers of the union may obtain a leave of absence not exceeding thirty days when such leave is necessary to perform their duties as union officers
5) All employees of the company may ride free on the company cars
6) All employees of the company have a right to join any reputable organization

7) Demerit register lists must not be made public

8) A day's run of ten or eleven hours must be made in a fifteen hour stretch

9) Straight runs must be made within twelve hours

10) Trippers working less than one hour will be paid for one hour

11) Regular men will have one day off in ten if desired

12) Bulletin boards for use of the union will be placed in all car houses

13) Motormen instructing students will be paid 25 cents a day extra

14) Men may purchase uniforms in the open market

15) The present wage scale will remain effective until January 1 or July 1 1907.[21]

Where none had existed before, the contract served to codify and secure for the carmen of Division 192 a specific set of entitlements and rights. It outlined a clear set of procedures by which motormen and conductors might address grievances, and it introduced new and actionable protections into the workplace.[22] To borrow from philosopher Henry Shue, the new contract established a set of "moral minimums" designed to protect workers from exploitation.[23] Against the demands of shareholders such as industrialist Francis "Borax" Smith—who had been the primary developer of the Key System—and against a competitive marketplace geared toward driving down wages and extending the working day, a contract was an important protection. Speaking at Grier Hall on the night of the strike vote, then-secretary of the State Labor Federation, James Bowling, captured the zeitgeist in no uncertain terms: "The trade unions stand between capital and slavery, and only by them can we hope for any freedom. . . . We belong to a union because we hate something and love something. We hate oppression and love liberty. Let us continue to show that we intend to uproot the one and demand the other."[24] In 1906, East Bay transit operators won a set of rights—the most important being recognition.

The Oakland Streetcar Strike of 1919

Disputes over the rights and working conditions of East Bay transit workers have not always been peaceful. In October 1919, the carmen of Division 192 grabbed national headlines in a strike notable for its violence.[25] Starting on October 1, and in the span of several days, what had begun as a not unusual labor dispute over working conditions quickly evolved into a city-wide riot leaving 6 people dead and 140 injured.[26] As had been partly the case in 1906, the conflict in 1919 was over working conditions. The chief demand of the union was an eight-hour work day. At least since 1906, carmen in Oakland and the East Bay had been expected to work anywhere between ten and twelve hours a day.[27] Additionally, if a carman happened to work a split run, as was common, it could mean a workday of up to fifteen hours. As the union was quick to point out, such long hours far exceeded those worked by carmen in cities such as Boston, Portland, Seattle, Chicago, and even San Francisco. In these cities an eight-hour workday was already the norm.[28] Having failed to impress this point upon their employers, the carmen of Division 192 called a strike on the morning of October 1. Thousands of East Bay residents prepared for the worst.[29] In preparation, Oakland's Mayor John Davies took the auspicious step of offering jitney licenses to anyone wishing to apply.[30] Similarly, special efforts were made by the Southern Pacific Railroad to increase ferry service to San Francisco.[31] The company, for its part, not only vowed to resume service on October 4 without unionized workers, but it also took the aggressive step of securing a federal injunction against the union. Perhaps in light of the chaos of the Seattle General Strike only eight months earlier, or the increasing specter of labor radicalism, the court's injunction was wide-ranging—prohibiting "speeches of intimidation," "trespassing," or using "abusive language to persuade any employee of the company from performing their duties."[32] On October 4 and 5 the injunction would have little effect. Throngs of carmen and their supporters emptied into the street intent on preventing streetcars from operating and on finding and harassing the many strikebreakers who had come from Los Angeles, Portland, and Seattle to take their jobs.

Over the next seven days, it is fair to say that the streets of Oakland belonged to the striking carmen of Division 192.[33] By October 4, attacks on strikebreakers had gotten bad enough that many of them had been moved from the city's downtown hotels to a ferry boat docked off the Key System pier.[34] Clashes with the police were common. On October 4, when the company attempted to run its first streetcar through downtown Oakland, it was met by riots, shouting crowds, and bricks. Even while flanked by armed police patrols, the streetcar was only able to make two trips on its first day back in service. The riots became particularly fierce at the corner of 13th and Webster after police escort George Underwood fired into the crowd—injuring two striking carmen.[35] On October 6, perhaps the worst day of the strikes, riots broke out on Broadway, Washington, 12th, and 13th streets.[36] At Alice and 13th, Police Captain William Wood and five others were injured after police escorts began trading fire with protestors.[37] In addition to pelting police escorts with stones, efforts to impede the progress of strike-breaking streetcars also took other forms. There were reports, for example, that strikers had placed a stolen steamroller on the tracks at 24th Avenue and East 14th, and that in other instances strikers had used automobiles as barriers.[38] By October 8 the situation had gotten so severe in Oakland that the general manager of the Key Route sent a telegram to then-governor William Stephens requesting that he "furnish whatever force may be necessary to establish order in the city of Oakland."[39]

Heeding the requests of the national union, the Oakland streetcar strike ended on October 11 when the carmen of Division 192 voted to submit their demands to an independent board of arbiters.[40] The strike had been costly. A full eleven days after it began, carmen had lost $55,000 in salaries, the traction company had lost $155,000 in revenue, and 140 people had sustained injuries.[41] From the perspective of the carmen, it may have seemed a total loss.[42] Ultimately, the arbiters would side with the company and reject the carmen's chief demand for an eight-hour day. The company, the arbiters argued, simply could not afford it.[43]

Despite this, and in retrospect, the strike had obviously succeeded in other ways. For one, it succeeded by demonstrating the growth of a certain postwar labor militancy in cities. Nationally, 1919 was a high-water mark with respect to strikes; the number of workers involved in work stoppages would be the highest recorded until 1946.[44] The streetcar strike of 1919 also served as an illustration of a maturing labor solidarity. Over the eleven days of unrest, the carmen had been joined in their fight by thousands of other workers. These workers, like the carmen themselves, believed that an eight-hour work day was a just demand. Moreover, they believed that a win for the carmen was a win for themselves. Near the height of the unrest—and after several reports of police brutality—leaders of the Central Labor Council, the Metal Trades Council, and the Building Trades Council had pledged their support for the striking carmen by threatening to issue a call that their workers take up arms.[45] Similarly, on October 10, the quite radical Electrical Workers Union No. 283 not only pledged their support for the carmen but also threatened a sympathy strike—promising to black out the entire East Bay.[46] If the strike had failed to secure the carmen an eight-hour workday, it had succeeded in demonstrating the potential power of labor to bring the city to a halt.

As with the crisis in 1906, the question was: What ought to constitute the rights of transit workers in the East Bay? Pointing to numerous other cities in which transit workers enjoyed more limited hours of work, the carmen's strike in 1919 was based on the belief that an eight-hour workday ought to be a right. Not only that, but the carmen believed that it was a right worth $55,000 in lost wages, that it was worth the cost of public inconvenience, and that it was worth potential bodily harm. For the Central Labor Council, it was a right worth sanctioning their fifty thousand workers to join in the struggle. Similarly, for the electrical workers of Division 283, the carmen's right to an eight-hour day was a right worth shorting the entire city. While the carmen would have to wait until 1925 for a provision guaranteeing an eight-hour day, the seeds of that provision were planted in 1919 and through a great deal of tumult.[47]

The 1946 General Strike and the 1953 Key System Strike

The longest recorded strike of transit workers in the East Bay occurred in 1953, lasting seventy-six days.[48] As in 1919, members of Division 192 found themselves at loggerheads with management over working conditions—this time over wages. Of course, a great deal had changed in transit between 1919 and 1953. The ownership of the Key System had switched hands. It was no longer a part of Francis "Borax" Smith's East Bay empire, and instead, by 1953, it was firmly the property of National City Lines, a company headquartered in Chicago.[49] Moreover, by 1953 streetcars and ferries were no longer the core of the East Bay transit system at all.[50] Instead, riders in Oakland and Richmond relied on a vast system of diesel buses and several commuter trains. Passengers, who in 1919 might have traveled to San Francisco by ferry, could now make that same trip using the Bay Bridge—a 4.5-mile stretch across the San Francisco Bay with two levels, one for automobiles and another below for Key System trains. In 1919, the Key System's major competitor was the Southern Pacific Company, which ran a parallel ferry service. By 1953, however, and with the postwar automobile explosion already underway, the Key System's major competition was the private automobile. Transit companies like the Key System were, by then, already losing riders and suffering the financial consequences of the new automobile age. Apart from such sweeping transformations, Division 192 had changed as well. In 1906, the contract for workers at Division 192 had fit on one page of the *Oakland Tribune*.[51] By 1953 the contract was at least fifty pages long and included provisions documenting every possible aspect of employment.[52] The contract read as both a palimpsest of past conflicts and a document of the times. New provisions had been added. The Key System was now a union shop that provided workers with sick leave.[53] Senior conductors and motormen— after a fourteen-day strike in 1947—now enjoyed a forty-hour week with two day's rest.[54] The eight-hour day, which had caused such a stir in 1919, was by 1953 not only a contractual provision but also a federal law. Real wages had increased as well. In 1915, a conductor for the Oakland Traction Company made 38 cents an hour. In 1953 the hourly wage of a bus driver was a $1.68—in real wages that marked an increase of 46 percent.[55]

The decades following World War II also saw their fair share of labor militancy. In 1946, Oakland had been ground zero for the Oakland General Strike— the last general strike in U.S. history. The history of the Oakland General Strike is well documented.[56] The city-wide work stoppage began on December 1 after the Oakland Police—armed with tear gas and gas masks—disbanded the pickets of striking workers at the Kahn's and Hastings department stores.[57] From the perspective of Oakland's labor movement, the interference of the police signified an unwarranted attack on the rights of department store workers to strike and picket, and it represented a direct threat to the rights of Oakland workers more generally. After all, if city authorities could blatantly break a wholly legal strike of private workers without repercussions, what would stop them from feeling emboldened enough to do it again? In the following hours and days, workers in Oakland would respond by ostensibly "cripp[ling] the commercial and industrial activities of their community."[58] Over the course of two days, what had begun as a minor strike of department store workers exploded into a city-wide crisis with more than a hundred thousand workers refusing to clock in. With respect to the impetus and impact of the Oakland General Strike, the carmen of Division 192 had a central role. Many, in fact, attribute the start of the more general strike itself to the moment Division 192 carman Al Brown abandoned his streetcar in the middle of Broadway and 17th Street, both refusing to cross the picket line at Kahn's and Hastings and then subsequently encouraging other carmen to do the same. As historian Phillip Wolman has argued, the Oakland General Strike reflected "a purging of emotions."[59] More specifically, it reflected the pent-up demand for wages and better living conditions that had built up during the war. These demands were widespread, and strikes were common. In fact, in 1946 alone there were a total of 4,985 strikes across the county, the highest number of strikes recorded in U.S. history.[60]

Not only did the Oakland General Strike reflect a broader set of postwar anxieties, but it ultimately succeeded in doing a great deal more. As Wolman argues, the Oakland General Strike laid the groundwork in Oakland for a progressive takeover of the Oakland City Council and a lasting set of reforms to the public sector.[61] In 1947, and as a direct outgrowth of the general strike, labor unions like the ATU 192 joined with the Oakland Voters League to support one of the most progressive platforms in the city's electoral history. That platform included the drafting of a new city charter, a repeal of a regressive city sales tax, an increase in assessments on downtown property owners, a call for city council neutrality during strikes, a repeal of anti-picketing and anti-handbilling ordinances, the creation of a civic unity commission to enforce equality in city employment, a call to maintain local rent control, a call to study the possibility of establishing a publicly owned transit system, an overhaul of the public health services, and, lastly, more money for public schools, public libraries, and public swimming pools.[62]

The carmen's dispute in 1953, by all accounts, was a more parochial matter. Nevertheless, the events of 1946 and the progressive platform that emerged in its wake would not have been far from memory—particularly the proposal for a municipally owned transit system. Moreover, the events of 1946 show that the ATU 192—having fought for their own rights in 1906 and 1919—saw themselves as part of something larger. Just as the electrical workers had done in 1919, members of the ATU 192 had in 1946 shown themselves willing to stand in solidarity with other workers, and to do so less out of obligation and more out of the belief that the fight for better working conditions for one was a fight for better conditions *for all*.

The longest transit strike in the history of the East Bay began on July 24, 1953. The chief dispute was over wages. At $1.68 an hour, carmen of the Key System rightly claimed to be some of the lowest paid transit workers on the Pacific Coast. Their pay of $1.68 an hour put them 18 cents below the regional average.[63]

Just across the bay in San Francisco, in fact, operators enjoyed a wage of $1.89 per hour for doing roughly the same job. After months of negotiations, however, ATU 192 president Vern Stambaugh and the Key System's negotiator, Harold Davis, had failed to find common ground. While the union had made some concessions on fringe benefits, such as overtime pay, the Key System's offer of 14 cents was not acceptable.[64] The company had made this increase contingent on a fare hike—which the union viewed as unnecessary. In addition to refusing the union's demand for a 20-cent increase, the company also refused to have the issue solved by binding arbitration.[65]

By late August, the strike was more than a month old, and the public's demand for a solution had become deafening. This took several forms: a short-lived and roundly ignored Oakland City Council resolution for "limited arbitration" and a more engaged effort by East Bay cities to facilitate the bargaining process themselves. On August 28, Mayor Clifford Rishell of Oakland took the forward step of convening a group he called the Citizen's Transit Emergency Committee.[66] The group's aim was to study the wage issue and then offer a fair contract on which both sides might agree. On August 31 the committee drafted a settlement that included an immediate 14-cent wage increase followed by a 7-cent pay bump six months later.[67] Not surprisingly, the recommendation was flatly rejected by the Key System. It exceeded management's offer by 7 cents, and as George Stanley, the manager of the Key System, stated acidly in a letter to Mayor Rishell, it gave "no consideration to the effect" a wage increase would have on either the agency's bottom line or the public's ability to pay higher fares.[68]

By September 21, the Key System strike was sixty days old. In terms of length, it had surpassed the 1951 record of fifty-nine days held by Detroit transit workers.[69] In September, and having exhausted all other means, citizens in the East Bay turned to the courts and to the efforts of one Fred Dubovsky. Described by one-time colleague and later AC Transit general manager Frank Nisbet as a "curmudgeon that operated out of his house and wore disheveled clothes," Dubovsky was an elderly lawyer based in Berkeley, who, in mid-August, took it upon himself to file a lawsuit on behalf of the citizens of the East Bay.[70] His suit argued that the Key System had "an obligation under its franchise to operate public transit whether or not they had a strike."[71] The Key System was an exclusive monopoly, with both fares and schedules set by the Public Utilities Commission, and its failure to operate transit service left the "entire community stranded and in a state of utter helplessness"; also, according to Dubovsky, this failure was wholly illegal.[72] Despite initial expectations, the lawsuit actually succeeded, and through a court-ordered writ of mandate, the Key System was ordered to resume service within seven days—lest it be held in contempt of court and put in receivership. With the union backing the courts, the Key System faced the unenviable choice of going into receivership or returning, head-bowed, to the negotiating table.[73] After resuming negotiations on Tuesday, October 5, and after only two days at the table, the carmen of the ATU 192 voted in favor of a new contract by a margin of 759 to 201—ultimately winning an 18-cent pay increase.[74]

The strike in 1953 lacked the violence of 1919.[75] Much like 1919, however, the strike of 1953 evidenced a similar degree of solidarity and public support for striking workers. Efforts by the Richmond City Council to contract out livery services during the strike had been killed by the Chauffeurs Local 923, which refused to sanction its workers as "strike breakers."[76] Greyhound Bus drivers of the ATU's Division 1225 made a similar pledge to striking workers, when the business agent of the Division 1225, H. B. Markely, assured Vern Stambaugh and the membership of Local 192 that Greyhound drivers would not pick up the slack.[77] This solidarity was reflected not only in the actions of other unionized transportation workers and in Mayor Rishell's admittedly pro-union "fair settlement," but in monetary contributions to the union's strike fund as well—including $500 received from the Building Service Employees Union Local 18, $25 received from the Bill Posters and Billers Local 44, and $50 received from the Optical Technicians Local 18791.[78] Numerous letters to the editor during the strike reflected a good deal of public support for the union, as well as a profound skepticism of the Key System and its parent company, National City Lines. Such skepticism was understandable. The company was a subsidiary of General Motors, and its commitment to public transit in the East Bay had always been questionable.[79] Apart from the length of the 1953 strike, it was important for other reasons. Most significantly, it galvanized much of the skepticism already attached to the Key System into a popular push for public ownership. Only two weeks into the strike, the sentiment was expressed succinctly in an editorial comment by local resident Sam Gorham: "The Key System is getting too much as is. We should own our own."[80] His wish eventually came to pass; by the fall of 1960, the East Bay had its own publicly owned transit system.

Proposals for a publicly owned transit system in the East Bay had appeared before—most notably in the years immediately following World War I.[81] It was the strike of 1953, however, that ultimately catalyzed the necessary legislative action to make that public system a reality. The ATU 192 was supportive of public ownership. After all, the idea of a wholly public bus system in the East Bay had been a prominent part of the progressive platform that emerged from the Oakland General Strike of 1946. Like riders, transit workers in the East Bay were frustrated with the Key System, and they also hoped that a publicly owned system might offer a solution to the labor and financial problems that had long come to plague regional transit. More viscerally, both transit workers and the riding public hoped that a publicly owned system might prevent strikes like those in 1953. As argued earlier, the public takeover of the Key System and the subsequent development of AC Transit came in response to the postwar urban transportation problems of congestion and the rapid increase in car ownership. At the same time, at least part of the catalyst for the development of AC Transit was also clearly linked to labor struggles—most clearly the labor struggle in 1953, and to a lesser degree the progressive platform of labor following the 1946 Oakland General Strike.

The ATU 192's Last Strike, 1977

Following 1953, labor disputes between Division 192 and management erupted in 1960, 1964, 1970, and 1974. These disputes arose over wages, cost of living adjustments, and pension contributions. Compared to the marathon work stoppage of 1953, however, these were relatively minor actions. It was not until 1977 that East Bay residents once again saw a strike of comparable significance. The strike in 1977 is notable for two reasons: for being the ATU 192's last strike and for largely being a failure. With respect to transit in the East Bay, a great deal had changed between 1953 and 1977. By 1977, urban transit in the East Bay was wholly public, serviced by both the AC Transit District and the Bay Area Rapid Transit District (BART).

These changes mattered for transit workers. At one level, by 1977 members of the ATU 192 were no longer private workers but public employees. Similarly, East Bay bus riders were no longer simply paying customers but rather "part owners." Management no longer hewed to a distant corporate board in Chicago but was now directed by seven democratically elected board members. At the immediate level, public ownership benefited workers in many ways. When the authority for a district was created in 1955, the state legislation had included explicit provisions ensuring collective bargaining.[82] AC Transit's first contract with the ATU 192 in 1960, in fact, included forty-three improvements to wages and working conditions. Between 1960, when AC Transit started service, and 1977, the year of the last strike, real wages for bus operators increased by 53 percent, and bus patrons in the East Bay enjoyed more service. Between 1960 and 1969 annual bus mileage at AC Transit increased from 19,713,149 miles to 25,187,613 miles.[83] All of which is to say that by 1977 the operators of the ATU 192 faced a different landscape and a far different set of challenges—challenges that would come into full view during the strike of 1977.

On November 21, 1977, the union voted down AC Transit's last offer by a margin of 697 to 397 and began what would be its longest strike since 1953.[84] The strike came after five months of deadlocked negotiations and centered on two points: pension benefits for retired workers and changes to the pay progression formula for new workers. Instead of new workers taking one year to reach full pay, AC Transit proposed to extend that period to thirty-six months. The counterproposal from the ATU 192—which included a 29-cent wage increase, greater pension payouts, and a new Employee's Anniversary Holiday—in many ways revealed what reporter Mike Libbey would deem both "the unrealistic expectations of the union's 1,883 members" and a certain degree of hubris rooted in the union's past successes.[85] As Libbey wrote, "the workers had become used to winning rich contracts which more than doubled their pay in the last 10 years." As such, the union's hard line in 1977 was not unexpected; they were simply used to winning.[86] The strike ended on January 27. While the union did manage to increase the contract's value from $10.8 million to $11.2 million over three years (excluding wages), the gain of $400,000 in pension benefits and pay progression savings paled in comparison to the nearly $6 million that local union members lost in wages during the strike.[87] Moreover, the strike actually saved the agency money.[88] While the agency lost $4.13 million in fares and contract services, it saved $8.7 million in wages, fuel, pension, and other costs.[89]

Many blamed the failure of the strike on the inexperience of then-ATU 192 president John Wesley, who had been a bus driver himself and had come into the position with high expectations but little experience. His "rash" decision making, as one reporter put it, was a hindrance.[90] Even with more attuned leadership, however, it is not entirely clear the union would have managed any better. The reality of the transit industry had changed, while the union's techniques had not.[91] By 1977, AC Transit's reliance on local and state tax revenue simply made striking more difficult. With almost 70 percent of its income coming from local and state taxes, and only 30 percent coming from fares, a work stoppage made little dent in the agency's revenues. Whether buses ran or not, tax revenue still flowed in. Suffice it to say, for agencies like AC Transit, losing a month's worth of fares but saving a month's worth of transit operating costs was increasingly a trade worth making.[92]

The Age of Proposition 13

That 1977 would be the last transit strike waged by the ATU 192 is unsurprising. The strike had largely been a failure. Even though workers had won a more favorable pay progression and a slight increase in pension benefits, they had forfeited a good deal more in wages. By 1978, however, the union was reeling from yet another challenge. In 1978, and through the ballot initiative process, California voters passed the Jarvis-Gann Amendment. Proposition 13, a property tax cap, was regarded as something of a "taxpayer's bill of rights." In real terms it functioned to limit the ability of public authorities like AC Transit to use their taxing power to generate new revenue. Following the passage of Proposition 13, the agency lost $17 million in subsidies.[93] The law not only had sizable impacts on AC Transit's service, but it also had a major effect on the working conditions of public sector workers. This had been part of its goal. As labor lawyer Harold

Coxson argued, Proposition 13 served "as a warning to public officials and union leaders that tax payers want greater efficiency and productivity for their tax dollars and they want a greater role in government decision making."[94] The law's message was clear: taxpayers were not getting their money's worth, and public sector unions were partially to blame. AC Transit bus driver David Lyons—who began work in 1980—recalls that the impacts of the law on East Bay transit drivers were wide ranging:

> I came [to AC Transit] in 1980 and that was right after Proposition 13. It had a huge impact—because at that time 60% of their subsidy revenue and 40% of their total revenue came from property taxes. From my opinion that tax cut mainly benefited the wealthy and the industrial and commercial property [owners]. Part of the response to that tax cut was the initiating of part-time work among bus drivers, which was a major attack on our conditions and the conditions that workers face. I was one of the last of the full-time class to go straight full-time. Part-timing at the time was a split shift, no benefits at all, just got paid for what you worked, no compensation for being available 13 hours a day and at the same time as there were declining conditions for workers, they began to cut service as well. Just an aside, we had a one year wage freeze as part of our first contract. That wage freeze would have cost me $1200 a year. My parents' home which was affected by Proposition 13— I didn't own a home at that time—they saved about $600 from that. So you can see just in one wage freeze alone, if I had owned a home, I would have lost more than I gained. At the same time in 1980 the fares went from 25 to 35 cents and the service began to be cut as a result of Proposition 13.[95]

Proposition 13 was explicitly aimed at reducing California's public sector expenditures. In direct contrast to the progressive proposals that emerged following the 1946 General Strike—which included proposals to increase public spending for schools, levy higher taxes on downtown properties, and repeal regressive sales taxes—Proposition 13 marked a stunning reversal of fortunes for working people in Oakland. According to AC Transit operators like David Lyons, Proposition 13 brought both losses in wages and fundamental changes to working conditions—most notably the introduction of part-time workers. In contrast to decades of gains, in both wages for workers and service miles for riders, Proposition 13 ushered in a new era for the union and a new era for AC Transit more generally. By limiting the power of AC Transit to levy taxes on real property within the district, both riders and drivers would have to do with less.

By 1974, the labor contract for East Bay transit workers had expanded from a one-page document to a seventy-four-page tome.[96] Whereas the rights of East Bay transit workers in 1906 had included the right to purchase a uniform on the open market, the right to free transportation, and the right to a maximum spread time of fifteen hours, by 1977 the rights of East Bay transit workers had expanded to include the right to three days of paid funeral leave, the right of workers to three weeks of vacation after five years of service, the right to a cost-of-living adjustment, the right to eight hours of work per day, and the right to a spread time of no more than ten hours.[97] These rights, of course, were not simply the product of management's good will. Rather, they were the products of struggle. In some instances, as in 1919, that struggle was a violent one, spilling out from the meeting rooms into the streets of Oakland. In other instances, as in 1977 and 1978, the demands of workers would fall short, run aground by the tides of a taxpayer revolt and a conservative backlash against labor more generally.

Transit workers in the East Bay have continued to fight to improve their working conditions—even as the political tides have shifted. Perhaps most recently, and alongside the perennial issues of wages and pensions, the ATU 192, in the last several years, has taken up the issue of bathroom breaks and the work rules that limit them. As many operators will attest, much of the challenge has hinged on the difference between what workers call *spot time* and *recovery time*. Per the contract, for every eight hours of work, AC Transit operators are entitled to a 50-minute lunch break. For operators who work an uninterrupted eight hours—rather than working a split shift—that 50 minutes often comes in the form of spot time. Per the contract *spot time* refers to the time that operators have at the end of each run to stretch, use the bathroom, and eat lunch. The amount of spot time depends on the length of each run. For runs between 30 and 60 minutes, drivers are entitled to 6 minutes of spot time. For runs that are 30 minutes or less, drivers are guaranteed a minimum of 5 minutes of spot time, and for runs that extend over an hour, spot time is set at a minimum of 12 minutes. Spot time is essential to securing operator well-being. *Recovery time*, by contrast, refers to the time built into the schedule to ensure that operators start their next run on time. In short, recovery time is built in the schedule as a buffer against traffic or other unforeseen delays—whether arising from directing tourists, breaking up a fist fight, or picking up a disabled passenger. In the last five years, one of the ATU 192's central critiques of AC Transit has been the tendency to blur the distinction between spot time and recovery time. With tighter budgets—especially after 2010—AC Transit management was increasingly allowing recovery time to devour spot time. For operators the most serious consequence was not so much losing time to eat as it was losing access to the bathroom. In 2010, Anthony Rodgers illustrated precisely this point.[98]

> In this last signup I was doing an 18 Line. It gave me—leaving from 14th and Broadway to 40th and Martin Luther King—I had six minutes. Six minutes from 14th and Broadway to the MacArthur BART station at 40th and MLK. A NASCAR driver couldn't do that! Let me take that back, you can do it in six minutes—if the traffic is clear, if you don't catch any lights, and if you don't waste your time picking up passengers . . .

Now let's say you're ten minutes late when you get to the end of the line and you have 15 minutes of spot time. That means you only have five minutes when you get there and the only restroom you know of at Marin and San Pablo is at the Albany City Hall, which is a block away. So you have five minutes to get off the bus, run over to the restroom [and] do what it is you have to do and run back.[99]

For Rodgers and other operators, AC Transit's scheduling practices increasingly denied operators the ability to accomplish the most basic of human functions—to go to the bathroom. In 2013, bathroom access was a key issue in contract negotiations. In one of the more memorable board meetings during contract negotiations, ATU 192 member Titus Warren addressed the AC Transit board as his alter ego—"the C220 ATU 192"—a fully equipped android for whom bathrooms, rest breaks, marital issues, and even contract negotiations were of little concern.[100] "I am," Warren declared, "the ATU 192 automaton!" The satire was not lost on the board, but the scheduling issue remained largely unaddressed in the final contract signed in December of the same year. In 2014, the ATU 192 partnered with Elana Kessler and Michelle Gonzalez—two interns working for the Occupational Health Internship Program—to publish a study entitled "Bus Operators and the Right to Access Restrooms."[101] In a survey of ninety-eight operators, the report found that 20 percent had accidently relieved themselves on the job. Of those surveyed, only 7 percent reported access to restrooms deemed safe and sanitary. Perhaps more startling, Kessler and Gonzalez noted that in the absence of facilities, a significant number of operators responded simply by "holding it." As the report notes, the act of simply "holding it" can increase the risks of urinary tract infections and renal damage, as well as traffic accidents as drivers lose the ability to focus on the road.[102] Alongside more common fights over wages and health benefits, the ongoing fight for a right to access bathrooms simply continues the union's long-standing commitment to improving the lives of transit workers and to further expand the rights and protection to which they are entitled.

Since 1906, the general function of the ATU 192 has changed very little. Like other unions, its role has been to negotiate contracts that secure for its members a set of rights and protections. These have been rights to fair wages, redress for grievances, and working conditions that are safe. While the goals of the ATU have not changed, the context in which the union has been forced to operate certainly has. When the carmen of Division 192 met in Grier Hall in the spring of 1906 to demand recognition and a written contract, they were in fact part of the larger unionization push at the turn of the century. Between 1900 and 1905 alone, union membership in the United States expanded from close to eight hundred thousand workers to nearly two million.[103] Against the competitive imperatives of capitalists like Francis "Borax" Smith, the carmen's insistence on a contract was based on the belief that workers needed a set of guaranteed

protections against exploitation. Similarly, in 1919, when East Bay transit workers took to the streets to demand an eight-hour work day, they embodied an
emergent labor radicalism characteristic of the years immediately following
World War I. In 1953, when East Bay transit workers struck for seventy-six days,
they did so only seven years after their pivotal role in the Oakland General
Strike of 1946. In 1953, the ATU 192 could count on a public and civic sphere in
which labor was still firmly entrenched.[104]

Workers and "the Public"

Today, as in 1977—the year of the last strike—members of the ATU 192 are no
longer private sector workers but rather public servants. Their struggles are no
longer against transit barons or traction capitalists, or even managers like Willis
Kelley, but against a democratically elected board representing the public itself.
Efforts to secure higher wages can no longer be framed as efforts at profit sharing. There is no profit to be had. If transit workers want shorter spread times,
more vacation days, or longer *spot time* minimums, such demands invariably
mean increasing public subsidies and raising taxes. To the degree that the ATU
192 attempts to secure the rights of workers, they secure them against the public
to which they are employees. Just as the streetcar strike of 1919 only makes
sense against the backdrop of a broader post–World War I labor radicalism, the
so-called sickout of AC Transit workers in 2010 can only be understood against
the evolution of the transit industry and the status of transit workers as public
sector workers at a time when such workers are increasingly under attack—in
ways that are little different than in the late 1970s.[105]

In this context, comments like those of Joyce Roy and Steve Geller are even
more important. As members of the East Bay's transportation justice movement, their skepticism of labor poses a set of rather sticky questions. How, for
example, should we understand the politics of the ATU 192, or other unions,
alongside the demand for transportation justice or the struggles of local riders
for better and cheaper transit? When we argue that public transit is important
for securing the rights to the city for the transit dependent—as we did in the
previous chapter—how do we understand the role of transit workers in that?
For transit activists like Roy and Geller, the answer was fairly clear. For them,
transit workers needed to "do more"—whether that meant contributing more to
their retirement or more to their healthcare plans. For both Roy and Geller, the
so-called rights of transit workers, if anything, were impediments to better transit service.[106] Why should transit riders support unionized workers who decline
to make any contributions to their healthcare plans—which most employers
require? How is it in the interest of the riding public to support transit workers'
rights to a spread time of ten hours rather than eleven or to a guaranteed eight

hours on the extra board?[107] Like many unions, the ATU 192 has clear provisions in its contract that give preference to senior workers when selecting pieces of work. The result is that the least-experienced drivers work the most difficult lines, while drivers with the most experience work far easier routes—often in the more affluent Oakland Hills.[108] How, we might ask, does this arrangement serve the interests of the transit dependent, the poor, or riders like Joyce Roy or Steve Geller? Where transit agencies struggle admirably to deal with peak-hour demand, why should such riders join unions like the ATU 192 in resisting the use of part-time workers?[109] When we define transit as a right, or when we take the additional step to argue that improved transit is central to securing a right to the city, how do we then understand the entitlements owed to transit workers? Should such entitlements simply be ignored or shunted aside?

In the context of a labor dispute, or when transit activists bemoan the generous salaries enjoyed by AC Transit workers, it is not at all self-evident that the rights of workers and the rights of the transit-riding public are at all commensurable. Indeed, it often seems just the opposite. For many workers, of course, this framing misses a broader point, namely, the degree to which workers are part of the public themselves and the degree to which labor can be central to creating the type of city that transit riders desire. This argument is an old one and hardly new to the East Bay. In fact, it was the argument that emerged in 1946 in the midst of the Oakland General Strike.

During that strike, the socialist paper the *Weekly People* published a stinging reply to the mayor of Oakland, who had reproached striking workers for endangering the public welfare.

Generally speaking, science has done a pretty good job on pixies, elves, fairies, spirits and similar supernatural imps, not to mention spooks and banshees. But there is one superstition that returns to haunt us no matter how often it is laid with scientific facts and logic. It is the mystic "public." Right now the public is suffering the tortures of the damned. We know this because every capitalist editor in the county tells us so both in screaming headlines and commiserating editorials. Especially is the "public" of Oakland California, suffering. According to the mayor of that city the "public" has been denied the right to "get food, to travel in any form of public transportation, to send their children to school where there are distances to be travelled, to have a daily paper." Resisting the impulse to let our hearts bleed for the "the public" of Oakland—and elsewhere—we move in for a closer look at this mysterious creature which always manages to be right in the middle in labor disputes. Who is the public? According to the editors, the "public" is all of us who are not directly involved in the dispute. Thus in Oakland, where there is a general strike as this is written, the public is the "public." Well who the hell is left when all the workers are on strike against the capitalist class of a city? . . . There isn't the slightest doubt that a lot of people suffer when there is a strike. But these people

are workers themselves, or the families of workers. They are members of the working class with interests in common with all other working men and women who
live on wages. . . . How convenient for the class of skinners, if only the workers of
this country, when not directly engaged in a skirmish with capital, would think
of themselves as the "injured" and "suffering public"! Why, then employers could
always count on a free hand in beating strikers to their knees. Nay they could count
on pressure from the "public" thinking workers to end the strike and to end on
terms favorable to the employer.[110]

For the editors of the *Weekly People*, the idea of a "long suffering public" missed
the point entirely. Striking workers *were* the public and not separate from it.
When a striker like Al Brown, for example, abandoned his streetcar, he did so
not out of spite for the public interest but on behalf of a public defined in explicitly class terms. Lest the term be co-opted, the editors of the *Weekly People*
sought to redefine the idea of the public in terms that emphasized a shared
struggle, that erased the distinction between workers and the public they
served, and that emphasized the degree to which the rights of workers were
more important than a temporary inconvenience. In 1946, the editors argued,
it made little sense to talk about the rights of the public "to get food, to travel
on public transportation" as separate from the rights of workers—workers *were*
the public.

In many ways, this was the same argument voiced by AC Transit workers
following their so-called sickout in 2010. As ATU 192 president Claudia Hudson
put it at the time, "The people who catch the bus, the people who drive the bus,
and the people who fix the bus are one and the same."[111] The riding public and
transit operators, she would add, are fighting for the same thing: "They are fighting for transportation dollars to keep transportation public and to keep it available for people to be able to utilize it. We are fighting for the same things but
we are also fighting to maintain our working conditions while we provide the
service."[112] The fact that the drivers might enjoy generous benefits or that they
might make more money than the people they carry was beside the point. As
East Bay bus drivers like David Lyons would suggest, generous benefits for
public sector workers are valuable not simply because they are generous, but
because they set a standard for other workers. For Lyons, the value of a class-
based argument could not be overstated: "I think the failure of a class approach
to labor struggle [is a problem]. . . . We do make more than a lot of people we
carry, but on the other hand if we lose, it doesn't mean they gain, in fact it's
usually the opposite. If you try and set a standard that other workers can shoot
for, they can point to [you] as they enter negotiations." After all, "the best safety
for bus riders, is a good contract for workers."[113]

Service reductions and fare hikes, one might argue, are not the fault of public
sector workers. They are the fault of bad policy. They are the fault of policies

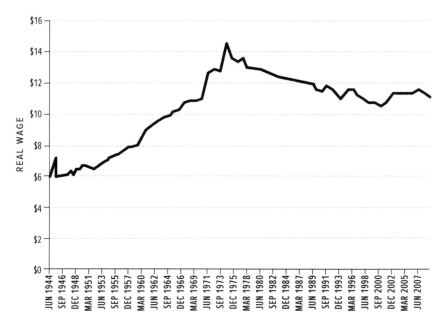

FIGURE 4. Real Wages for East Bay Bus Operators. Compiled by author from wage data available at the San Francisco State University Labor Archives and Research Center, Amalgamated Transit Union 192 Records, Box 12, Folder 3. The graph is not a record of nominal wages, but of wages in real dollars based on the San Francisco–Oakland Consumer Price Index for 1982–84.

that have gutted the public sector in favor of private and commercial property owners. Even if they might disagree momentarily—as during the sickout—bus riders like Joyce Roy and members of ATU 192 like David Lyons arguably have an equal stake in finding ways to reverse such policies. In direct contrast to the idea that riders and drivers have opposing interests, one need only look at the striking effects of Proposition 13. Between 1960 and 1978 drivers enjoyed real wage gains almost each successive year (Figure 4). During that same period transit passengers enjoyed gains as well—both decreases in real transit fares (Figure 5) and an expansion of service miles. Proposition 13 reversed all that. Following its passage, not only did service become more erratic, but real wages for transit workers fell (Figure 4) and real fares began to trend upward (Figure 5).[114] This change of fortunes was the result of a clear legislative choice to gut the public coffers. In this context, Claudia Hudson's argument that "the people who catch the bus, the people who drive the bus, and the people who fix the bus are one and the same" not only seems less glib but an appropriate assessment of the degree to which "the people who ride the bus and the people that drive the bus" have each gotten a raw deal.[115]

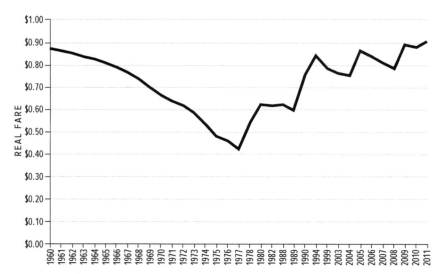

FIGURE 5. Real Fares at AC Transit. Compiled by author from fare data available at AC Transit, based on AC Transit's single zone fare—the cheapest fare available. The graph is not a record of nominal fares, but of fares in real dollars based on the San Francisco–Oakland Consumer Price Index for 1982–84.

Claudia Hudson's argument extended yet further. For Hudson, transit workers were also a key tool in the fight for a more just city. As evidence, Hudson cited the example of Parchester Village. Sitting just north of downtown Richmond, Parchester was developed in the 1950s as one of the few suburban areas open to black residents. Despite being pitched as a "community for all Americans," by the 1970s it was almost entirely black.[116] Hemmed in by the San Francisco Bay to the west, the Richmond Parkway to the south, Giant Highway to the east, and by a state park to the north, Parchester was largely cut off from the rest of the East Bay. According to Hudson, for much of the 1960s bus service to Parchester Village was limited to skirting the outskirts. Instead of venturing into the enclave itself, AC Transit would pick up passengers on a busy road on the area's perimeter. In the late 1970s this began to change, and according to Hudson, it was largely due to the advocacy of black bus drivers working in AC Transit's Richmond division. It was bus drivers, Hudson remarked, "who led the fight to have Parchester Village serviced actually on their streets."[117] For Hudson, the role of transit workers in serving the residents of Parchester Village was indicative of something larger. In the face of public disinvestment and in the wake of Proposition 13, it indicated that drivers and riders were committed to a similar vision of the city. That vision was one in which working-class residents in places like Parchester Village were part of the public and had a right to the city. More broadly, it was a vision that held out the promise of a working-class city made in the image of working-class people—whether they were behind the wheel of a bus or waiting patiently for a bus to arrive.

In the midst of sickouts like those in 2010, it is easy to bemoan the impact of labor disputes on the riding public—especially when that public is composed of the transportation disadvantaged and the poor, as is the case in the East Bay. Where "resources are scarce," and where service levels have long been compromised, demanding that public sector workers "do more" is understandable. Of course, such arguments miss a great deal. As Figures 4 and 5 indicate, they miss the degree to which "scarcity" itself is a product of both politics and a concerted effort to gut the public sector. To return to the *Weekly People*, it also misses the degree to which workers are themselves part of the public. Most importantly, however, it shortchanges the history of unions such as the ATU, which has long been at the forefront of defending policies that benefit the poor and the working class. That history includes the union's struggle for an eight-hour workday in 1919, its demand in 1947 for a forty-hour work week, and its role as codefendant in the civil rights lawsuit *Darensburg v. MTC*. It includes the ATU 192's role in bringing service to Parchester Village. Perhaps the high point of this advocacy came in the wake of the Oakland General Strike of 1946. Following that strike, the ATU 192 and other local unions took on a range of progressive initiatives aimed at remaking Oakland and the East Bay: repealing anti-picketing and anti-handbilling ordinances; increasing expenditures on public schools, public libraries, and public swimming pools; overhauling public health services; and creating a civic unity commission to enforce equity in city hiring.[118] To the extent that transportation justice advocates, or activists like Geller and Roy, ignore this history, to the extent that they forget that transit's perennial "funding crises" are a product of political choices rather than worker greed, or to the degree that they define the public in ways that exclude workers, they not only embrace a rather narrow view of the public, but they also obscure the degree to which transit workers can play a central role in creating a more just city—as they have in the past.

CHAPTER 4

Alternatives in Transit

It's 100% a dream, there's no reality to it, it may look like it's official, but that's because I am very good at making things look official, but all it is, is one lunatic—that's me—coming up with the idea, making a whole route map, designing it as if it were a real bus system and then just announcing that it's real and having public meetings. . . . If enough people assume that it's real—then it becomes real—that's how things happen in the world.

—Kristan Lawson, creator of the B-Line, December 7, 2010

In late October 2010, any number of residents in Berkeley or Oakland might have stumbled upon a rather peculiar document—a map of an otherwise fictitious transit system called "The B-Line." On the back of each glossy map (see Figure 6)—and amid a jumble of bullet-point declarations—there was an explicit call to action: "The time has come for us, the residents of Berkeley, to set up our own transit system—a modest fleet of electric small buses or trolleys running through the city on a network of routes designed with riders' needs in mind." A new transit system, according to the flyers, would "transform Berkeley into the public transit paradise it deserved to be. . . . Existing bus riders will get vastly improved service, with buses going exactly where we want them to go, more frequently and less expensively than with AC Transit."[1] According to the flyer, the B-Line would have seven separate routes. Route B1 would run from Berkeley's renowned "Gourmet Ghetto" to the top of Telegraph Avenue near People's Park. Route B2, nicknamed the "North Berkeley Circle Line," would serve the areas of North Berkeley, as well as San Pablo Avenue. Route B3 would connect downtown Berkeley with the Fourth Street Business District—an upscale shopping area west of San Pablo Avenue and east of Interstate 80. Running through south Berkeley, Route B4 promised to offer a link to yet another popular business district in Emeryville. The B-Line's Route B5 would run along Telegraph Avenue before ending at the Claremont Hotel. For connections to the rather affluent Berkeley Hills and the Tilden Regional Park, route options

FIGURE 6. "The B-Line: Berkeley's Municipal Transit System." Kristan Lawson, 2010. https://berkeleytransit.wordpress.com/route-map/. Map courtesy of Kristan Lawson.

would include both B6 and B7. For many familiar with Berkeley, the proposed system may have raised some immediate red flags. The absence of any routes through the historically working-class and minority areas of South Berkeley, for example, and the obvious emphasis on upscale shopping areas were notably conspicuous. For those less familiar with the area, however, the map may have raised a simpler question: Why did Berkeley need its own transit system?

In some respects, the idea of a new transit system in California's East Bay made perfect sense. As of October, the year 2010 had proved a horrible one for transit. Over the course of nine months, AC Transit had cut service by nearly 15 percent and had undergone a prolonged labor dispute that had left riders stranded for two weeks; in September, its board of directors had voted to cut most weekend service altogether.[2] Whatever the B-Line promised, there was little doubt that it would be an improvement. Of course, for just as many in the East Bay, the idea of the B-Line was laughable. The nine-county Bay Area already had twenty-seven separate transit agencies. Martha Lindsey, of the environmental advocacy group Transform, argued that "people riding transit already have to keep track of [too] many different transit agencies."[3] What was the point of adding yet another? Even more disqualifying than the logistics of adding a new system was the issue of the B-Line's origins. The idea of the B-Line, after all, was not the product of some popular referendum. Neither was it the result of some prolonged transit study. Rather, the B-Line was the brainchild of a middle-aged nonfiction writer from the Berkeley Hills named Kristan Lawson—a man with no planning credentials, and whose primary claim to fame was as a coauthor of a children's book on Darwinian evolution. By his own admission, Lawson had drawn up the map of the B-Line in less than a fortnight. When asked about what had prompted the B-Line, Lawson's response hardly engendered any additional confidence:

> In 1994, I got an incredibly great deal on a house way up on the top of the Berkeley hills, something I normally couldn't afford. One of the deciding factors in buying this house was that there [were] two AC Transit bus lines one block away from the house. One was the 65 and the other was 8 line. . . . And then two years after I moved, they canceled the 8 line. . . . Then they started downgrading the 65 service. And the thing that spurred me on was that four months ago they said they're going to cancel the 65 entirely on the weekends and possibly have it once an hour on the weekdays, which basically makes my life a living hell. . . . So I said why doesn't someone make a better bus system. And I am one of these entrepreneurial people, and I said: "Why don't I make a better bus system," and so I took the bull by the horns.[4]

Even if the B-Line began as little more than a knee-jerk reaction to AC Transit cutting the bus line to his house, at the heart of Lawson's B-Line was something wholly genuine. As Lawson explained in an interview with the *Daily Californian*, the goal of the B-Line was simple: to offer an alternative. The idea was to imagine a transit system more "in tune with local community needs" and more in line with "the hopes and dreams" of people chastened by perennial service cuts, fare hikes, and unpredictability.[5] More than this, the goal of the B-Line was to open up a conversation. While Lawson's original map included seven clearly defined routes, these lines, he assured people, were not set in stone. Instead, he explained, they were merely the opening gambit in what he hoped to be a broader debate over the type of transit system people in Berkeley actually wanted.

I understand that everyone is going to come out and say "this [should] go there" and "this line is stupid" or "my house is there" and everyone is going to argue. I don't care about the details. I just wanted to get it going. And if you all want to wrestle about the details or how it's funded, fine. Wrestle away. If the City of Berkeley says we'll give $20 million to make the B-Line a reality, then great; throw away my idea about it being privately financed. I was just trying to come up with alternatives.[6]

To the degree that Lawson saw the B-Line as an invitation to debate an alternative to AC Transit, he was also clear to note that this debate had little if anything to do with "transportation justice," rights, or even a discussion on the type of city people want to live in. If anything, Lawson hoped to avoid such discussions altogether. According to Lawson, the idea of transportation justice was a nonstarter.

The problem is that in Berkeley and probably other places, transit becomes politics. Everything gets intertwined with all these political agendas, and I just wanted to stay away from that. . . . I'm not doing this for transit justice. . . . I know when someone says "transit justice," [what] they're talking about is much more hyperpartisan than they're revealing. . . . They want to penalize the wealthy people at the expense of the poor people. Eight years ago, they were considering canceling the 65. . . . And so I made the mistake of going to one of their public comment meetings. . . . There were about three other people there who were also going to complain about the 65 being canceled. . . . Before I even had a chance to say anything, other people got up and complained about their bus lines, and then the 65 people got up and complained, and the other bus advocates were shouting them down. "Privileged people don't need a bus. Just jump in a car, you rich millionaire asshole!" . . . And this is the divisive attitude. It's not like these bus advocates would even want there to be buses to the hills. . . . I live in the hills, which identifies me as privileged, even though I bought that house with my last dime and I'm totally broke because of it. And I know all my neighbors are what I call "house-poor." . . . The hills are filled with old people, disabled people. And the rich people have children, teenagers who go to school. They have maids, home care workers. There's hundreds of homecare workers who take care of old people in the hills, and there's no way to get to these people's houses.[7]

According to Lawson, the transportation justice movement in the East Bay had written off the Berkeley Hills and thus had written off transit riders like himself as well as the array of people in the Berkeley Hills who were just as reliant on transit as riders in the East Bay. Lawson's critique of the idea of transportation justice went further still. The problem with transportation justice was that it was often less interested in transit itself than transit as a political tool.

When people say "social justice," it's just a euphemism. They don't really want universal bus coverage, they want it as, like, an implement of the revolution. They want to drain the coffers of the privileged and give it to the underprivileged for some revolutionary purposes. Berkeley is filled with all sorts of political things. Not that I'm against that, but that's not what I'm talking about here. I'm saying to everyone, "If we make the bus system universally applicable, then everybody will want to take it equally, and it will achieve universal equality and universal diversity, since everyone will be taking the same transit system. Isn't that what we all want?"[8]

The B-Line was not an "implement of the revolution," nor was it designed to drain the coffers of the wealthy. It was not even an invitation to imagine a better society. In contrast to the East Bay's "social justice warriors," Lawson "simply wanted buses for everyone." He did not "care about politics." "People need buses," he argued, not a revolution. Of course, everything covered in this book militates against this view of transit. Debates over transit are inherently political and are inextricably connected to broader debates over what type of city we want to live in as well as what rights we afford workers, riders, and taxpayers. What is perhaps most curious is that Lawson himself seemed well aware of this fact. He simply wished that the reality were different.

> Already . . . I've got all these people emailing me going, "There's not enough buses that go to South Berkeley. I see three buses that go to North Berkeley and only two buses that go to South Berkeley. What are you, some kind of Klan member?" . . . So I know that as neutral as I try to be, and as pragmatic as I try to be, and as helpful as I try to be, it will be torn to shreds by all these competing factions who all want social justice this, social justice that, and the end result is, it'll never happen, and the earth will burn up because no one's riding buses. What do you want me to do? I can't change the world.[9]

Of course for most people—Kristan Lawson notwithstanding—the question of whether or not politics ought to matter in how we think about transportation policy is a mute one. Debates on transportation are inevitably political— whether we like it or not. The more important question is how we think about those politics and how we make sense of political conflict. In this vein, the work of Jason Henderson is invaluable. As Henderson argues in his book *Street Fight*, the political conflicts that define urban transportation policy are almost always ideological and often take the form of three competing visions—a conservative vision that defends automobility, a neoliberal vision that celebrates market competition in all its forms, and a progressive vision that values social equity and environmental stewardship and that is skeptical of too much mobility—especially as measured in vehicle miles traveled (vmt).[10] In the spirit of the B-Line, and drawing direct inspiration from Henderson's work, this chapter examines three of the most promising ideas in transit innovation in the East Bay: Transit Oriented Development (tod), Complete Streets, and bus rapid transit (brt). As becomes clear in the discussion, while Henderson's work is helpful in making sense of both the politics that drive such initiatives and the politics that drive opposition to them, it is less helpful in other respects. It is not only less helpful in explaining the material realities that constrain ideology but also in critically assessing what type of progressive politics is necessary for lasting change.

The Alternatives

Over the last fifty years, the Bay Area has produced its fair share of Kristan Lawsons—individuals who have taken it upon themselves to draft often radical transit alternatives. In 1969, former Stanford University transportation technologist Howard Ross famously regaled the AC Transit Board of Directors with the promise of a revolutionary new idea in personal transit—a system consisting of small, personalized transit capsules made to glide frictionlessly on a "linear accelerated guide way." Using a compressed air system technology, Ross argued, the system would whisk passengers from one end of the East Bay to the other at speeds previously unimaginable (Figure 7). The "AC" in AC Transit, writers for the *Oakland Tribune* quipped, would now stand for "Air Cushion."[11] In 1967, from the Palo Alto headquarters of Tube Transit Inc., a Lockheed engineer named L. K. Edwards proposed the construction of an underground pneumatic vacuum tube running from Marin County in the north to San Jose in the south. Gravity Vacuum Transit (GVT), as Edwards called it, would allow passengers to travel underground at speeds of up to ninety-five miles per hour.[12] While these transit proposals are perhaps less famous than BART, they speak with equal force to the Bay Area's long tradition of fomenting transit experimentation.[13] In the last two decades, efforts to promote transit in the East Bay have congealed around Transit Oriented Development (TOD), Complete Streets, and bus rapid transit (BRT). While each offers slightly different solutions to the transit problems afflicting cities, they share a belief in the importance of linking debates over transit with debates over general land-use policy. For proponents of such initiatives, lasting improvements to transit require a wholesale transformation in how cities and municipalities design streets, direct traffic, and prioritize how land is used. In the East Bay, this view of transit has best been expressed in AC Transit's *Designing with Transit: Making Transit Integral to East Bay Communities*.[14]

Published in 2004, *Designing with Transit* was authored by AC Transit planner Nathan Landau and was written with a specific aim: to provide a blueprint for how to better integrate transit concerns into the East Bay's land-use planning process. *Designing with Transit* begins by stating the problem in broad terms:

> The American transportation system has become unbalanced, excessively reliant on the automobile. For decades, the system has developed to encourage mobility

FIGURE 7. "Ross's Test Vehicle," 1969. Reprinted from *AC Transit Times* 11, no. 9, cover. Courtesy of AC Transit.

by auto, with transit an afterthought at best. . . . As a result, sprawling, low density development that can only be effectively served by automobiles has proliferated. Bus transit came to be seen by many as "last resort" transportation for the "transit-dependent," an image that further discouraged ridership and helped stimulate a spiral of decline. The outcome is that Americans take more of our trips by car than citizens of any other developed country, including Canada. The East Bay does not escape this automobile dominance. Yet there are foundations here for transit to build on. The older communities of the East Bay were initially developed around transit. . . . This history has meant that many of these communities continue to have land use patterns that make effective transit service possible.[15]

At the heart of *Designing with Transit* is a simple argument: public transit is most successful when communities plan their streets and land use in ways that prioritize transit service.[16] Connected to this is the belief that improving public transportation is too important and too complex a task to be left to transit planners alone. Instead, that task requires input from community members, real estate developers, zoning board members, and elected officials. To this end, *Designing with Transit* contains a range of recommendations and policy suggestions that—while differing both in focus and scope—all aim at encouraging a range of actors to adopt land-use policies that facilitate transit. *Designing with Transit* highlights three specific areas of land use reform that serve to do this: developing transit-based communities, developing better pedestrian corridors, and improving street and traffic flows (read: TOD, Complete Streets, and BRT, respectively).

Transit Oriented Development

Designing with Transit defines "transit-based communities" as areas in which "residents, workers, and other users of the area can meet their daily needs by using transit and walking."[17] These are areas with high levels of transit service and a mix of both commercial and residential uses.[18] With an intent to encourage cities to develop "transit-based communities," reports such as *Designing with Transit* offer a list of "best practices," which include scrapping or reducing parking requirements for new builds; relaxing zoning limits on high-density projects; clustering housing, restaurants, and civic facilities in areas associated with high-transit connectivity; and simply identifying the types of developments that are most appropriate for areas with potentially heavy transit usage. In many ways, the arguments for such "best practices" are obvious. Where parking is free or cheap, there will be little incentive for people to leave their cars at home. In areas where drive-through restaurants, car dealerships, and big box stores predominate, promoting transit will be that much harder. Similarly, in the absence of dense residential neighborhoods with a mix of retail options (grocery stores, pharmacies, and restaurants are particularly important) not only will bus transit be ineffective, but people will have little option but to use cars to meet their daily needs.

As many planners have noted, there are a number of areas in the East Bay that can already be classified as transit-based communities. These include the areas around Berkeley's downtown BART station, the area surrounding Oakland's downtown bus transfer station and, most famously, Oakland's Fruitvale Transit Village. These areas are all defined by mixed retail and residential developments, a high density of land uses, and excellent transit connectivity. Of course, there are also large swaths of the East Bay where more is needed. Perhaps *Designing with Transit*'s most important observation is that there is a need in the East Bay to be more creative in developing transit-based communities. While a great deal of attention has been paid to projects like the Fruitvale Transit Village and other BART stations, there is no reason that transit-oriented communities cannot develop around AC transit's five major trunk routes. These are the areas along International Boulevard, MacArthur Boulevard, Broadway Street, Foothill Boulevard, and San Pablo Avenue. Arguably, these corridors, which carry 40 percent of all AC Transit riders, are extremely well situated to become thriving, transit-oriented communities.[19]

Complete Streets

In the effort to revive transit in the East Bay, the promotion of TODs represents only one effort among many. Another focus has been on the idea of walkability—an issue to which AC Transit's *Designing with Transit* dedicates an entire chapter. Of course, the immediate question is, what does walkability have to do with transit? The answer, in many ways, is obvious. Where streets are unsafe, where walking is discouraged, or where using bus transit means crossing a possibly dangerous intersection to board or transfer, fewer people will endeavor to take buses. There is no scarcity of areas in the East Bay to which these conditions apply. As in most cities, high traffic speeds, uncontrolled intersections, and narrow sidewalks are simply part of urban life in the East Bay. Where these conditions persist, encouraging transit is difficult. The question for planners in the East Bay has thus been a rather simple one: How can sidewalks and streets be designed in ways "that are [both] safe for pedestrians and functional for buses and other vehicle traffic"?[20] How can streets be designed in ways that allow pedestrians to move safely between bus stops and various activity centers? To these questions, *Designing with Transit* offers a number of suggestions: integrating transit stops into activity centers, installing sidewalk furniture, widening pedestrian walkways, and making sure that sidewalks are "visually interesting" so as to attract rather than repel users. Additionally, planners should be making sure that bus stops are located in areas with adequate lighting, that pedestrian crossings are clearly demarcated, and that traffic speeds are not excessive.[21] All such policies will not only make walking safer but will also make it easier for people to take advantage of transit. Of course, as noted in chapter 1, planners must enact such policies in ways that do not open themselves up to even greater tort liability.

In recent years, many of these same policy suggestions have coalesced around the idea of the "Complete Street," a term first coined in 2003 by writer and transportation consultant Barbara McCann. A Complete Street is one that has been "designed to be safe for drivers, bicyclists, transit vehicles; and pedestrians of all ages and abilities."[22] For its proponents, the logic of Complete

Streets could not be any clearer. Experience has proven that streets designed for cars only "limit transportation choices by making walking, bicycling and taking public transportation inconvenient, unattractive and too often dangerous."[23] While Complete Street advocates have latched onto any number of policy suggestions, much of the practical emphasis of Complete Streets' advocacy has centered on traffic-calming policies—particularly on urban arterials. In their essay "Complete Streets: We Can Get There from Here," John Laplante and Barbara McCann focus on narrowing travel lanes from twelve feet to eleven or ten feet, tightening turning radii, eliminating free right turns, and installing landscaped center medians.[24] By slowing traffic, these policies have been proven to promote pedestrian safety and walkability—both essential elements to promoting transit ridership.

The idea of promoting pedestrian safety is not new to the East Bay; Oakland and Berkeley have long been at the forefront of such efforts. Oakland was one of the first cities in the county to develop an explicit plan to support pedestrian travel. In 2004, Berkeley passed a "Pedestrian Charter"—committing itself to promoting safe, convenient, and comfortable walking conditions.[25] Given what many planners have argued, these pedestrian-friendly policies should be embraced not only by those who care about pedestrian safety but also by those interested in promoting transit ridership.

Bus Rapid Transit

To this already rich discussion, there is yet another popular focus of transit advocates in the East Bay—namely, improving the speed and efficiency of transit service itself.[26] When buses cannot remain on schedule, or when they are slow and inefficient, efforts to promote high-density TODs or safe pedestrian walkways will mean very little. Bus delays and inefficiencies arise from any number of sources. They can stem from the time passengers need to embark and disembark, or the time buses spend waiting at traffic lights or navigating congested streets. In tackling these challenges, reports like *Designing with Transit* have offered planners a number of strategies, such as reducing on-street parking; implementing proof-of-payment systems; making certain that signal timing is supportive of bus operations; placing bus stops at safe, efficient, and convenient locations; and wherever possible implementing priority treatment for transit on key corridors.[27] In many ways, these policy suggestions constitute the backbone of a specific concept that is conspicuously absent from *Designing with Transit*, namely, the idea of Bus Rapid Transit (BRT). The National Bus Rapid Transit Institute defines BRT as an integrated system using "buses or specialized vehicles on roadways or dedicated lanes to quickly and efficiently transport passengers to their destinations."[28] The most common image of BRT is of a grade-separated or otherwise distinguishable "transit-way" in which transit vehicles can travel uninhibited by traffic. In addition to exclusive "transit-ways," BRTs often utilize level boarding platforms and proof-of-payment systems— which save time by both eliminating the need for buses to "kneel" and the need for drivers to collect fares. Perhaps the most famous examples of successful BRT systems are in Curtiba, Brazil, and Bogota, Colombia, cities that have designed their entire urban transit systems around these principles. Successful BRT projects have arisen in Los Angeles, Miami, Cleveland, and numerous other cities and have often been followed by increased ridership.[29]

The first public effort to develop a BRT system in California's East Bay emerged in 2007, after AC Transit released a Draft Environmental Impact Statement for a proposed BRT route running from San Leandro to Berkeley. The three cities to be affected—Berkeley, San Leandro, and Oakland—immediately hosted a series of public debates on the proposal. This 2007 proposal actually built upon the earlier findings of a federally mandated Major Investment Study (MIS) that the agency had undertaken in 1999.[30] That study focused on improving service along AC Transit's major transit corridors and weighed the possibilities offered by light rail, express buses, and a BRT route. The study found that a north–south BRT route ultimately offered the best balance between cost and efficiency. BRT, the study noted, had "the potential to offer rail like service without the expense of rail."[31] Drawing directly from this study, the AC Transit's 2007 BRT proposal was quite specific.[32] The proposal called for the constructing of a transit corridor in two segments—one segment along Telegraph Avenue between Berkeley and Oakland and a second segment on International Boulevard between Oakland and San Leandro. Apart from bus-only lanes—which would be the system's key innovation—the proposal also included the construction of median stations with level boarding, the establishment of transit signal priority, the development of a proof-of-payment system, the construction of shelters, and the development of a real-time traveler information system. Since 2007, this original BRT proposal has been amended numerous times, and in almost every case it has been scaled back.[33] Most notably, in 2010 the Berkeley City Council voted against allowing dedicated bus lanes in the Berkeley section of the BRT route. Despite hurdles, construction on the BRT began in early 2017.[34] When completed, the BRT will be the most ambitious attempt since the construction of BART to increase the speed and overall efficiency of transit in the East Bay.

Transit-oriented neighborhoods, better pedestrian corridors, and BRT projects have been proposed in places like the East Bay as a way to rebalance an inarguably unbalanced urban transportation system. With over seventy years separating us from the end of World War II, the legacy of the postwar automobile boom remains an inescapable reality—as do its attendant problems of congestion, pollution, and waste. Partly addressing these problems, TODs, Complete

Streets, and BRT can be seen as the latest and best efforts toward an alternative. While these strategies differ in emphasis, each shares a fundamental insistence on improving transit's viability by transforming the city itself. In many ways, cities like Oakland and Berkeley have been at the leading edge of these alternative visions for transit. Oakland's Fruitvale Transit Village has become a nationally recognized example of a successful TOD. Berkeley's dedication to pedestrian safety and accessibility is manifest in its "Pedestrian Charter" and its generous regulations regarding clear-path sidewalk clearance for the disabled. The East Bay's first BRT line along Broadway and International Boulevard is currently under construction. Initiatives like TOD, BRT, and Complete Streets, however, have not been without their problems. At the local level, some of these challenges have been financial. More commonly, however, these challenges arise from both the limitations of the street itself and the difficulty of building community "buy-in."[35]

The Paradox of the Complete Street and BRT

One of the central demands of Complete Streets' advocates is for slower traffic speeds. As advocates Laplante and McCann have argued: "Speeds much over 30 mph in urban areas are incompatible with pedestrians and bicyclists, if not downright dangerous."[36] In attempting to make streets more user friendly for pedestrians, reports like AC Transit's *Designing with Transit* have proposed a range of strategies, including everything from minimizing the width of roadways and installing center medians to adding signals where none existed before. Even minimal efforts to slow traffic speeds, so the argument goes, not only have a significant impact on reducing automobile fatalities,[37] but they can also enhance the willingness of residents to walk and use transit. While there are certainly costs to slower traffic, these costs, many argue, are far outweighed by the benefits to livability. Laplante and McCann give us the following situation: "For a 5 mile trip along an arterial corridor with a 45 mph travel speed, the added travel time with a reduced speed of 30 mph would be 2.5 minutes. In the overall scheme of things, how important is this potential delay when compared to the proven safety benefits and the city livability advantages that come with slower traffic speeds?"[38] In 2010, a senior planner at AC Transit offered a far less rosy picture of Complete Streets. Despite supporting the general idea, the planner noted a fundamental tension between the benefits of lowering traffic speeds and the required speed needed to operate transit effectively:

> Slower is great. Slower is safer, right? But slower also means that our buses are traveling slower, which has a number of [implications]: one, it probably is going to cost more for us to meet our set frequencies. If we have a bus route that has a 30-minute

frequency and it's 10 miles long, we probably operate that service with eight buses, or something like that. Well, if they start looking at slowing down those streets our buses are going to go at a much slower speed. We need to put many more buses out there to maintain the frequency, and that is not a cost that a regular driver [of a private automobile] sees—maybe they are late to work, maybe they have different opportunity costs, but there's not [the] direct dollar cost that we have. And so that is a big problem that we see with Complete Streets. There's ways that you can probably make Complete Streets work and still get transit some priority, but the local jurisdictions don't want to put in that type of development.[39]

For planners at AC Transit, the idea of Complete Streets thus presents a catch-22. On the one hand, the aim of Complete Streets is to produce street-level conditions that serve transit better by giving special attention to both pedestrian safety and walkability. On the other hand, these same conditions can also result in transit delays and greater costs. While reports like those of Laplante and Mc-Cann might argue for the importance of adding bike lanes, widening sidewalks, and adopting traffic-calming strategies, these same propositions can have the unintended consequence of actually making transit slower and more costly to operate. In 2000, for example, the Oakland City Council voted to install bike lanes on a one-mile stretch of MacArthur Boulevard. To do so the council eliminated two lanes of traffic.[40] While Macarthur Boulevard might now be called a Complete Street, the change has actually functioned to make transit along that stretch far less cost efficient. As the senior planner explained:

> We used to have two lanes in each direction, and those are places where we want to put out a limited-stop service, like a rapid bus service, and we can't. Because the rapid bus can't pass the local bus, because there is only one lane of traffic, we can't give people express bus type of service that is equivalent to the car because we can't get our buses to go that fast. . . . We used to be able to stop, and cars could go around in the other lane, cars could pass us, and now we are all in just one lane, with a total vehicle speed that's maybe five miles slower than it used to be, and so we have more costs. It's weird because those are things that are positively perceived in community planning these days, but they are not taking into consideration the delays on transit, and that has a real cost to us.[41]

For agencies like AC Transit, service delays come with additional operating costs—whether those delays are, ironically, the result of a more "complete street" or something else. Increased delays not only impose more fiscal constraints; more importantly, they undermine transit's ability to attract new riders. In the 1960s, John Meyer, John Kain, and Martin Wohl noted in *The Urban Transportation Problem* that any "substantial diversion" of commuters from automobiles to transit hinged upon a very clear metric: transit's ability to provide commuters similar or shorter "home-to-office travel times."[42] Where transit service is characterized by unreliable, slow, or uncomfortable travel, there is little hope that any such diversion is possible. In many ways, the idea of BRT has aimed at addressing this exact problem—offering to attract riders with faster service.

Like Complete Streets, however, BRT projects present their own paradoxes, contradictions, and challenges. The case of BRT in Berkeley is a case in point. In 2010 the Berkeley City Council voted against allowing dedicated lanes along Telegraph Avenue in Berkeley. The vote came after sustained resistance from a number of individuals and groups concerned with increased congestion and losses of on-street parking. By the BRT functionally reducing four lanes of automobile traffic on Telegraph Avenue to two, the proposed effects on parking were particularly contentious. Roland Peterson, the executive director of the Telegraph Avenue Business Improvement District, argued that preserving on-street parking was crucial to the local business community. He argued that not only do on-street parking spaces matter for businesses who rely on customers being dropped off in cars, but these same parking spaces provide a necessary staging area for delivery trucks.[43] Joyce Roy, a long-time transit activist—but staunch opponent of BRT—noted that with less on-street parking and fewer lanes, surrounding neighborhoods might be inundated with unwanted cars searching for a place to park.[44] However beneficial BRT might be for transit riders, a significant number of people in Berkeley believed that the BRT would not just slow auto traffic and take away street parking, but it would fundamentally "mar the character of Berkeley neighborhoods."[45] While a good deal of resistance to the BRT in Berkeley came from business owners and neighborhood groups, resistance also came from less predictable places. One example is Chris Mullen of Berkeley's Center for Independent Living (CIL). As a transit trainer for the East Bay's disabled and elderly, Mullen's concerns were with the BRT's ability to meet the needs of his clients. With the aim of increasing transit speeds and frequency, the BRT planned to relocate a number of bus stops along Telegraph. Instead of the customary one bus stop every 1,000 feet (1/5 mile), the BRT's plans would amend that to one stop every 1,636 feet (1/3 mile).[46] As Mullen was speaking on behalf of the East Bay's disabled community, his critique of the BRT was understandable: "If they are going to make bus stops from two blocks to four block apart, that really hurts the population [I work with], two blocks is not that big a deal if you can walk . . . but two blocks in a manual wheelchair might as well be a mile, that's a long way to go." The problem with BRT was not only that it would eliminate parking spaces but also that it would mark a reduction in the total number of bus stops, and thus make it harder for the elderly and the disabled to use public transit.[47]

Advocacy for both Complete Streets and the BRT in the East Bay has been aimed at accomplishing much the same thing—increasing transit ridership and promoting more sustainable neighborhoods. Both initiatives start from the same premise; namely, that there is little point in pumping more money into transit without demanding more fundamental changes in land use. For boosters of BRT and Complete Streets, transit's success can only be achieved by reconfiguring the street and the city itself. However, what this reconfiguration should look like can be rife with contradictions and unintended outcomes. As with Complete Streets, the emphasis on traffic-calming measures may encourage walking, but it may also mean costly delays for transit. While projects like BRT might make transit faster and more attractive to use, they may also impose costs on surrounding businesses and neighborhoods. Ironically, the BRT's emphasis on speed and quicker headways might also have the effect of rendering transit less accessible to the disabled and the elderly—the very population for whom transit is a fundamental lifeline.

How, we might ask, do transit planners and proponents of Complete Streets or BRT understand such paradoxes? For some transit planners, part of the problem is simply that streets cannot accommodate everyone—there is simply not enough space. As one senior planner at AC Transit stated:

> One problem—especially in older neighborhoods—is that you just don't have enough property to meet everyone: you do not have enough to have a bike lane, a bus lane and traffic and parking. You can't fit it all into one street, and that's the challenge we are facing.[48]

In the East Bay, almost every inch of the street is spoken for. Buses traditionally need at least 11 to 12 feet of lane width to operate effectively; safe bike lanes require at least 5 to 6 feet; and in accordance with the accessibility guidelines of the Americans with Disabilities Act and the Architectural Barriers Act, sidewalks and other publicly accessible routes must have a minimum 4 feet of clearance width—enough for one wheel chair to operate without difficulty (ADA/ABA, 2004).[49] In sum, when efforts are made to expand sidewalks, or add a bus stop, or when efforts are made to widen bike lanes or create dedicated transit lanes, planners find that there is simply not enough space to do it all. For other planners, however, spatial limitations are only part of the problem. Transit planners face a much larger and far more challenging predicament. As one AC Transit senior planner noted: "The biggest challenge that we have in planning is that we don't own the streets. . . . So in order for us to get anything done, we have to talk to the city and that means [for] anything: that means all that ADA stuff, if we want to put a new bus stop in, if it requires the removal of parking, well we have to work with the city; we don't have that control."[50] The problem in the East Bay—to borrow the language of riders like Joyce Roy—was "[that] the streets of Oakland belong to the people of Oakland" and *not* to transit planners.[51] The problem was not simply one of insufficient space; it was also a lack of control. It was not only that the street had been parceled off, but that any effort to change that arrangement meant coming up against a political reality in which any demand to improve transit confronted yet other demands—for more parking, for wider bicycle lanes, for less automobile congestion, and so on.

The Paradox of Transit Oriented Developments

If the story of Complete Streets and BRT is one of unintended consequences and contradictions, the story of Transit Oriented Development is little different. Like proponents of Complete Streets or BRT projects, TOD enthusiasts start from the premise that to make transit more attractive and more efficient, cities must dramatically change their land-use priorities. According to the national non-profit Reconnecting America—a nationally recognized leader in advocating for TODs—successful TODs include "a mix of uses that makes it possible to get around without a car, a greater mix of housing types and transportation choices, an increased sense of community among residents and a heightened sense of place."[52]

Oakland is home to one of the nation's more successful TODs—the Fruitvale Transit Village. The Fruitvale Transit Village was initiated in the late 1990s by The Unity Council, an Oakland-based community development corporation that works closely with East Oakland's Latino community. Completed in 2004, the Fruitvale Transit Village has served to connect BART with the rest of the community and has added to the neighborhood's stock of retail, residential, and public space.[53] While Fruitvale Village has been hailed as a success, in truth it has done little to assuage increasing concerns that TODs might reinforce some of the same patterns they have been developed to ameliorate—particularly when they result in gentrification.

These concerns have been expressed in such reports as *Mapping Susceptibility to Gentrification: The Early Warning Toolkit; Maintaining Diversity in America's Transit-Rich Neighborhoods;* and *Case Studies for Transit Oriented Development: Case Studies That Work.*[54] Each of these reports points to a paradox: "the people who are attracted to transit-rich neighborhoods—and have the money to pay more to live there don't use transit as much as less affluent people who can get priced out."[55] In *Maintaining Diversity in America's Transit-Rich Neighborhoods* Stephanie Pollack, Barry Bluestone, and Chase Billingham trace the all-too-common and all-too-unfortunate life cycle of TODs. New transit stations lead to increased land values and accelerated housing turnover. The typically higher-income households that take up residence around or near the station are less likely to use transit and more apt to use private motor vehicles. In some of the neighborhoods included in Pollack's study, new transit stations actually led to falling rates of transit ridership.[56] Thus, there is a deep irony to TODs. Rather than rewarding communities that have long been doing the right thing—living in dense urban areas and using public transit—TODs can punish these communities, banishing the former residents to lower-cost exurbs where car ownership is almost a necessity.

In the East Bay, transit alternatives like Complete Streets, BRT, and TODs represent the latest efforts toward addressing persistent and familiar problems. They demonstrate efforts to reverse urban sprawl, to encourage urban environmental sustainability, and to catalyze what Jane Jacobs called the desperate need for "automobile attrition."[57] To the degree that such policies have been implemented in the East Bay, progress has been slow. Such policies have not only faced outright hostility and opposition, but they have come up against the physical limits of the street itself.

The Limits of Ideology

One way to understand the East Bay's experience with TOD, Complete Streets, and BRT initiatives is to borrow from the work of Jason Henderson and to frame that experience as one of competing ideologies. For Henderson, ideology refers to the "system of ideas and representations that dominate the minds of individuals and groups."[58] As Henderson observes, debates over the provision of urban transportation in cities like San Francisco have not only been deeply ideological but have often broken along three separate ideological lines—progressive, conservative, and neoliberal. In each case, individuals and groups approach questions of mobility in ways that reflect a broader set of values. Where *progressives* "conceptualize mobility as a systemic problem" and treat the dominance of the private automobile as a fundamental threat to the environment and social equity,[59] *conservatives* take almost the opposite tack. Not only do they champion the automobile as an embodiment of personal freedom and safety, but they also are deeply skeptical of government efforts to promote public transportation, walkability, and urban public life more generally. *Neoliberals* approach mobility in yet a different way. Neoliberals, Henderson suggests, tend to treat mobility as a commodity whose provision ought to be dictated by market competition alone. Not unlike conservatives, they are also deeply skeptical of the public sector and its ability to solve transportation challenges cost-effectively.[60]

Henderson's schema is a useful one and pushes those engaged in transportation debates to move beyond the easy fiction that has long dominated public perception of transportation planning—namely, the fiction that transportation planning is apolitical, objective, and merely a reflection of "common sense." Of course, as a self-described progressive, Henderson is also interested in engaging a debate on what *ought* to be done and what advancing a more progressive mobility agenda ought to involve.[61] Henderson's own answer is a revealing one. For progressives, he argues, the first step, in many ways, is to look in the mirror.[62] As Henderson observes, while there are many self-described progressives who are critical of automobility, there are far fewer progressives who are willing to change their own habits and to "embrace a lifestyle that is car free."[63]

In this regard, San Francisco is the prototypical example: "In San Francisco the broad progressive discourse might support transit first and bicycle space conceptually, but when it comes to the specific transformation of a particular street or to eliminating what is perceived to be an entitlement to parking, many progressives invoke a staunchly conservative essentialization of automobility. Every time a stretch of street is considered for change, angry motorists line up at city hall to protest the change."[64] Where "resistance to change is expected from conservatives, who essentialize automobility, and from neoliberals, who seek profit," in San Francisco it is often progressives themselves who pose the most significant barrier to a pro-transit future.[65] To the degree that progressives resist stricter parking measures, "defend what they perceive as their entitlement to high speed car space," and defend motoring, "they are acting in a contradictory manner," and they stand in the way of the very agenda to which they subscribe.[66] In advancing a progressive mobility agenda, the first thing required, Henderson argues, is for progressives to ask themselves "why they are still driving."[67] In Henderson's schema, the East Bay's experience with TOD, Complete Streets, and BRT is thus hardly surprising. It has been an experience in which the conflict has been between a progressive commitment to public transportation and a conservative defense of off-street parking and "neighborhood character." Indeed, If Berkeley's experience with BRT proves anything, it proves that the progressive hypocrisy so endemic in San Francisco is no less obvious in the East Bay.

There is, of course, yet another way to view the East Bay's experience with Complete Streets, TOD, and BRT, and that is to return to the implicit question raised by AC Transit planners: Who owns the streets? Or, rather, who should? For planners at AC Transit, the very changes required to make transit work—altering the city's land-use priorities—are ones over which they have little control. When, for example, AC Transit wants to install dedicated bus lanes, timed signals, or even a new bus stop, they must seek the permission of the municipality and navigate a complex landscape of municipal codes, community groups, and an array of legal rights. While mixed-use developments and higher-density residential projects along AC Transit's five major transit corridors might help AC Transit ridership, the fate of such a project will have little to do with the goals of a progressive transit planner. Instead, its fate will hinge on the actions of private land owners, on the approval of municipal councils and zoning boards, on investment from private developers, and on the consent of neighborhood associations. Whether these groups self-identify as progressive, neoliberal, or conservative, how they decide on issues of parking or "road dieting" may have very little do with ideology. When Joyce Roy and Roland Peterson oppose the loss of parking space associated with BRT, they do so not as progressives, conservatives, or neoliberals but as individual property owners who have a material interest in the status quo. For the latter, less parking means a potential loss in business. For the former, less main-street parking means more neighborhood traffic and a potential loss in the resale value of their house. When private developers of TODs fight against affordable housing set-asides, they do so to increase their "return on investment." Whether they are self-professed progressives will have little do with it.

Even progressive transit planners may approach initiatives like Complete Streets with trepidation. Where Complete Streets often come with slower traffic, for some planners the costs (in labor alone) associated with maintaining appropriate headway times may lead them to oppose such initiatives. In making sense of the transportation landscape in cities, Henderson's emphasis on ideology remains important. Of course, the emphasis on ideology alone comes with risks. One risk is that we begin to ignore the material interests that often drive people like Roland Peterson or Joyce Roy to take the stances they do. Another risk—and this is perhaps the more important one—is that a focus on ideology means we advance a politics focused solely on the "ideas that dominate the minds of individuals and groups participating in the politics of mobility." The barriers to progressive mobility are not simply attitudinal or psychological—they are also economic. While pushing progressives to drive less or to "rethink automobility" remains important, advancing a politics aimed at more structural changes will be just as important.[68]

Returning to the B-Line, Lawson's complaints are worth revisiting. For Lawson the challenge facing the B-Line and any other transit alternative remained the same. The problem was "that in Berkeley and probably other places, transit becomes politics." Everything "gets intertwined with all these political agendas," and ultimately nothing gets done. For Lawson, the problem was not simply the inescapability of politics but, worse still, the constant demand in Berkeley for social justice. As he argued, such demands distracted from the real goal: universal bus service for everyone.

> When people say "social justice," it's just a euphemism. They don't really want universal bus coverage, they want it as, like, an implement of the revolution. They want to drain the coffers of the privileged and give it to the underprivileged for some revolutionary purposes. . . . Not that I'm against that, but that's not what I'm talking about here. I'm saying to everyone, "If we make the bus system universally applicable, then everybody will want to take it equally, and it will achieve universal equality and universal diversity, since everyone will be taking the same transit system. Isn't that what we all want?"[69]

Where this book has sought to frame public transportation as a "right to the city" issue, in many ways it has thrown its support in the direction of the social justice warrior described above. Namely, it has suggested that fights for better public transportation are important to the degree that they fit within a broader struggle for a more just city. To the extent that this book advances this view, it does so under the presumption that the very things that riders like Lawson want—universal bus coverage, universal equity, and better service for everyone—will require embracing the very types of politics to which they are most resistant. That is a politics that is explicitly radical and that aims at mobilizing those with a material and a class interest in a better transit system. This means embracing a politics aimed at organizing the transit dependent, the elderly, the young, and the 72 percent of AC Transit riders defined as low income. These are riders with a direct interest in quicker and more affordable transit, and for whom transit improvements are the most impactful. When transit service is threatened, the stakes for these groups cannot be higher. At stake are their rights to participate fully in society, to engage in the democratic process, and to connect with other residents in ways that ward against isolation. Ultimately, the argument is thus a simple one. Where the goal is "universal bus coverage" (to quote Lawson) or "transit first policies" (to borrow from Henderson), an effective politics will focus less on convincing individual progressives to get out of their cars and to live by their principles, and more on "draining the coffers of the privileged" so as to create a city in the image of those traditionally excluded from it—the poor, the transit dependent, and the working class. As Henderson's work makes clear, while there are few people in the East Bay or San Francisco who may oppose—on principles alone—the idea of a Complete Street or the idea that transit ought to serve everyone, those principles often disappear at the very moment that people stand to lose materially. A politics that does not address this fact can only be so successful.

From Civil Rights to a Right to the City

Whether it is food security, housing, healthcare or education, the right of
transportation is the most integral to each.
   —Karen Smulevitz, September 22, 2010

The idea of framing something in terms of a right is extremely complex. . . . How do
we exercise that right? How do we legislate it? Say we want to recognize it. You [try
to] write the law—it isn't easy. . . . The ones we're used to now, everyone understands
and nobody challenges, but . . . when you start inventing new ones. . . . It's hard to
talk about things in terms of rights. I would almost rather just say: let's just try and get
a better transit system for everyone.
   —AC Transit board member, November 12, 2010

In the fall of 2010, and for the third time in one year, the AC Transit Board of
Directors convened to vote on yet another round of service cuts. Coming on the
heels of reductions in March and October, the proposed cuts—which included
thirty-four of fifty-one weekend bus lines—threatened to push AC Transit service down to levels not seen in thirty years.[1] Perhaps predictably, the events of
2010 elicited a good deal of finger-pointing. For some, the blame lay with California lawmakers, who in the previous year had raided $532 million from the
State Transit Assistance program—a program established to provide operating
support to the state's transit systems.[2] For others, it lay squarely with AC Transit's
mismanagement and its choice in 2000 to approve the purchase of a new fleet of
costly buses from the Belgian Van Hool company.[3] For still others, however, AC
Transit's real problems lay elsewhere—namely, with the riders themselves. This
was, in fact, the conclusion drawn by one of AC Transit's own board members:

> [AC Transit] is heavily comprised of transit-dependent people. We have very few
> middle-class riders on our buses. Even riders that are not transit dependent are
> not middle class. And one of the things that has happened because of that is that

we do not have the overarching political support. Without [that] support, you are nowhere. AC Transit has continued to focus more and more on transit-dependent ridership and . . . it is causing problems. . . . Middle-class people demand quality transit. You cannot give them poor service. So when you don't have them as riders, your service tends to deteriorate. An attitude sets in that says: "Well, what choice do they have?" And it's not as if we promote that attitude. But it comes. "We are poor people's transit." "We are a social service." And I'm not sure that's healthy in the long run, because [transit] becomes a "program," and in this country "programs" don't live long. What lives long are things that have a widespread appeal so, politically, I think transit is in danger all across the country.[4]

According to the board member, the problem with AC Transit was all but apparent. With 72 percent of its riders defined as "low income," and with an additional 62 percent defined as "transit dependent," AC Transit's problem was that it had become "poor people's transportation"—welfare on wheels.[5] Bereft of the "overarching political support" that might come with more middle-class riders, AC Transit was a "program for the poor" in a country where "programs" and social services "don't live long."

In the same year, Steve Gerstle—a transit activist and a long-time resident of the East Bay city of Alameda—offered a similar take:

Local riders are people riding in Oakland, Berkeley, Richmond and [Alameda] and that group tends to be poorer . . . and people who are poorer tend not to have a voice . . . they do not have time to get involved. Even if they did, what would they say? What would they do? Who would they talk to? . . . I mean people who are wealthy have connections, have money, have education, and they know how things work. They know who to contact. They know what strings to pull. People who are taking public transit tend to be on the other end of the spectrum. They don't have those things and they don't have the same power if they are busy just trying to survive.[6]

For Gerstle, the problem with AC Transit was not simply that its riders lacked political influence. The problem went deeper yet. Even *with* political influence, Gerstle asked, what would such riders say? What would they do? What, in short, would be their argument? While this book has largely declined to weigh in on the cause of AC Transit's woes, it has gone some way in addressing a set of broader questions. How should we defend public transportation? If not as a "program for the poor," then as what instead? What should struggles to improve or preserve public transportation entail? Moreover, how should we frame those struggles? To these questions, and in almost every instance, this book has responded with some version of the same answer—namely, it has echoed riders like Karen Smulevitz in presuming that public transportation is both a right and a public good central to securing other rights—especially the right to the city.

As should be clear from this book's opening chapter, there is, of course, nothing simple about rights. Rights are complex. They defy easy application, and they hinge on moral questions that are not only difficult to resolve but even more difficult to interpret. The immediate concerns facing transit agencies often *appear* to be logistical and technical. Rights, on the other hand, seem to move in precisely the opposite direction—toward ever higher levels of abstraction. Given all this, for any number of people, the temptation to simply avoid rights talk altogether is a real one. Of all the arguments developed in this book, however, perhaps the simplest is the argument for not only fighting this temptation but for rejecting the related view expressed by the AC Transit board member cited in the epigraph above—namely, a view that advises transit advocates to ignore rights and to simply focus on getting "a better transit system for everyone." As hopefully every chapter has shown, rights and rights talk are largely inescapable. Rights intrude in debates on where to place a bus stop, on how much funding ought to go to rail versus bus service, and on whether bus companies are liable when passengers are injured in a fist fight. Rights become central for transportation justice organizations—whether in their efforts to redirect transit investment or to redress the needs of minority riders. Rights appear in contract negotiations between management and transit operators, and they become the source of tension in times of budget cuts. As much as transit policy makers or aspiring ones like Kristan Lawson may dread being drawn into some prolonged ethical debate on people's rights, the practical task of administering transit means doing just that. And here the argument is perhaps the clearest: while rights and rights talk may slow the wheels of "progress," the alternative is far more frightening. Where moral questions are off-limits, and where rights talk is deemed out-of-bounds, the very questions that should matter fall from view. These are questions of justice, of what public transit is for, and of what its role ought to be in a democratic society.

Of course, for many transit advocates, the above argument may seem a hopelessly basic one. To say that "rights matter" is not only to state the obvious, it is to find little disagreement with anyone familiar with urban transit's workings. The more important question is how we understand rights, how we talk about them, and how we decide which rights and which *kinds* of rights are worth championing. As many may note, within much of the literature on transportation justice and transportation equity this question is already settled. In this literature—which is rife with rights talk—the focus is almost exclusively on civil rights. These are rights to equality under the law, equal treatment, and freedom from discrimination—especially of the racial variety. Given the history of the United States, this focus is understandable. As events like the Montgomery bus boycott remind us, for much of the twentieth century racial discrimination in the provision of public transportation was commonplace. In cities across the country, African Americans were routinely denied equal access to mass transit and also to the social and economic benefits that transit services inevitably provided. While the overt racism that once defined cities like Montgomery has largely disappeared, racial disparities remain in how we invest in transportation. As authors Robert Bullard, Thomas Sanchez, Ricardo Marcantonio, and Aaron Golub have all convincingly argued, today's discrimination is less the product of explicit racial animus than of ostensibly color-blind policies that inadvertently reproduce historic inequities.[7] For such authors, the fight for transportation justice has been a fight not only to unmask such policies (see *Darensburg v. MTC*) but also to realize the promise of the postwar civil rights movement—a promise that remains unfulfilled.

Where much of the literature on transportation justice has focused on civil rights, the cases explored in the preceding chapters speak to issues that clearly remain outside the traditional civil rights ambit. This was purposeful. These were issues related to the rights of transit labor, the broad ambitions of such groups as the Alliance for AC Transit, and the conflicts that arise over the space of the city street itself. Given these cases, and in light of the failure of civil rights lawsuits like *Darensburg v. MTC*, one of this book's goals has been to suggest the need to think about rights in broader terms. For many scholars, of course, one way of broadening our discussion of rights and public transportation is to turn to the work of liberals such as Jeremy Waldron or Isaiah Berlin—that is, to defend public transportation as a positive socioeconomic right or a so-called welfare right.[8] Such "second generation" rights—as they are sometimes deemed—refer to the general entitlements people have to basic material goods like food, housing, health care, or a fair wage. These are rights to resources regarded as central to sustaining a dignified life. The argument in defense of such rights, whether from Waldron or others, often begins by placing them in relation to the less controversial rights associated with civil liberty. These are the rights we have to private property, to free speech, and against state interference into private matters. As defenders of socioeconomic rights often point out, for those individuals unable to feed or clothe themselves, the promise of such civil liberties—whether to free speech or to security from state overreach—is often an empty one. Such individuals require food and clothes before they can take advantage of those freedoms. Indeed, even "equality under the law" can appear an empty gesture to those who—borrowing from Anatole France's dictum—are forced by poverty to steal bread or to live on the streets.[9] In short, socioeconomic rights are important because they give substance to the promise of freedom and liberty in a world in which people's basic needs too often go unmet. For many, public transportation falls in the same category as other basic needs like housing or health care. As members of the East Bay Center for the Blind might note, public transportation can mean the difference between a life lived in isolation and a life lived with the rest of the public. Indeed for others—like Chris Mullen's client—public transportation means the difference between getting to the polls to vote or staying home and simply watching the returns on TV.

There is little in this book that has denied the importance of public transportation as a civil rights issue. There is even less that has denied the importance of defending it as a basic socioeconomic entitlement. Even with that said, however, the book has chosen to advance a yet different notion of rights. More specifically, it has advanced a notion of rights culled from the work of Henri Lefebvre. Writing in the late 1960s, Lefebvre coined the "right to the city" phrase in response to what he saw as the wholesale remaking of French urban life.[10] As Lefebvre observed, the French city of the postwar period had become a profoundly alienating one. In the wake of urban renewal, not only had the city's poor been decanted to the "new towns" and housing projects of the urban periphery, but the very places of social encounter and exchange that had given the city its organic unity had been paved over or demolished.[11] For Lefebvre, building on Marx, the class struggles of modern France were not simply struggles over the traditional factory but over the street itself and the production of daily urban life. In this context, the right to the city, as a slogan, marked Lefebvre's attempt to rally a defense of a city that was quickly disappearing—a city defined by places of encounter and exchange and in which radical politics had not yet given way to the privatized isolation of the suburb.

In the last two decades activists and scholars across the globe have taken up the right to the city as a cry and a demand for more just cities. As these activists and scholars have argued, cities the world over continue to be organized in ways that disenfranchise the poor and that limit their ability to enjoy the benefits of urban life. For many, the causes are clear. According to David Harvey, for example, many of the gross inequities that continue to define cities have been driven by the broader forces of capitalist urbanization.[12] Where globalization has made capital more mobile, not only have cities—through increased interurban competition—been forced to be more entrepreneurial in their hunt for investment, but they have also been forced to adopt policies that often run directly counter to the interests of the poor.[13] These policies include land giveaways, tax write-offs, the enclosure of public land, slum removal, speculative real estate investments, and urban policies focused more on attracting investment than attending to the material needs of their residents. As Don Mitchell and others have argued, such policies also include the aggressive policing of urban public space—whether through laws banning panhandling or new forms of surveillance.[14] As Mitchell notes, the goal of such aggressive policing—not unlike the goal of slum removal—has been to remake cities in ways that not only serve elite interests but that remove anything threatening exchange value—even if that includes removing the homeless and poor themselves. In both the developing and developed world the result of continued capitalist urbanization has been clear: the production of cities defined by ever more extreme forms of inequity. In this context, the right to the city, for many, has been as much a right to housing or to public space as it has been a right against the political economy itself and the very processes that have compelled cities to enact policies so at odds with the interests of their most disadvantaged citizens.

One of the reasons that this book has sought to place Lefebvre's right to city at the center of how we think about public transportation—and thus to go beyond both the strictures of civil rights or socioeconomic rights—is that it assumes that any discussion of public transportation, and especially transportation justice, cannot afford to ignore the questions that those demanding a right to the city have made central. These are questions related to the political economy of cities, the nature of class power, and for whom and what purpose cities are designed. Of course, the history of transit in the East Bay is rife with these questions. As noted in the introduction, it is largely impossible to understand the early development of the East Bay's Key System—the private transit system that AC Transit eventually replaced—without making reference to its roots in the real estate speculation of industrialists such as Francis "Borax" Smith. It is no less difficult to understand the history of BART without some reference to the Bay Area Council (BAC)—the coalition of local CEOs that not only backed BART but that saw BART as a way to shore up the value of their downtown real estate holdings. Indeed, the development of AC Transit—along with Washington, D.C.'s Metro and the passage of the Urban Mass Transportation Act of 1964—cannot be separated from broader national anxieties around urban disinvestment and the devaluation of property in the central city.[15] For many, the recent battle over the Oakland Airport Connector (OAC) has touched on the same issues. While its detractors have condemned the project as a waste of money, its proponents have touted its potential in marketing the East Bay to global investors and thus improving Oakland's competitive position vis-à-vis other municipalities. If making sense of the East Bay's transit history means raising questions that deal directly with the issues of interurban competition, class power, and for whom cities are designed, then such issues continue to be relevant.

Even more recently, the Bay Area has become the epicenter of an ongoing national debate on gentrification and housing affordability. Where residents across the region continue to wrestle with the rapid surge in rental prices, many have come to lay the blame on a seemingly unlikely source, the "Google bus"— shorthand for the fleet of private shuttles used to cart elite technology workers from San Francisco and the East Bay to tech jobs in San Jose's Silicon Valley.[16] The focus on these shuttles is not unwarranted. In 2014, the anti-eviction mapping project released a study that showed that 69 percent of no-fault evictions from 2011 to 2013 were within four blocks of Google bus stops.[17] The report's conclusion was clear: with new tech workers flooding the city—an influx aided by corporate shuttles—local property owners were responding as might be expected: namely, kicking out older residents and raising rents. In this context, the wave of "anti-Google bus protests" that rocked San Francisco and Oakland in 2013 came as little surprise. In December 2013, forty protestors prevented a shuttle owned by Apple from leaving the San Francisco Mission district for thirty minutes. Parading around the bus, the protestors held banners reading "Eviction free San Francisco" and "San Francisco: a tale of two cities." Addressing the crowd from the back of a pickup truck, one protestor declared: "We want the ruling, which is becoming the tech class, to listen to our voices and the voices of the folks being displaced."[18] A week earlier, a similar protest in Oakland led to a Google bus with a cracked windshield after a protester hurled a stone. "Fuck Google," one sign read.[19] For many protestors, of course, the Google bus was simply the most visible symptom of a much larger problem—namely, the transformation of the city itself. The Bay Area, as Rebecca Solnit put it, was becoming a place where a whole class of people had not only been "deemed too valuable to use public transportation" but were also driving up rents, taking over the central city, and consciously alienating themselves from the wider public.[20]

By placing Lefebvre's idea of the right to the city at the heart of how we think about public transportation and transportation justice, we advance not only a notion of rights that is explicit in raising questions dealing with the political economy of cities and the nature of class power but one that allows us to draw connections between ostensibly distinct transportation struggles. To start with a right to the city is to note that what the Google bus protestor wants is not too different from what the OAC protestor demands. Each aims to reject the elite takeover of "public transportation" and the affront such modes represent to the city's poor. To start with a right to the city is not only to take seriously the lesson from Parchester Village but to see it as an example of labor's role in producing a society that, to quote Lindsay Imai, "cares for all communities equally well and that ensures a level playing field."[21] Indeed, to start with a right to the city is to see the Alliance for AC Transit and its fight to prevent the relocation of the city's bus hub as both a direct rebuke to downtown property owners and an attempt to retake the city from the same business interests represented by the BAC. At its most simple, the right to the city allows us to see struggles over transportation as directly related to struggles against gentrification, overpolicing, and other urban policies that reflect the interests of capital rather than those of workers or the poor.

There is, of course, one additional argument for placing Lefebvre's right to the city at the heart of how we think about public transportation and transportation justice—and especially in regions like the East Bay. Where the goal of "enhancing global economic competitiveness" remains the top priority of the MTC—as revealed in the Darensburg decision—or where projects like the OAC proceed despite vocal opposition, appeals to civil rights alone seem to misgauge the threat at hand. Civil rights, of course, *are* deeply important. To the extent that they work to secure the political equality of individuals and to defend minorities against majoritarian tyranny, they remain essential tools for achieving a just society. For Karen Smulevitz, however, and for surely many others, the problems facing public transportation are often less a result of majoritarian tyranny than they are the tyranny of the political economy itself. This is the tyranny of the OAC, the Google bus, and those eager to revitalize downtown Oakland by moving bus riders out of public view. It is a tyranny that produces cities that are defined by isolation, alienation, and idiocy. More simply still, it is the tyranny concomitant with those forces keen to redesign cities and mass transit in the interests of the affluent alone. Such forces not only run counter to the civil rights of minorities but also run against even the most milquetoast assertion of public transportation as a basic socioeconomic right. To place the right to the city at the center of how we think about public transportation is to advance a notion of rights that takes this reality seriously. Put another way: to secure the world demanded by scholars like Robert Bullard, or litigants like Sylvia Darensburg, or unionized transit operators like David Lyons, or even to secure the world imagined by transit scholars like Jason Henderson, not only must we critique the political economy of the city itself, but we must adopt a notion of rights that can give that critique moral and political clarity.

Reflecting on the events of 2010, East Bay rider and activist Steve Gerstle made an interesting point. The problem facing AC Transit was not simply that its riders lacked the right political connections but rather something far more invidious. Even if they had such connections, Gerstle asked, what would they say? What would they do? What would be the nature of their demands? This book has shown that there are any number of individuals and organizations in the East Bay for whom the answer is clear enough. For many, that answer begins and ends with some version of the argument advanced by Karen Smulevitz: the argument for seeing public transportation as a right. For those sympathetic to this claim, this book has advanced what I argue is an important addendum: there are different types of rights, and those differences matter. Those differences not only shape how we debate transportation issues—and what concerns rise to the top—but they also shape how we focus our politics. To the degree that we organize our politics around civil rights, the focus of our political engagement will take a particular form—it will focus on identifying and rooting out discrimination, questioning the legality of policies like Resolution 3434, and fighting for the rights of racial and other minorities. To the extent that we organize our politics around demanding public transportation as a socioeconomic right or a welfare right, the focus of our political engagement will be yet different. It may, for example, mean fighting to readjust how we fund public transportation at the federal level—specifically, by shifting the balance of surface transportation funds dedicated to mass transit versus highways, of which only 20 percent goes to mass transit and 80 percent to highways. It may also mean adopting service minimums at the local level—whether measured in platform hours or ridership miles.[22] Struggling for rights on these terms remains essential.

At the same time, however, this book has suggested that the politics necessary for real change requires adopting rights of a different order. These are rights aimed less at countering majoritarian tyranny than in intervening in the ongoing struggle over what and for whom cities are designed. On one side of that struggle are those whose vision of the city remains tied to the image of the Google bus, of the Oakland Airport Connector, and where transportation policies are gauged—again borrowing from the MTC—by their ability to promote "global economic competitiveness." On the other side of this struggle are those advancing a vision of a city that is more democratic and less alienating. It is a city with lower VMTs and where unionized transit operators are considered members of the same working-class public as those they carry—rather than alienated from them. It is a city, most importantly, that reflects the needs of the poor and transit dependent. When riders like Karen Smulevitz assert their right to transportation, this book's argument to those already committed to transportation justice is that there remains a desperate need to advance those rights that can work toward the second city sketched above rather than the first.

NOTES

Introduction. For Rights

1. For more on the transit cuts, see Michael Cabanatuan, "AC Bus Cut Hits Sunday—More in December," *San Francisco Chronicle*, October 30, 2010, C1. See also "General Managers Memo to the Board: Consider the Adoption of Resolution 10-045 Approving the December 2010 Service Reduction Plan, Pending Receipt of a Final Title VI Disparate Impacts Study" (GM-memo 09-217j, Oakland, Calif., September 22, 2010).

2. For more on STA funds, see Mike Rosenberg, "Running on Empty—Bay Area Transit in Trouble," *San Jose Mercury*, January 10, 2010, 1A; "Transportation Development Act Guidelines" (Placer County Transportation Planning Agency Report, Placer County, Calif., August 2011).

3. In its 2010 report, "Impacts of the Recession on Public Transportation Agencies," the American Public Transportation Association (APTA) noted that 84 percent of all transit agencies in the country had been forced to either cut service, raise fares, or consider other cost-saving measures in 2010. See "Impacts of the Recession on Public Transportation Agencies" (American Public Transportation Association, Washington, D.C., 2010), 2.

4. For more on the historic nature of service reduction, see "General Managers Memo to Board"; Michael Cabantuan, "AC Transit May Whack Service Yet Again," *San Francisco Chronicle*, September 23, 2010, C2. Also see Urban Habitat, "Riders and Drivers Share the Pain, December Cuts Postponed," flyer, http://urbanhabitat.org/files /11.9.10%20Report%20Back.doc. According to the Urban Habitat flyer, the proposed cuts would have resulted in 24,016 riders losing weekend service.

5. AC Transit's overall financial health had been declining long before the crisis in 2010. Indeed, service levels and overall bus speeds had tracked a downward course since the late 1980s. By 2009, the agency's fare box revenue ratio—the percentage of operating costs covered by fares—had dropped to 18 percent; that is, less than one-fifth of the system's revenues were generated from fares. See "Short Range Transportation Plan (SRTP) 2010–2020" (AC Transit Report to MTC, Oakland, Calif., April 28, 2010).

6. AC Transit provides audio recordings of all public hearings online. The quotes from Smulevitz were transcribed from the audio of an AC Transit Board meeting held on September 23, 2010. The audio of the meeting can be accessed at http://www .actransit.org/about-us/board-of-directors/board-memos/.

7. Marcuse, "From Critical Urban Theory," 192.

8. Burke, *Reflections on the Revolution*, 67.

9. Ibid., 55.

10. Glendon, *Rights Talk*, 14.

11. AC Transit board member in discussion with author, November 12, 2010.

12. Tushnet, "Critique of Rights."

13. Ibid., 1371.

14. Marx, *On the Jewish Question*, 24.

15. Tushnet, "Critique of Rights," 1364.

16. Marx, *Capital*, 344.

17. Ibid.

18. Mitchell, *Right to the City*, 25. Also see Blomley, "Mobility, Empowerment." As Patricia Williams writes, for minorities, "rights are islands of empowerment. To be un-righted is to be disempowered, and the line between rights and no-rights is most often the line between dominators and oppressed." Williams, *Alchemy of Race and Rights*, 233.

19. The distance between these two claims is not insignificant. To say that rights are a force themselves is to flirt with a certain level of idealism. To say, on the other hand, that rights organize force, is to adopt an argument that recognizes the power of discourse but that avoids ascribing rights an "independent force." As Don Mitchell writes: rights can "provide a valuable tool for restraining power or for justifying it in particular ways. That is precisely what 'rights' do: they provide a set of instructions about the use of power." See Mitchell, *Right to the City*, 27.

20. See Fried, *Right and Wrong*, 108. Yet another way to think about the relationship between rights and morals is to turn to Dworkin's work on the law. When Dworkin argues that there are moments when individuals have a moral right to break the law, he is offering an account of rights that treats them as moral entities above and beyond utilitarian law. Acts of civil disobedience are defensible precisely because they appeal to moral rights that have yet to be recognized by legal institutions. While this view of rights is not without its critics—Jeremy Bentham being the most famous—it remains a core principle of those who advocate for the legitimacy of universal human rights. See Dworkin, *Taking Rights Seriously*. Also see Jones, *Rights*.

21. Shue, *Basic Rights*, ix.

22. Ibid.

23. Dworkin, *Taking Rights Seriously*, 205.

24. See Marjorie Cohn's "Human Rights Hypocrisy: US Criticizes Cuba," *Marjorie Cohn* (blog), March 18, 2016, http://marjoriecohn.com/human-rights-hypocrisy-us -criticizes-cuba/.

25. Waldron, *Liberal Rights*, 24.

26. Ibid. For more on the distinction between negative and positive rights see Fried, *Right and Wrong*, 110.

27. Berlin, *Four Essays on Liberty*, 124.

28. For a lengthy discussion of the civil rights movement's links to public transpor-tation, see Bullard, "Anatomy of Transportation Racism," 15–33; also see Kelley, *Right to Ride*.

29. Of course, historically, the idea of public transportation as a civil rights issue has hardly been limited to race. As Mary Johnson and Barrett Shaw have shown, the national fight for wheelchair lifts on public buses played a central role in galvanizing

the passage of the Americans with Disabilities Act (ADA). See Johnson and Shaw, *To Ride the Public's Buses*.

30. Bullard, "Addressing Urban Transportation Equity," abstract; Sanchez and Brenman, "Transportation and Civil Rights," 6.

31. Bullard, "Anatomy of Transportation Racism," 20.

32. Sanchez et al., in *The Right to Transportation*, make this same point, as they write: "Transportation equity is rooted in environmental racism and environmental justice and, over the last several years, has focused primarily on racial discrimination" (95). For many scholars and activists committed to advancing transportation equity, one of the most significant organizations of the last thirty years has been the Los Angeles Bus Riders Union (BRU). Founded in 1991, the BRU gained national attention in 1996 after winning a major settlement against the Los Angeles County Metropolitan Transportation Authority (MTA). At issue in the settlement was the MTA's alleged violation of Title VI of the 1964 Civil Rights Act—a law prohibiting recipients of federal funding from discriminating on the basis of race, color, or national origin. As the BRU argued, between 1993 and 1994 the MTA had put forward budgets that simultaneously pledged to expand service for white commuters while raising the fare on bus services used largely by the city's minority population. In winning the settlement, the BRU pointed to the power of both local organizing around transportation equity and the power of appealing to civil rights legislation. See Mann, "Los Angeles Bus Riders Union," 33–49.

33. Sanchez et al., *Right to Transportation*, 111.

34. Litman and Brenman, *New Social Equity Agenda*, 2.

35. Ibid.

36. Bullard, "Addressing Urban Transportation Equity," 1186.

37. Litman and Brenman, *New Social Equity Agenda*, 5.

38. Ibid., 13.

39. For a detailed look at the costs of automobile ownership for the poor, see Lutz and Fernandez, *Carjacked*.

40. Henderson, *Street Fight*, 196.

41. See Jacobs, *Death and Life*, 364.

42. Marcuse, "From Critical Urban Theory," 192.

43. The right to the city concept has produced an ever-growing body of literature. On participatory planning and the right to the city, see McCann, "Urban Citizenship, Public Participation," 25–32. On the right to the city and political organizing, see Purcell, "Citizenship and the Right." On the right to the city and debates over urban development, see Chaskin and Joseph, "Positive Gentrification, Social Control." On the right to the city and public space, see Mitchell, *Right to the City*. On the right to the city and affordable housing, see Sinha and Kasdan, "Inserting Community Perspective Research." For a critical discussion, see Attoh, "What *Kind* of Right?"

44. Lefebvre, *Writings on Cities*, 178.

45. Ross, *Fast Cars, Clean Bodies*, 4.

46. Scargill, *Urban France*, 8; United Nations, Department of Economic and Social Affairs, Population Division, *United Nations World Population Prospects: The 2014 Revision*, https://esa.un.org/unpd/wup/Country-Profiles/.

47. Tony McNeill, "Les Trente Glorieuses: 1945–1975," *Comminqué*, 1998, http://eserve.org.uk/tmc/contem/trente1.htm.

48. Tuppen, "Development of French New Towns"; McNeill, "Les Trente Glorieuses."

49. Price, *Concise History of France*, 292.

50. Scargill, *Urban France*, 176.

51. For a richer discussion of Lefebvre's life, see Merrifield, *Henri Lefebvre*.

52. Gough, "Brief History of the Right."

53. Ross, *Fast Cars, Clean Bodies*, 11.

54. Marx and Engels, *Communist Manifesto*, 55. For discussion of "rural idiocy," see Draper, *Adventures of the Communist Manifesto*, 123. As Hal Draper argues, Marx and Engels used *idiocy* in the classical sense—from the Greek word *idiotai*. *Idiocy* is thus more similar to the words *idiosyncratic*, *idiolect*, and *idiographic* than to words more commonly seen as synonyms—such as *stupid*. Also see Attoh, "Public Transportation."

55. Engels, *Condition*, 3–4.

56. Gough, "Brief History of the Right," 418.

57. N. Smith, foreword to *Urban Revolution*, vii–xxiii; Burgess and Park, *City*; Castells, *Urban Question*.

58. As Andrew Merrifield has noted, Lefebvre's relationship with the French Communist Party (PCF) was always rather strained. His critique of Stalinism, his critique of "everyday life," and the eventual publication of *Problemes Actuels du Marxisme* in 1958—in which Lefebvre criticized the PCF refusal to de-Stalinize—all culminated in his expulsion from the party in June 1958. After breaking with the party, Lefebvre embarked on a deep rethinking of Marx and Marxism—some of which was expressed in a new interest in cities and urban life. See Hirsh, *French Left*, 92–104. Also see Merrifield, *Henri Lefebvre*.

59. For a deeper discussion of this concept, see Greenberg and Lewis, *City Is the Factory*.

60. See United Nations Human Settlements Programme, *Challenge of Slums*; Davis, "Planet of Slums."

61. Fernandes, "Constructing the 'Right.'"

62. Ibid., 212.

63. For a critical take on the institutionalization of the right to the city, see M. Mayer, "Right to the City," 368. The right to the city has even appeared as a central component of the United Nations' Habitat program—a program aimed at promoting participatory governance in cities throughout the developing world. For critical commentary, see Merrifield, *Henri Lefebvre*.

64. This has certainly been the view of the U.S.-based Right to the City Alliance—a coalition of community-based organizations engaged in issues ranging from foreclosures to immigrant rights. For them, the right to the city functions less as a legal demand than as a "radical credo" useful in advancing economic and racial justice. See Fischer et al., "We Are Radical," 160; Harmony Goldberg, "Building Power in the City: Reflections on the Emergence of the Right to the City Alliance and the National Domestic Worker's Alliance," *In The Middle of a Whirlwind* (blog, *Journal of Aesthetics and Protest*), 2008, 3, https://inthemiddleofthewhirlwind.wordpress.com/building-power-in-the-city/.

65. Marcuse, "From Critical Urban Theory," 192.

66. Harvey, "Right to the City," 37.

67. Harvey, *Rebel Cities*, xvi. This rather broad appeal to the "heart" has had its critics. Among others, Susan Fainstein has been notably critical of what she sees as the absence of any programmatic description of the type of city theorists like David Harvey demand. In response, Fainstein has developed the notion of the "just city" as a way to move beyond mere critique and toward a set of clear criteria through which to measure urban policies. For Fainstein, a just city is one in which urban policies have been geared toward furthering equity, diversity, and democracy. See Fainstein, *Just City*.

68. Marcuse, "From Critical Urban Theory," 192.

69. Dworkin, *Taking Rights Seriously*, 205.

70. See Mitchell, *Right to the City*.

71. For a twentieth-century history of the East Bay, see Self, *American Babylon*; Rhomberg, *No There There*.

72. See Andrew Merrifield's discussion of Navarrenx in *Henri Lefebvre*.

73. "BART Board Approves New Oakland Airport Connector Funding Plan," *Bart.gov*, July 22, 2010, https://www.bart.gov/news/articles/2010/news20100722.

74. Juliet Ellis and Frank Sterling, "BART Cannot Afford to Build Oakland Airport Connector," My Word, *East Bay Times*, May 8, 2009, http://www.eastbaytimes.com/2009/05/08/my-word-bart-cannot-afford-to-build-oakland-airport-connector/.

75. Ibid.

76. AC Transit board member, interview by author, November 12, 2010.

77. In 2008 and 2009, 53 percent of AC Transit's ridership was defined as "very low income"—or as earning below 50 percent of the Oakland Freemont HUD median income ($86,100 per year). See "2008/2009 On-Board Rider Survey—System-Wide Results," prepared for Alameda-Contra Costa Transit Division of Long Range Planning by the Public Research Institute, San Francisco State University, Public Research Institute, San Francisco, October 2010, 12.

78. Carolyn Jones, "Oakland Council Leans against BART Airport Line," *SFGate.com*, October 6, 2008, http://www.sfgate.com/bayarea/article/Oakland-council-leans-against-BART-airport-line-3284465.php#ixzz0TAwGst8p.

79. Bay Area News Group, "Future for Oakland Airport Looks Bright," *East Bay Times*, June 17, 2011, http://www.eastbaytimes.com/2011/06/17/future-for-oakland-airport-looks-bright/.

80. Marx Greene, "Transcript of Testimony before the California Railroad Commission in Application 2985" (transcript of hearing, Oakland, Calif., 1917), 1761–62; Adler, "Political Economy of Transit," 57; Smythe, "Economic History," 104; for more context, see "Brocek Says Key System Faces Failure," *Oakland Tribune*, May 29, 1918, 6.

81. Smythe, "Economic History," 104.

82. For the most famous critique of BART see Webber, "BART Experience."

83. Whitt, *Urban Elites and Mass Transportation*, 76.

84. These corporations included Bank of America, American Trust Company, Standard Oil of California, Pacific Gas and Electric, Bechtel Corporation, and U.S. Steel. See Whitt, *Urban Elites and Mass Transportation*.

85. Ibid., 44.

86. Ibid., 73.

87. For a history of D.C. Metro, see Schrag, *Great Society Subway*. For yet another look at this period, see Sawers, "Political Economy."

88. For a history of D.C. Metro, see Schrag, *Great Society Subway*. In 1978 California voters passed Proposition 13—a ballot initiative that reduced tax rates on real property and that limited any future increase to 2 percent per annum. Following its passage, AC Transit immediately lost $17 million in revenue. See John Wesley, "Internal Memo: To the Membership of the Local 192," (1978) Amalgamated Transit Union Local 192 Records, Box 5, Folder 4, Labor Archives and Research Center, San Francisco State University. As many have argued, some of Proposition 13's strongest support came from corporate real estate interests. See Clyde Haberman, "The California Ballot Measure That Inspired a Tax Revolt," *New York Times*, October 16, 2016, https://www.nytimes.com/2016/10/17/us/the-california-ballot-measure-that-inspired-a-tax-revolt.html?_r=0.

89. See Jordan Crucchiola, "SFS Tech Bus Problem Isn't about Buses. It's about Housing," *Wired.com*, February 12, 2016, https://www.wired.com/2016/02/sfs-tech-bus-problem-isnt-about-buses-its-about-housing/.

90. See Dworkin, *Taking Rights Seriously*, 205.

91. Berlin, *Four Essays on Liberty*, 124.

92. See the introduction in Waldron, *Liberal Rights*.

Chapter 1. Torts, Transit, and the "Majestic Equality" of the Law

1. Tocqueville, *Democracy in America*, 310.

2. AC Transit board member, interview by the author, November 12, 2010.

3. Prosser, *Handbook of the Law of Torts*.

4. In an ideal world, the TCRP report concluded, "state tort laws would balance the rider's rights to be made whole by the negligence of public transit systems [with] the fiscal concerns of taxpayers." Thomas and McDaniel, "State Limitations on Tort Liability," 3.

5. See "factual background" in both Appellate and Supreme Court cases: *Bonanno v. CCCTA*, 89 Cal. App. 4th 1398 (Cal. Ct. App. 1st Dist., 2001); *Bonanno v. CCCTA*, 30 Cal. 4th 139 (Cal. 2003).

6. Senior planner at AC Transit, interview by the author, October 13, 2010.

7. Following the passage of the California Torts Claim Act of 1963, both Cal. Gov. Code § 830 and Cal. Gov. Code § 835 have functioned to specify one major area of government tort liability, namely, that surrounding "dangerous conditions of public property." For more on the California Torts Claim Act, see Nellis, "California Governmental Tort Liability."

8. See "Analysis" section in *Bonanno v. CCCTA*, 2003.

9. See "Factual Background: Section C" in *Bonanno v. CCCTA*, 2001.

10. See "Analysis" section in *Bonanno v. CCCTA*, 2003.

11. *Bonanno v. CCCTA*, 2003 (Baxter, J. Dissenting), see page 3 of dissent.

12. Ibid., 4.

13. Ibid., 5.

14. Ibid., 3.

15. In 2003, hundreds of transit agencies in California sponsored Assembly Bill 2737. The bill sought to overrule the majority opinion in *Bonanno v. CCCTA* and to

"immunize any public entity or public employee for injuries caused by the location of, the condition of public property not owned by or controlled by the public entity." The bill's sponsors argued that the majority ruling promised to saddle public agencies with the onerous duty of ensuring the safety of all routes to and from their properties. Public transit agencies like AC Transit would be required to review the egress and ingress patterns of hundreds if not thousands of stops. Where necessary, such stops would have to be moved. While the beneficiaries of the bill were clear, the bill also had its detractors. These included the California Nurses Association, the Congress of California Seniors, the Older Women's League, and the Consumer Federation of California. The bill was never passed. See California State Assembly, *Immunity Government Tort Liability*, May 4, 2004, Hearing (AB 2737), Sacramento, Calif. Analysis prepared by Saskia Kim.

16. Senior planner at AC Transit, 2010.

17. See "Opinion" in *Lopez v. Southern Cal. Rapid Transit District*, 40 Cal. 3rd 780 (Cal. 1985).

18. See text of Cal. Civil Code § 2100.

19. See text of Cal. Gov. Code § 845.

20. See text of Cal. Gov. Code § 815.2; Cal. Gov. Code § 820.2.

21. In its defense, the SCRTD also cited a set of more practical concerns. The SCRTD argued that nothing short of an armed security force might assure that riders remain safe at all times. With 220 bus lines and 2000 buses, the defense complained that protecting passengers from each other promised to be an onerous, if not an impossible, task.

22. *Lopez v. Southern Cal. Rapid Transit District*, 1985.

23. For a fairly readable discussion of the "special relationship doctrine," see Sandt, "Schools' Duty to Protect Students."

24. *Lopez v. Southern Cal. Rapid Transit District*, 1985.

25. The seven largest transit operators in the Bay Area are AC Transit, BART, Caltrain, Golden Gate Transit, MUNI, SamTrans, and Santa Clara Valley Transit Authority. Of these seven, MUNI (~220 million), BART(~101 million), and AC Transit (~65 million) have the highest annual ridership. See discussion of "Transit Operators" in *Darensburg v. MTC*, 611 F. Supp. 2d 994 (N.D. Cal. 2009). See the unpublished document "Findings of Fact and Conclusions of Law following Court Trial" (Ordered by Elizabeth Laporte in *Darensburg et al. v. MTC*, N.D. Cal., March 27, 2009), 15.

26. In a class action lawsuit, Sylvia Darensburg was the representative plaintiff for a class of individuals consisting of black, Hispanic, Asian, or Pacific Islander, as well as American Indian or Alaskan Natives, who were patrons of AC Transit. Apart from Sylvia Darensburg, the "named plaintiffs" in the original suit included Vivian Hain and Virginia Martinez, also East Bay minority bus riders. In addition to these three individuals, the case also included two organizational plaintiffs: the Amalgamated Transit Union Local 192 (ATU)—a labor union representing AC Transit drivers—and Communities for a Better Environment (CBE)—a self-described social justice organization focused on issues of environmental health. See discussion of "Plaintiffs" in *Darensburg v. MTC*.

27. See text of Cal. Gov. Code § 11135.

28. See "background discussion" in *Darenbsurg v. MTC*.

29. The history of disparate impact discrimination is an interesting one and begins with the Supreme Court's decision in *Griggs v. Duke Power Co.*, whereby the court found that the use of an IQ test by a power company for job applicants—while facially neutral—stood in violation of Title VI of the 1964 Civil Rights Act because of its disparate impact on minority applicants. See *Griggs v. Duke Power Co.*, 401 U.S. 424 (1971). The Supreme Court has since limited the private right of action under Title VI to intentional discrimination—namely, in *Alexander v. Sandoval*, 532 U.S. 275 (2001). These same limitations, however, do not extend to the corresponding California statute, Government Code 11135, where the private right of action in disparate impact claims remains intact. It was under this statute that the Darensburg case was tried.

30. See Siegel, "Discrimination in the Funding," 114–19.

31. G. Mayer and Marcantonio, "Bay Area—Separate and Unequal," 20.

32. *N.Y. Urban League v. Metropolitan Transportation Authority*, 905 F Supp., 1266 (S.D. N.Y., 1995); Siegel, "Discrimination in the Funding."

33. In 1995, the federal government eliminated all federal operating aid to local transit agencies. This prompted a national wave of service cuts and fare hikes. The New York MTA was no exception. See Alan Fram, "Congress Passes GOP's Landmark Budget Balancing Plan," *Contra Costa Times*, June 30, 1995, B01; Melinda Henneberger, "Budget Plan Holds Big Cut in Money for Transit," *New York Times*, February 6, 1995, A22.

34. Siegel, "Discrimination in the Funding," 112–14.

35. Ibid., 112; Marcantonio and Jongco, "From the Back," 10.

36. As an indication of BATLUC's particular prominence, a common refrain in the transit advocacy community was, "If we didn't have BATLUC, we wouldn't have any luck at all." John Katz, interview by the author, November 29, 2010. In their 2006 report, *MTC, Where Are Our Buses?*," Urban Habitat argued that the Darensburg case "represented an important tool in the long struggle for equity in Bay Area transportation funding." The report also warned against a narrow focus on the courts, suggesting instead that the work of lawyers could only be successful with the support of organized communities. See Urban Habitat, *MTC, Where Are Our Buses?*, 5.

37. In addition to Loni Hancock and Barbara Lee, signatories on this letter included George Miller (congressman), Don Perata (state senator), Johan Klehs (assemblyman), William Chan (assemblyman), Keith Carson (Alameda County supervisor), and John Gioa (Contra Costa supervisor). See Loni Hancock, "Dear Chairman Rubin" (letter to MTC, Oakland, Calif., September 12, 2005).

38. Hancock, "Dear Chairman Rubin." The range of supporters also included the American Civil Liberties Union (ACLU), which in 2005 filed an amicus curie on behalf of Darensburg. See ACLU, "Brief on behalf of plaintiff in opposition to defendant Metropolitan Transportation Commission's motion to dismiss" (San Francisco, November 29, 2005). In 2005 as well, both the Berkeley and Oakland City Councils passed resolutions in support of increased financial support of AC Transit. See Berkeley City Council, "Resolution 69888 NS: Supporting Increased Financial Support of AC Transit for the Equitable Benefit of its Passengers by the Metropolitan Transportation Commission" (Berkeley, CA, July 12, 2005). Also see Oakland City Council, "Resolution 79555 CMS: Supporting Increased Financial Support of AC Transit for the Equitable Benefit of its Passengers by the Metropolitan Transportation Commission" (Oakland, Calif., November 1, 2005).

39. For the district court decision, see *Darensburg v. MTC*, 611 F. Supp. 2d 994 (N.D. Cal. 2009); for 9th Circuit decision, see *Darensburg v. MTC*, 2011, 636 F. 3d 511(9th cir. 2011).

40. Siegel, "Discrimination in the Funding," 108.

41. Uncommitted or "Track 1" funds like CMAQ are restricted—save for a few exceptions—to capital expenditures. The use of STP funds is generally less restricted. While the MTC has not traditionally used STP funds for preventative maintenance or operating expenses, the plaintiffs argued that there was nothing barring MTC from doing so. This fact was corroborated during the trial by expert witness Therese McMillan—then serving as the deputy director of policy at the MTC. See Therese McMillan, "Testimony for Prosecution in *Darensburg v. MTC*" (Trial Transcript, Testimony before the Honorable Judge Laporte of the United States District Court, Northern District of California, Reported and Transcribed by Debra L. Pas [court reporter], October 2, 2008, 224).

42. Bill Lann Lee, "Opening Statement in *Darensburg v. MTC*" (Trial Transcript, Statement before the Honorable Judge Laporte of the United States District Court, Northern District of California, Reported and Transcribed by Debra L. Pas [court reporter], October 1, 2008), 6.

43. McMillan, "Testimony for Prosecution in *Darensburg v. MTC*," 284.

44. Lee, "Opening Statement," 6.

45. By definition, committed funds are "dedicated by law, ballot measure or prior MTC programming actions to specific transportation investments." State-committed funds include those passed through statewide ballot measures like Proposition 1B, Assembly Bills like A.B. 664, and Regional Measure 1, all of which direct toll bridge revenue to the MTC. See discussion of committed funds in *Darensburg v. MTC*, 2009.

46. In the Bay Area, FTA formula funds (also called section 5307 and 5309 funds) are administered by the MTC using the Transit Capital Priorities (TCP) program—a scoring system that ranks projects on a scale from 8 to 16. Projects scoring 16 are normally funded, while projects scoring 8 are usually not. The FTA administers these grants as formula grants based on population and population density. Following the passage of the Transportation Equity Act in 1998, section 5307 funds have become eligible to be used for some operating costs if defined as "preventative maintenance." Along with section 5307 and 5309 funds, there are also a set of even more restricted pots of money. These include the funds associated with the Job Access and Reverse Commute (JARC) program, as well as grants for improving the accessibility options for the disabled. At the state level, committed funds take the form of Transportation Development Act (TDA) funds. These funds are derived from a ¼ percent tax on all retail sales. Committed funds also take the form of State Transit Assistance (STA) funds. STA funds provide a major source of operating aid to AC Transit. See discussion of 5301 and 5309 funds in *Darensburg v. MTC*, 2009.

47. The process by which STIP funds are allocated involves the collaboration of both local MPOs and county-level congestion management officers. Together, both MTC officials and congestion managers compile a list of priority transportation projects. This list is then funded or denied by the California Transportation Commission on the basis of need and competing demand. See discussion of STIP funds in *Darensburg v. MTC*, 2009.

48. Resolution 3434 was passed in 2001 as the successor to Resolution 1876. Through the 1990s, Resolution 1876 saw the implementation of a number of high-profile projects under its banners. These included the BART extension to Pittsburg/Bay Point, Dublin/Pleasanton, and the BART extension to the San Francisco Airport. See discussion of Resolution 3434 in *Darensburg v. MTC*, 2009.

49. The plaintiff's attack on Resolution 3434 relied on a different set of comparisons than were used in earlier arguments. Here the plaintiffs were not comparing AC Transit riders with BART or Caltrain riders, but rather they were comparing Bay Area rail riders with Bay Area bus riders. With respect to Resolution 3434, they based their disparate impact claim on the fact that 51.6 percent of rail passengers in the Bay Area were minority while 66.3 percent of bus riders in the Bay Area were minority. See discussion of "Prima Facie case against Resolution 3434" in *Darensburg v. MTC*, 2009.

50. This overrepresentation was largely a function of the fact that the MTC held higher standards for funding bus projects as compared to rail projects. Resolution 3434, for example, stipulated that any "bus-only" project included in the RTP must "effectively address congestion relief by proving a clearly attractive alternative to single occupancy vehicles." This same requirement was not extended to rail projects. As MTC's Therese McMillan testified, it was simply assumed that rail projects would have this effect. See discussion of Resolution 3434 in *Darensburg v. MTC*, 2009. See also McMillan, "Testimony for Defense in *Darensburg v. MTC*" (Trial Transcript, October 21, 2010), 1256–58).

51. McMillan, "Testimony for Defense in *Darensburg v. MTC*."

52. Over the course of the month-long trial, the defense acknowledged the difficulties of AC Transit's minority riders, but it also countered that many of the problems at AC Transit were outside of the MTC's control. The MTC argued that they had been more than generous in their support of AC Transit. Apart from criticizing expert witnesses like Thomas Rubin for exaggerating AC Transit's deficit problems, the defense pointed out that in the case of both committed and uncommitted funds, pumping more money into AC Transit amounted to taking it away from elsewhere—whether that was from bridges, other carriers, or capital refurbishment needs. Despite the plaintiff's claims that the MTC and the RTP process treated AC Transit unfairly, the MTC cited a number of examples in which the MTC had done exactly the opposite—namely, instances in which the MTC had rededicated federal formula grants to AC Transit in the form of preventative maintenance. In response to the plaintiff's critique of Resolution 3434, the defense used a different tact. The MTC argued that the plaintiff's distinction between high-minority systems like AC Transit (78 percent) and low-minority systems like BART (53 percent) was an arbitrary one. Moreover, in terms of absolute numbers, a system like BART actually surpassed AC Transit with respect to minority ridership. Where the plaintiffs argued that Resolution 3434 favored rail projects over bus projects, the MTC argued that such rail projects were just as beneficial to minorities as bus projects. See discussion of "committed funds" in *Darensburg v. MTC*. See also Thomas Rubin, "Testimony for Prosecution in *Darensburg v. MTC*" (Trial Transcript, Testimony before the Honorable Judge Laporte of the United States District Court, Northern District of California, Reported and Transcribed by Debra L. Pas [court reporter], October 8, 2008), 517.

53. See discussion of "MTC's burden," *Darensburg v. MTC*.

54. Ibid.; also see United States Code governing Urban Transportation Planning, 23 U.S.C § 134.

55. See Kimon Manolius, "Opening Statement in *Darensburg v. MTC*" (Trial Transcript, Testimony before the Honorable Judge Laporte of the United States District Court, Northern District of California, Reported and Transcribed by Debra L. Pas [court reporter], October 1, 2008), 41.

56. As Manolius argued: "The 26 operators within the nine county area do not operate in 26 individual vacuums. They interconnect. This is a regional transportation system. They coordinate. AC Transit and SamTran buses feed BART. BART pays AC Transit to run those feeder buses. Santa Clara's VTA [Valley Transportation Authority] is the project sponsor for the BART expansion to San Jose, and through Freemont. SamTrans helped build and operate BART from San Mateo County. There are so many examples of this interconnection and coordination." Manolius, "Opening Statement," 29.

57. Ninth Circuit Court of Appeals, 2011, *Darensburg v. Metropolitan Transportation Commission*, Opinion, February 16, 2011, 2258, http://www.ca9.uscourts.gov/datastore /opinions/2011/02/16/09-15878.pdf.

58. Ibid., 2574.

59. Golub, Marcantonio, and Sanchez, "Race, Space, and Struggles," 700.

60. Karner and Niemeier, "Civil Rights Guidance," 131.

61. Michael Cabanatuan, "AC Transit May Whack Service Yet Again," *San Francisco Chronicle*, September 23, 2010, C2.

62. "General Manager's Memo to the Board: Consider the Adoption of Resolution 10–045 Approving the December 2010 Service Reduction Plan, Pending Receipt of a Final Title VI Disparate Impacts Study" (GM-memo 09-217j, Oakland, Calif., September 22, 2010).

63. The quotes from Greg Harper were transcribed from the audio of an AC Transit Board meeting held on September 23, 2010. The audio of the meeting can be accessed at http://www.actransit.org/about-us/board-of-directors/board-memos.

64. See "2008/2009 On Board Rider Survey: Prepared for Alameda-Contra Costa Transit Division of Long Range Planning by the Public Research Institute San Francisco State University" (Public Research Institute, San Francisco, October 2010) 10.

65. Ibid., 22.

66. For yet another reading of *Darensburg v. MTC*, and one that engages both the appellate court's decision and the history of race and transit in the East Bay, see Golub, Marcantonio, and Sanchez, "Race, Space, and Struggles."

67. Marx, *On the Jewish Question*, 24.

68. Karner and Niemeier, "Civil Rights Guidance," 129.

69. France, *Red Lily*, 95.

Chapter 2. Transportation Justice and the Alliance for AC Transit

1. Armand Emamdjomeh, February 1, 2010 (12:43 p.m.), "Could $70 Million for the Oakland Airport Connector Be Better Spent?," Bay Area (blog), *New York Times*, http://bayarea.blogs.nytimes.com/2010/02/01/could-70-million-for-the-oakland -airport-connector-be-better-spent/; Malia Wollan, "U.S. Blocks $70 Million for Rail Line in Bay Area," *New York Times*, February 17, 2010, A13.

2. Peter Rogoff, letter to Steve Heminger and Dorothy Dugger, January 15, 2011, http://transbay.files.wordpress.com/2010/02/fta_oac_02122010.pdf.

3. Wollan, "U.S. Blocks 70 Million," A13.

4. Richard Marcantonio and Marc Brenman, "Transportation Victory for Social Equity," *Planetizen* (blog), February 22, 2010 (5:00 a.m.), http://www.planetizen.com /node/42991.#123#.

5. To recall, John Rawls's theory of justice began by imagining a hypothetical scenario in which people must make decisions about social arrangement behind a so-called "veil of ignorance." Without the benefit of knowing a priori one's "class position, or social status," Rawls suggested that people would ultimately choose principles of justice that prioritized "liberty, opportunity and constraints on inequality." Given an equal chance of being poor or wealthy, the rational person, Rawls suggested, would choose a social arrangement that insured equality of opportunity, and that put a floor on human suffering. A defense of transportation justice can begin from much the same premise. Behind a veil of ignorance, and without the benefit of knowing a priori one's place within a network of urban roads, or bus routes, a rational person would, following Rawls, invariably choose a transportation system that insured equal access and equal mobility regardless of one's social standing or geographic location. Thus, from a Rawlsian perspective, in those instances where transportation funds are limited, such funds should be directed in ways that benefit the least advantaged and that ensure them equal access and equal mobility. Litman, *Evaluating Transportation Equity*. See discussion of Rawls in D. Smith, *Geography and Social Justice*; see also Rawls, *Theory of Justice*.

6. One additional criticism of the OAC was the limited extent of the proposed service. Despite running through a working-class area, the OAC's elevated train included no intermediate stop. Additionally, a one-way trip on the OAC was predicted to cost riders $3 more than the current fare for the same trip on an airport shuttle. See Marcantonio and Brenman, "Transportation Victory for Social Equity."

7. At least since the late 1970s—when it was slated to be called the "Amelia AirBART"—city boosters in Oakland and the East Bay have argued for a higher-profile connection to the Oakland Airport. George Raine, "BART Oakland Airport Plan Revived—Light-Rail Link among 3 Proposals under Study," *San Francisco Chronicle*, January 9, 2001, A19; Guy Span (Bay Area public transportation examiner), "MTC Wants to Build a Monument with Oakland Airport Connector," *San Francisco Examiner*, January 28, 2010.

8. For more on San Francisco highway revolt, see Issel, "Land Values, Human Values." For more on highway revolts in general, see Mohl, "Stop the Road."

9. Rodriguez, "Rapid Transit and Community Power."

10. For more on impact of BART protests, see Merewitz, "Public Transportation"; Stokes, "Bay Area Rapid Transit."

11. See Frieden, "Independent Living"; Pelka, *ABC-CLIO Companion.*

12. This was, in fact, precisely the case in downtown Oakland, whose business district suffered following BART's development. BART, as it was discovered, simply made it easier for East Bay commuters to bypass downtown Oakland on their way to San Francisco. See Webber, "BART Experience."

13. Tara Shioya, "AC Transit Struggles as Budget Shrinks," *San Francisco Chronicle*, November 20, 1995, A13.

14. Shioya, "AC Transit Struggles," A13; see also Cohen and Crabbe, *Cutting Transit Eliminating the Economy*, 6–10.

15. Renita Sandosham, "100 March against Cuts Planned by AC Transit," *West County Times*, June 15, 1996, A03.

16. John Katz, interview by author, November 29, 2010.

17. "Look at Us," *Alliance for AC Transit Omnibus* 2, no. 2 (1998): 3.

18. Before September 1999, the Alliance and Bus Riders Union maintained two separate membership lists, even though their affiliation began in fall 1997. The cost of an annual membership was $5 for the Alliance and $2 for the Bus Riders Union. In 1998 the Bus Riders Union had 1,051 dues-paying members. "Look at Us," 3; Catherine Bowman, "Bus Riders Won't Stay Seated—AC Transit Passengers Want a Say in Service," *San Francisco Chronicle*, March 31, 1997, A1.

19. Karen Ackerman, "Formation of Groups Advocating for AC Transit: A Chronology" (unpublished document, Oakland, Calif., April 4, 1998).

20. "The Mission of the Alliance," *Alliance for AC Transit Omnibus* 5, no. 1 (2002): 2.

21. Stuart Cohen, "Letter to MTC Chair Dianne McKenna and Commissioners," September 11, 1996.

22. This campaign was led by the Bay Area Transportation and Land Use Coalition (BATLUC)—which later became TransForm. The campaign focused on the MTC's inclusion of several highway expansion projects in the 1998 Regional Transportation Plan. Following several months of protests, the MTC board took the unprecedented step of ignoring their staff and adopting the suggestion of local transit advocates—revising the 1998 RTP to cut funding from six environmentally destructive highway projects and rededicating the money. Sam Diaz, "Panel Promises Transit Funding," *San Jose Mercury News*, October 10, 1998, 1B.

23. Chris Tribbey, "AC Transit Unveils Plan to Double Ridership by 2010," *Oakland Tribune*, October 9, 2001, Local.

24. Sean Holstege, "AC Transit Riding on Property Tax Measure," Headline News, *Alameda Times Star*, November 1, 2002.

25. "New! How-to Guide Helps Save Time, Money, Environment, on the Bus" (press release, Oakland, Calif., October 25, 2001); *Bus Riding 101: A Guide for Discerning Travelers* (Oakland, Calif.: Alliance for AC Transit, 2001).

26. "Downtown Oakland Development Issues: A Report by the Broadway Corridor Committee to the Oakland Chamber of Commerce" (Oakland, Calif.: Oakland Chamber of Commerce, February 3, 1997), 2.

27. In opposing efforts to move the transfer station, the Alliance cited the failure of a similar effort in Kansas City, Missouri. A new and less-central transit facility would reduce transit ridership by inconveniencing riders and would also do little to solve the problems of crime and loitering that prompted the proposal in the first place—indeed, it would simply move those problems elsewhere. "Downtown Oakland Transfer Center—Critique and Alternate Proposal" (Oakland, Calif.: Alliance for AC Transit, 1998).

28. Joyce Roy, "Bus Stops for Broadway," My Word, *Oakland Tribune*, December 1, 1998.

29. Thaai Walker, "Controversial Bus Stop Staying Put—Oakland Council," *San Francisco Chronicle*, September 3, 1998, A25.

30. "Downtown Oakland Development Issues"; "Downtown Oakland Transfer Center."

31. Katz, interview by the author.

32. "Bus Riders Bill of Rights Endorsed," *Alliance for AC Transit Omnibus* 4, no. 1 (2000): 3; Bus Riders Bill of Right Action Plan (Oakland, Calif.: Alliance for AC Transit, 2000).

33. Bowman, "Bus Riders Won't Stay Seated." For more on the tension between transit advocates and environmental groups in the East Bay at this time, see Cohen and Hobson, "Transportation Choices."

34. Grant Proposal (Oakland, Calif., Alliance for AC Transit, 1999); Marc Albert, "How Berkeley Can a Year Get? 1999 in Review," *West County Times*, January 3, 2000, A31.

35. These tensions were most pronounced in the differences between the Bus Riders Union and the Alliance for AC Transit. While the Bus Riders Union embodied a more grassroots and confrontation component of the partnership, the Alliance for AC Transit often emphasized cooperation with transit planners and directed its attention toward regional policy concerns. As John Katz recalls, the members of the Bus Riders Union were much more ready to "fire off an angry missive to AC Transit" than were the leaders of the Alliance for AC Transit, who were more interested in working with the agency. In fact, Alliance members like Victoria Wake and Aaron Priven were eventually hired by AC Transit. See Joyce Roy, interview by the author, September 27, 2012, and Katz, interview by the author. In some ways, this was a product of each group's membership: the Bus Riders Union attracted transit-dependent riders and seniors on fixed incomes; the Alliance for AC Transit was largely composed of white professionals.

36. Katz, interview by the author.

37. "Transportation Justice," *Urban Habitat*, http://www.urbanhabitat.org/policy-advocacy/transportation; Lindsay Imai, interview by the author, October 19, 2010.

38. Bob Egelko, "Getting on the Bus Is Half the Story," *San Francisco Chronicle*, April 20, 2005, B1; Josh Richman, "MTC Sued for Race Bias in Funding," Tri-Valley, *Oakland Tribune*, April 20, 2005; G. Mayer and Marcantonio, "Bay Area—Separate and Unequal."

39. One of Urban Habitat's goals has been to persuade the MTC to adopt better internal mechanisms that ensure regional transit equity. Although the MTC has included an equity analysis in every RTP since 1998, Urban Habitat and others have criticized the MTC's methodology. Despite an overemphasis on rail projects that benefit more affluent communities, the MTC has defined such projects as equally beneficial to minorities since such projects often run through minority neighborhoods. Over the years, Urban Habitat has attempted to formulate better methods of measuring equity and has worked with the MTC's various public bodies to persuade the MTC to adopt such methods.

40. "Our Approach," TransForm, http://www.transformca.org/landing-page/our-approach; "Oakland Airport Connector Options Analysis," report prepared for TransForm (Portland, Ore.: Kittelson and Associates, August 2010), http://www.transformca.org/sites/default/files/Oakland%20Airport%20Connector%20Options%20Analysis.pdf.

41. "Mission," Genesis, https://www.genesisca.org/.

42. Denis Cuff, "Coalition Urges Free Bus Passes for Students in Bay Area," *Contra Costa Times*, March 17, 2010, 4A.

43. Genesis organizer, interview by the author, November 12, 2010.

44. At least in 2010, there were few evident links between the Alliance for AC Transit and Bus Riders Union and the ACCE Bus Riders Union. If the comments of former Alliance member Joyce Roy are at all representative, the remaining Alliance members viewed the ACCE Bus Riders Union with some degree of skepticism, perhaps partly due to ACCE's origins. Many of the key organizers for the ACCE Bus Riders Union were neither from the East Bay nor rooted in the East Bay's activist community. The ACCE Bus Riders Union was merely one component of a much larger statewide organization. As a result, not only did its goals seem more contrived, but its annual membership fee far exceeded that of the Alliance. This was due largely to the overhead associated with having a paid staff and statewide presence. See Joyce Roy, interview by the author, October 11, 2010.

45. Joe Garofoli, "California's Acorn Branch Splits from National Group," *San Francisco Chronicle*, January 14, 2010, A4.

46. Alliance of Californians for Community Empowerment (ACCE), "About," http://www.acceaction.org/about.

47. In other ways, ACCE and the Alliance were quite different. As part of a statewide progressive organization, ACCE's organizers often drew from the members in the Bus Riders Union in fights that had little to do with transit. For example, in 2010 many members of the ACCE Bus Riders Union were recruited for ACCE's voter registration drive and its campaign to support youth violence-prevention programs in Oakland.

48. See Rawls, *Theory of Justice*. Also see discussion of Rawls in D. Smith, *Geography and Social Justice*, 78.

49. Litman, *Evaluating Transportation Equity*, 4.

50. Ibid., 4.

51. Groups such as Urban Habitat, TransForm, and Genesis have not been alone in this approach. Indeed, there is a whole body of scholarship dedicated to exploring the uneven distribution of transit subsidies and the disparate impact of transit projects on poor communities—whether it is work on cross-subsidization, the distribution of costs and benefits associated with new projects, racial discrimination, or the relationship between transportation and generalized income inequality. See Pucher, "Who Benefits from Transit Subsidies?"; Hodge, "Fiscal Equity"; Lewis, *Divided Highways*; Bullard, Johnson, and Torres, *Highway Robbery*; Kain and Meyer, "Transportation and Poverty."

52. Katz, interview by the author.

53. Imai, interview by the author.

54. Since 1994, bus riders' unions have materialized in cities across the United States—in such cities as Anchorage, Oakland, Atlanta, Baltimore, Memphis, Tucson, Portland, Long Island, and Laredo, Texas. In each city, of course, bus riders face a different set of challenges, and thus each BRU often differs in focus. In 2011, a public accountability nonprofit called Good Jobs First, with the support of the Amalgamated Transit Union's president Larry Hanley, published *Organizing Transit Riders: A Manual*. Drawing from examples across the country, the manual offers a how-to guide

for organizing bus riders. If anything, the guide is a testament to the popularity of the bus riders' union model. See LeRoy, *Organizing Transit Riders*.

55. Janet Gilmore and David Bloom, "Court Backs Order against Bus Fare Hike," *Daily News of Los Angeles*, September 9, 1994, N4; James Sterngold, "Improve Bus Service and Soon, Blunt Judge Tells Los Angeles," *New York Times*, September 25, 1999, A11.

56. Mann et al., "Environmental Justice Strategy."

57. Mann, *New Vision for Urban Transportation*, 3.

58. Ibid.

59. Since around 2005, TEN operated under the aegis of the Gamaliel Foundation and worked to fulfill Gamaliel's larger social justice mission. It functioned as both a policy clearinghouse for member organizations and a forum in which smaller-member groups could learn about broader trends in federal transit policy advocacy. TEN's platform included demanding increased federal funding for public transportation, increased community and democratic control over local transportation planning, greater support for Transit Oriented Development, and the greater representation of minorities and women in the transportation construction industry. See Transportation Equity Network, "One Nation, Indivisible: The TEN Vision for America," http://www.transportationequity.org/images/stories/TEN-vision.pdf.

60. Transportation Equity Network, "One Nation, Indivisible," 5.

61. Rebecca Schein, "Free Transit and Movement Building," *Bullet: Socialist Project*, E-Bulletin no. 438 (2010), http://www.socialistproject.ca/bullet/438.php.

62. Bus Riders Union, "Mission Statement," https://busridersunion.weebly.com/mission-statement.html.

63. Steve Geller, interview by the author, October 5, 2010.

64. Fran Haselsteiner, interview by the author, October 1, 2010.

65. East Bay Center for the Blind, focus group conducted by the author, November 9, 2010.

66. Chris Mullen, interview by the author, November 19, 2010.

67. Lefebvre, *Writings on Cities*, 173.

68. See Merrifield, *Henri Lefebvre*.

69. Marx and Engels, *Communist Manifesto*, 55.

70. Draper, *Adventures of the Communist Manifesto*, 220. Also see Attoh, "Public Transportation."

71. Engels, *Condition*, 222.

72. Lefebvre, *Writings on Cities*, 179.

73. Ibid., 159.

74. The comments of bus riders like Steve Geller suggest that in many places a right to the city—whether understood as a right to participate or a right to centrality—may require public transportation.

Chapter 3. The Rights of Transit Labor

1. The timeline of events leading up to the rash of absences on July 19 goes as follows: Contract negotiations between AC Transit and its workers began on April 1, 2010. Despite at least ten state-mediated sessions, no agreement was reached by the June 30 deadline—the expiration date for the previous labor contract. On June 22

the ATU 192 requested binding interest arbitration—whereby an outside committee would draft a contract. On June 27 AC Transit rejected this request. On June 30, having reached the deadline without an agreement, the AC Transit Board of Directors voted to impose their last and final offer. This contract was to be effective starting July 18 and would save the agency $15.7 million. At least since 1960, binding arbitration has been the preferred method for resolving labor disputes between AC Transit management and the ATU 192. On June 16, and after an earlier petition by the union, the court compelled AC Transit to submit to binding arbitration. On August 2, and after an earlier and separate petition, Judge Ford ordered AC Transit to return to the previous contract until the arbitration process produced a new one, writing, "the ATU has sufficiently established that AC Transit's imposition of new terms under the 'last best and final offer'" violated its duty to bargain in good faith and to continue collective bargaining rights under these statutes. See "Order Granting Motion for Relief from Stay and Granting Preliminary Injunction" in *ATU 192 v. AC Transit*, Case Number: RG10522627 (California Superior Court, District 1, August 2, 2010), 10. See also Mary King, "Protecting AC Transit's Future Requires Cooperation Now from Labor," My Word, *Alameda-Times Star*, July 3, 2010.

2. Somewhat unbelievably the union blamed the absences on a confusion surrounding system signups. Despite this, much of the reporting on the event assumed the absences were part of a protest. See Daniel Borenstein, "AC Transit Faces Risky Situation," editorial, *Oakland Tribune*, July 25, 2010; Claudia Hudson, "Press Release: We Are at Work, There Is No Sickout," *Berkeley Planet*, July 21, 2010. With buses idle and with absences continuing into the week, accusations flew. AC Transit management accused workers of abandoning their duties to "working-class riders," students, and the disabled. Conversely, AC Transit operators and mechanics accused management of negotiating in bad faith. Workers argued that the imposed contract was an affront to decades of collective bargaining and an assault on their rights as workers. How, drivers asked, could they accept a contract that imposed a three-year wage freeze, a new two-tiered pension plan, one fewer paid holiday, larger medical co-pays, and cuts into operators' overtime compensation? The president of ATU 192, Claudia Hudson, went as far as to argue that the imposed contract was more "about busting our union than necessarily about saving money." See Claudia Hudson, interview with author, December 8, 2010. Both Hudson and drivers such as Anthony Rodgers even suggested that management had hoped to provoke a strike like that of 1977—a strike in which the union had actually lost wages. For media coverage on the impact on the poor and disabled, see Joanna Lin, "Riders Left Waiting in AC Transit Labor Dispute," *California Watch*, July 23, 2010, http://californiawatch.org/dailyreport/riders-left-waiting-ac-transit-labor-dispute-3460 (unavailable); Heather Ishimaru, "More Finger Pointing in AC Transit Labor Dispute," *East Bay News*, July 22, 2010, http://abc7.com/archive/7570142/. For more on contract stipulations, see "General Manager Memo to the Board: Report on the Options Available for Further Cost Reduction Strategies" (GM memo 10-210, Oakland, Calif., September 2010). For driver reactions, see Claudia Hudson, interview by the author, December 8, 2010; Janis Mara, "Breaking News: Bay Area's AC Transit Bus Service Disrupted as Imposed Contract Continues," *Alameda-Times Star*, July 20, 2010.

3. AC Transit board member, interview by the author, November 12, 2010.

4. East Bay bus operators, as it was revealed, made an average of $50,000 a year. They received an additional $45,000 a year in pension and healthcare benefits. Although not a glamorous job, bus operators, one could argue, certainly made a lot more than many of the bus patrons they carried. Borenstein, "AC Transit Faces Risky Situation."

5. Joyce Roy, interview by the author, October 11, 2010.

6. Steve Geller, interview by the author, October 5, 2010.

7. For a rare exception, see Greenberg and Lewis, *City Is the Factory*.

8. Freeman, *In Transit*.

9. It is not clear when exactly the ATU 192 ceased to be referred to as the Carmen's Union. Most likely, this change occurred in the years following World War II. This chapter uses both interchangeably. "Union Men Meet," *Oakland Tribune*, March 29, 1906, 3.

10. Ibid.

11. Ibid.

12. "Vote to Go Out If Company Persists," *San Francisco Chronicle*, March 30, 1906, 16; "Union Men Meet," 3.

13. "Will Not Recognize Union of Street Carmen," *Oakland Tribune*, March 19, 1906, 1.

14. Even before the votes, the Oakland Traction Company had already begun to take precautionary measures. In the lead-up to the strike, rumors swirled that hundreds of non-union strikebreakers were primed to arrive from as far as Chicago and Los Angeles. See "Carmen Will Await Result of Monday Conference," *San Francisco Chronicle*, April 1, 1906, 1.

15. Ibid.

16. "Vote to Go Out," *San Francisco Chronicle*, 16.

17. "Carmen Will Await Result of Monday Conference," *San Francisco Chronicle*, April 1, 1906, 1.

18. Ibid.

19. Division 192's own "Certificate of Affiliation" indicates that Division 192 was incorporated on June 1, 1901, although the first reference to the incorporation appears in May of the following year. See "Car Men Organizing," *Evening News* (San Jose), May 19, 1902, 1. One earlier reference notes a failed attempt to organize a union in October 1901; see "Union Men Not Wanted," *Oakland Tribune*, October 22, 1901, 2.

20. "Wage Scale Unchanged," *Oakland Tribune*, April 4, 1906, 2.

21. "Strike Prevented by Concessions," *Los Angeles Times*, April 5, 1906, 13; "Carmen Gain Victory," *Oakland Tribune*, April 4, 1906, 1.

22. Many of the provisions outlined in the carmen's first contract appear in most labor contracts irrespective of the industry. These include provisions on wages and the use of company property. Other provisions, however, are more particular to the transportation industry. Provisions restricting operators from working a spread of over fifteen hours, for example, are quite specific to the transportation industries. Many provisions in the 1906 contract of Division 192 employees, in fact, remain a part of the current contract. Apart from limits on spread time or the use of company property, benefits for conductors and motormen such as free travel on Key Route trains and ferries are still part of the contract.

23. Shue, *Basic Rights*.

24. "Union Men Meet," *Oakland Tribune*, March 29, 1906, 2.

25. "Strike Terror Grips Oakland," *Los Angeles Times*, October 8, 1919, 13.

26. "Five Shot in Oakland Riots," *San Jose Mercury Herald*, October 7, 1919, 1; "Mass Meeting in Oakland Results in Vote to Return," *San Francisco Chronicle*, October 12, 1919, 1.

27. "Traction Men Give Demand to Arbiters," *Oakland Tribune*, December 19, 1919, 1–2.

28. Ibid.

29. The actual strike vote took place on September 28, with the union voting 1008 to 16 in favor of a strike. It was only on October 1 that the last attempt by the company to offer arbitration was formally rejected. See "Strike Lasting for Ten Full Days, Disorder and Riots Mark Conflict, Eight-Hour Day Is Final Issue," *Oakland Tribune*, October 12, 1919, 5.

30. "Workers Will Make Decision at 3 a.m. Today," *San Francisco Chronicle*, October 1, 1919, 1.

31. "Key Route Men Out on Strike," *Los Angeles Times*, October 2, 1919, 16.

32. "Federal Judge Orders Union Halt Coercion," *San Francisco Daily Chronicle*, October 4, 1919, 1.

33. "Eight Hurt, Fifteen Jailed in Outbreaks, Police among Injured," *Oakland Tribune*, October 5, 1919: 2; "Federal Judge," *San Francisco Daily Chronicle*, 1.

34. "Strike Lasting for Ten Full Days, Disorder and Riots Mark Conflict, Eight-Hour Day Is Final Issue," *Oakland Tribune*, October 12, 1919, 5.

35. "Eight Hurt," 1.

36. "Strike Lasting for Ten Full Days," 5.

37. "Five Shot in Oakland Riots," *San Francisco Chronicle*, 1.

38. The greatest number of fatalities occurred on October 7 when six people were killed after a streetcar collided with an automobile. There were rumors that the brakes of the car had been tampered with. "Speeding Train Hits Auto; Six Are Killed, One Is Believed Dying," *Oakland Tribune*, October 7, 1919, 1–2: "Eight Hurt," 1.

39. "Executive of State Coming to Bay Cities," *Oakland Tribune*, October 10, 1919, 1–2.

40. "Strike Terror," *Los Angeles Times*, 13.

41. "Traction Platform Men Approve Plan for Arbitration and Return to Work," *Oakland Tribune*, October 11, 1919, 2.

42. In retrospect, the demands of the union in 1919 actually appear quite bold. In addition to an eight-hour day, they had also demanded a spread time for split runs of ten hours, a minimum pay for men working the extra board, and a 70/30 straight to split run ratio. Just as a comparison, bus operators in 2010 could only count on an eleven-hour spread and 60 percent straight runs. "Carmen Win Wage Increase, but Not Eight-Hour Day," *Oakland Tribune*, January 20, 1920, 1–2; for rates in 2010, see "Summary of Savings: Last but Final Offer" (Oakland, Calif., District's final proposal to ATU 192, June 30, 2010).

43. Between 1912 and 1919, the Key System paid no dividends to its shareholders, operating revenue dropped by $272,000, and starting in the early part of 1919, the company was in default on several bonds. An eight-hour day, the board argued, "would make it impossible for the company to maintain its current standard of

service," to keep fares low, to pay workers a "fair living wage," to meet its bottom line, and to adequately deal with peak-hour loads. See "Key Route Men Told Why New Scales Denied," *Oakland Tribune*, September 20, 1919, 3; "Carmen Win Wage Increase," 1–2; "Another East Bay Car Strike, Plan," *San Jose Mercury Herald*, January 14, 1920, 3; "Oakland Car Strike Ended," *Los Angeles Times*, October 12, 1919, 10.

44. Seidman, *American Labor from Defense*, 275.

45. "More Rioting in Oakland, 50,000 to Arm," *San Jose Evening News*, October 8, 1919, 1.

46. The carmen's decision to arbitrate meant that a blackout would not be needed.

47. In 1925 the carmen of Division 192 would win both an eight-hour workday and a thirteen-hour spread time restriction. Even in 1925, when these provisions were added, they were fiercely opposed by the company, which argued that such a change would "wipe out the entire net income of the economy," and that the burden of the increase "will be passed on to the public." "Key Carmen Win," *Oakland Tribune*, December 3, 1925, 1.

48. In fact, it would be the longest transit strike in U.S. history until the 1983 strike of Philadelphia's SEPTA workers. See William Robbins, "Last Union Reaches Agreement to End 108-Day Philadelphia Commuter Rail Strike," *New York Times*, July 1, 1983, A6.

49. National City Lines Inc. was a Chicago-based holding company financed by Firestone Tire and Rubber Co., Phillips Petroleum Corp., Standard Oil of California, and General Motors. In 1953, National City Lines operated transit systems in fifty-two other cities. Demoro, *Key Route*, 120.

50. Streetcars were eliminated in 1948. Under the ownership of National City Lines, starting in 1945, the management of the Key System slowly began replacing streetcar lines with General Motors diesel buses. Demoro, *Key Route*, 122.

51. "Carmen Gain Victory," *Oakland Tribune*, April 4, 1906, 1.

52. "Agreement between Key System and Division 192" (June 1, 1949), Amalgamated Transit Union Local 192 Records, Box 20, Folder 14, Labor Archives and Research Center, San Francisco State University.

53. Per Taft Hartley, this meant that workers were required to join the union within thirty days of hiring.

54. "Union Rejects Key Offer of 8 Cent Raise," *Oakland Tribune*, June 17, 1947, 1; "Agreement between Key System and Division 192."

55. The 38 cents was for interurban conductors in their first year. It was 30 cents for traction conductors in their first year. See "The Key Route and the Carmen's Union: A Plain Statement of a Controversy Affecting the Vital Public Interest" (Oakland, Calif.: Board of Directors, San Francisco–Oakland Terminal Railways, October 2, 1915), 9–10. For Key System wage rates in 1953, see "Agreement between Key System," 1953. Amalgamated Transit Union Local 192 Records, Box 20, Folder 14, Labor Archives and Research Center, San Francisco State University.

56. Wolman, "Oakland General Strike of 1946"; Self, *American Babylon*; Rhomberg, *No There There*.

57. Wolman, "Oakland General Strike of 1946," 154.

58. Ibid., 147.

59. Ibid., 175.

60. Ibid., 149.

61. Ibid., 174.

62. Ibid., 174.

63. Vern Stambaugh, "Speech to A.F.L. State Federation Convention," August 12, 1953, Amalgamated Transit Union Local 192 Records, Box 16, Folder 1, Labor Archives and Research Center, San Francisco State University.

64. "No Buses in Sight as Key Talks Are Rushed," *Oakland Tribune*, August 30, 1953, 1.

65. The company's last best offer of 14 cents was roundly rejected by the union, which noted that such an increase wouldn't even bring workers' wages up to the regional average. Similarly, the company balked at the union's 20-cent wage demand and refused to submit anything to binding arbitration. Stambaugh, "Speech to A.F.L State Federation Convention."

66. "Compromise Fails to End S.F. Bridge Tie Up," *Los Angeles Times*, September 3, 1953, 12.

67. Ibid.

68. Oakland Mayor Rishell subsequently called the Key System's negotiation committee "a bunch of Charlie Macarthys." See "Key under Fire from Mayor, Citizen's Committee Head," *Oakland Tribune*, September 3, 1953, 3; George Stanley, "Letter to Mayor Rishell," September 2, 1953, Amalgamated Transit Union Local 192 Records, Box 16, Folder 1, Labor Archives and Research Center, San Francisco State University.

69. "Key System Set Length Mark," *Bakersfield Californian*, September 21, 1953, 17.

70. Robert Nisbet, "From Private to Publicly Owned Transit in the Bay Area: Reflections of the Attorney, Lobbyist and General Manager of the Alameda Contra Costa Transit District, 1950's to 1980's," an oral history conducted in 2000 by Laura McCreery, Regional Oral History Office, Bancroft Library, University of California, Berkeley, 2003, 20.

71. Ibid., 28.

72. "East Bay Cities Seek Solution to Key Strike," *Oakland Tribune*, August 15, 1953, 2.

73. Nisbet, "From Private to Publicly Owned," 30.

74. "Bay Area's Carmen OK Strike End," *Long Beach Independent*, October 7, 1953, 15.

75. Apart from one minor act of malicious mischief against the house of an alleged strikebreaker, over much of the seventy-nine-day strike there was little to no violence to report. See Sergeant Lewis, "Letter to Lieutenant Bernstein," September 24, 1953, Amalgamated Transit Union Local 192 Records, Box 14, Folder 13, Labor Archives and Research Center, San Francisco State University.

76. "New Key Peace Recesses in Deadlock," *Oakland Tribune*, August 28, 1953, 1.

77. H. B. Markley, "Letter to the membership," July 23, 1953, Amalgamated Transit Union Local 192 Records, Box 16, Folder 1, Labor Archives and Research Center, San Francisco State University.

78. "1953 strike received donations," October 9, 1953, Amalgamated Transit Union Local 192 Records, Box 16, Folder 1, Labor Archives and Research Center, San Francisco State University.

79. In 1949, National City Lines had been convicted in an antitrust lawsuit alleging that it had conspired with General Motors, Firestone, and Standard Oil to monopolize trade and commerce. Demoro, *Key Route*, 128. As of September 9, 1953, the Key System owed the city of Oakland $1,350,000 for track removal. The Key System's unwillingness

to engage in arbitration, for many observers, might have seemed parallel to its unwillingness to follow through on its agreement with the city of Oakland to remove its streetcar tracks from city streets, having abandoned the operation in 1948. "Daily Knave," *Oakland Tribune*, September 9, 1953, 25.

80. Sam Gorham, "Fares Too High," editorial, *Oakland Tribune*, August 3, 1953.

81. Demoro, *Key Route*; Wolman, "Oakland General Strike of 1946," 174.

82. It was the first public agency in California to include a provision ensuring collective bargaining. This was a major and substantive win for the members of the ATU 192. At the federal level such protections would not take effect until 1964 with the passage of the Urban Mass Transportation Act's section 13(c). See Nisbet, "From Private to Publicly Owned," 20.

83. "AC Transit History 1960–1970," April 1970, Amalgamated Transit Union Local 192 Records, Box 17, Folder 38, Labor Archives and Research Center, San Francisco State University.

84. "How to Negotiate a Contract!" 1977, Amalgamated Transit Union Local 192 Records, Box 16, Folder 8, Labor Archives and Research Center, San Francisco State University.

85. Mike Libbey, "AC Transit Strikers the Big Money Loser," *Oakland Tribune*, February 8, 1978, 1; see also clippings in Amalgamated Transit Union Local 192 Records, Box 18, Folder 16, Labor Archives and Research Center, San Francisco State University.

86. Ibid.

87. Winner/Wagner & Associates, "Report Submitted to Hon. Frank Vicencia on Impact of 1977 Strike," March 13, 1978, Amalgamated Transit Union Local 192 Records, Box 23, Folder 2, Labor Archives and Research Center, San Francisco State University.

88. The strike of 1977 was not the first instance in which a labor strike had actually improved AC Transit's financial position. In fact, in a notable sixty-two-day-long strike over driver wages in 1974, much the same thing happened, and AC Transit's financial picture improved markedly. In the midst of the strike, Lance Williams of the *Hayward Daily Review* wrote: "Each week the AC Transit strike continues the transit district's projected budget deficit of $4.5 million is reduced by $125,000. Thus, the 50 day strike has actually improved, on paper, the district's financial prospects by reducing the operating deficit by more than $2 million. According to a district spokesman, if AC Transit buses had been carrying passengers since the strike began July 1st the district would have lost $325,000 per week. This is because the district's sources of income—$10.5 million annually in property taxes and $4.8 million in gasoline taxes—are almost $4.5 million less than the estimated operating expenses for the year. Because the district has provided no service during the strike, these operating losses have not occurred. The district continues to receive income from the gasoline sales tax and other minor sources and when the district board sets the property tax rate later this month the district will also receive funds from that source for the period during which no service is provided." See Lance William, "Strike Trims AC Transit Deficit," *Hayward Daily Review*, August 20, 1974, 17.

89. Winner/Wagner and Associates, "Report Submitted," 1978.

90. Libbey, "AC Transit Strikers," *Oakland Tribune*.

91. Ibid.

92. Winner/Wagner and Associates, "Report Submitted."

93. John Wesley, "Internal Memo: To the membership of the Local 192," 1978, Amalgamated Transit Union Local 192 Records, Box 5, Folder 4, Labor Archives and Research Center, San Francisco State University.

94. Coxson, "Impact of Proposition 13."

95. David Lyons, interview by the author, December 1, 2010.

96. "Agreement between Alameda Contra Costa Transit District and Division 192," August 27, 1974, Amalgamated Transit Union Local 192 Records, Box 20, Folder 15, Labor Archives and Research Center, San Francisco State University.

97. Ibid.

98. See Kafui Attoh, "Dead Labor on a Dead Planet: The Inconvenient Truth of Worker's Bladders," June 11, 2014, *Monthly Review Zine*, http://mrzine.monthlyreview .org/2014/attoh061114.html.

99. Anthony Rodgers, interview by the author, November 19, 2010.

100. Titus Warren, "Testimony before AC Transit Board" (Oakland, Calif., AC Transit Board Meeting, June 26, 2013), http://www.actransit.org/about-us/board -of-directors/live-and-archived-audio-for-board-of-directors-and-standing -committee-meetings/.

101. Elana Kessler and Michelle Gonzales, "Bus Operators and the Right to Access Restrooms" (Oakland, Calif., Occupational Health Internship Program, Summer 2014).

102. Ibid., 11.

103. United States Department of Labor, *Brief History of the Labor Movement*, 16–17.

104. In 1953 over seventeen million workers belonged to a union—32.3 percent of all waged and salaried U.S. workers. See Gerald Mayer, *Union Membership Trends*, 23.

105. Just as in 1978, state legislators across the country drew increasing attention in 2010 to what they saw as the excessive rights of public sector workers, the exploding of pension and healthcare costs, and growing deficits in state budgets. In states such as Wisconsin these debates would become quite dramatic.

106. One example, at the operations level, that clearly shows the degree to which antagonisms can develop between AC Transit operators and riders is the issue of recovery time. In much of the transit industry, drivers are not entitled to a full thirty-minute lunch break. Instead schedules are cut for drivers so as to provide them five to ten minutes after every run in which to eat and rest. While this time is at least nominally sufficient, it is predicated on being on time. The simple time costs of picking up one or two disabled riders can thus eliminate whatever break a driver is entitled to. While disabled riders have a right to transit, secured by the Americans with Disabilities Act, it can come at the expense of a driver's right to a break. At the financial level economists like Kenneth Chomitz and Charles Lave have long noted the costs of restrictive and union-friendly provisions on spread time and part-time labor. These provisions have costs, and they are costs, Chomitz and Lave argue, that are born by riders in higher fares and inefficient service. See Chomitz and Lave, "Forecasting the Financial Effects."

107. The extra board refers to a list of workers who are on call but who are not given regular assignments.

108. Anthony Rodgers, interview by the author, November 19, 2010.

109. After years of resistance, part-time workers began working at AC transit in 1980. After initially fighting for as few benefits for part-time workers as possible—hoping no one would apply—by 2010, the ATU 192 had won benefits for part-time workers equiv-

alent to full-time workers. Ironically it meant eliminating the costs savings associated with part-time workers. David Lyons, interview by the author, December 1, 2010.

110. "Rumblings of Revolt," *Weekly People*, December 14, 1946, 1.

111. Claudia Hudson, interview by the author, December 8, 2010.

112. Ibid.

113. David Lyons, interview by the author, December 1, 2010.

114. The unintended consequence of Proposition 13 has been wage stagnation and an increasing reliance of paying workers through credit—namely pension contributions. Of course, when the stock market falters, then such pension investments became increasingly seen as underfunded entitlements.

115. Ibid.

116. Rona Marech, "Of Race and Place: Parchester Village/Richmond's Global Village/Neighborhood Finally Nearing Multiracial Goal," *San Francisco Chronicle*, May 3, 2002, 2.

117. Hudson, interview by the author.

118. Wolman, "Oakland General Strike of 1946," 174.

Chapter 4. Alternatives to Transit

1. Kristan Lawson, "The B-Line: Berkeley's Municipal Transit System, Proposed Route Map," Berkeley, October 25, 2010, https://berkeleytransit.wordpress.com/route-map/; Kristan Lawson, "AC Transit's Service Cuts Leading to Ridership Decline and Downward Spiral," December 24, 2010, https://berkeleytransit.wordpress.com/.

2. Michael Cabantuan, "AC Transit May Whack Service Yet Again," *San Francisco Chronicle*, September 23, 2010, C2.

3. Nina Brown, "Alternative Bus Line to Be Discussed October 25 in Community Forum," *Daily Californian* (blog), October 25, 2010, http://blog.dailycal.org/news/2010/10/24/alternative-bus-line-to-be-discussed-oct-25-in-community-forum/ (unavailable).

4. Kristan Lawson, interview by the author, December 7, 2010.

5. Brown, "Alternatives Bus Line."

6. Lawson, interview by the author.

7. Ibid.

8. Ibid.

9. Ibid.

10. Henderson, *Street Fight* 9.

11. "AC Transit Could Mean 'Air Cushion,'" *Oakland Tribune*, March 15, 1969, 4E.

12. "Tube Trains Proposed on Peninsula," *San Mateo Times*, March 2, 1967, 29.

13. Of course, the most famous example of such experimentation is the Bay Area Transit District itself. In 1962, voters in three Bay Area counties voted to issue a $792 million bond to build the Bay Area Rapid Transit District. As Bill Stokes, BART's first general manager, wrote in 1973, BART was more than a transit system—it was "the partial embodiment of a new way of urban living." Coinciding with Lyndon Johnson's Great Society programs, BART came to capture a similar sense of optimism. BART was not without its critics, and economists such as John Meyer, John Kain, and Martin Wohl would dedicate much of their 1975 classic *The Urban Transportation Problem* to warning state and local officials from further large-scale investments in transit. See Stokes, "Bay Area Rapid Transit"; Meyer, Kain, and Wohl, *Urban Transportation Problem*.

14. Nathan Landau, *Designing with Transit: Making Transit Integral to East Bay Communities* (Oakland, Calif.: AC Transit, 2004), http://www.actransit.org/wp-content/uploads/designing-with-transit.pdf.

15. Ibid., 1–3.

16. *Designing with Transit* begins with an important observation—that for much of the twentieth century, transit was not only a central component of urban life in the East Bay, but that the region, in fact, grew up and developed around transit. Whether people were using Key System streetcars or whether they were using ferries operated by the Southern Pacific, the East Bay's urban landscape—up to the 1950s—was a landscape shaped and designed around the needs of the transit rider and the walking commuter. In many ways, the question at the heart of *Designing with Transit* is thus: how might the East Bay get back to that? See Landau, *Designing with Transit*, iv.

17. Ibid., 3-8.

18. *Designing with Transit*'s definition of "transit-based communities" and the definition of what I call "Transit Oriented Developments" are interchangeable.

19. Ibid., 3-16.

20. Ibid., 4-2.

21. Ibid., 4-17.

22. Laplante and McCann, "Complete Streets."

23. "What Are Complete Streets?" *National Complete Streets Coalition*, https://smartgrowthamerica.org/program/national-complete-streets-coalition/what-are-complete-streets/.

24. Laplante and McCann, "Complete Streets," 26.

25. City of Berkeley, Office of Transportation, *Berkeley Pedestrian Master Plan*, final draft, prepared by Alta Planning + Design, January 2010, http://cityofberkeley.info/uploadedFiles/Public_Works/Level_3_-_Transportation/Optimized%20Final%20Document%20January%202010.pdf.

26. Between 1989 and 2004 average speeds at AC transit fell by 15 percent. Inefficient transit and service delays not only represent a waste of resources but also "annoy passengers and discourage them from riding buses." As *Designing with Transit* noted, each hour of bus operation at AC Transit costs $82; the ability to pick up more passengers per hour and offer quicker service not only benefits customers but also benefits the agency's bottom line—allowing the agency to expand service elsewhere. See Landau, *Designing with Transit*, 5-7.

27. Some of these policies have included ensuring that transit streets have the appropriate characteristics for bus operations, assuring that road width is adequate but not excessive; making sure that bus stops are located to balance speed and convenience concerns (one thousand feet apart recommended); providing curbside bus stops; installing bus hubs where necessary; and painting the curb at bus stops red. See Landua, *Designing with Transit*, 5-7.

28. National Bus Rapid Transit Institute, *Bus Rapid Transit*.

29. Ibid.

30. "Adopt Resolution 10–033 Selecting the East Bay Bus Rapid Transit Locally Preferred Alternative for Study in the Final Environmental Impact Statement/Final Environmental Impact Report" (GM Memo 10-144, Oakland, Calif., June 9, 2010).

31. "AC Transit Berkeley/Oakland/San Leandro MIS: Summary Report," prepared for AC Transit by Cambridge Systematics with Parsons Transportation Group, Nelson\ Nygaard Consulting Associates, Hausrath Economics Group, Montoya Communications, and Carney Hammond Filmore, September 9, 2002), 39, http://www.actransit .org/wp-content/uploads/BRT_Summary.pdf.

32. Rachel Gordon, "Hearings Set for East Bay Transit Plan," *San Francisco Chronicle*, May 6, 2007, final ed.; "Adopt Resolution 10–033," 2010.

33. In 2010, the Berkeley City Council voted against the inclusion of dedicated bus lanes along Telegraph Avenue. In 2012, city council members in San Leandro and Oakland also voted to limit the use of dedicated bus lanes. While the original proposal had called for 18 miles of dedicated bus-only lanes, by 2013, the most BRT advocates could expect was 9.5 miles. See Phil Matier and Andy Ross, "East Bay Express Bus Line Plan Hitting Some Bumps in the Road," *San Francisco Chronicle*, April 1, 2013, C1.

34. "Adopt Resolution 10–033"; Matier and Ross, "East Bay Express Bus Line."

35. At the national level, support for initiatives like TOD, Complete Streets, and BRT has only grown—taken up by such groups as Smart Growth America, PolicyLink, the National Complete Streets Coalition, and the National BRT Institute. Support for such initiatives has even come from the federal government. In 2009, the United States Department of Housing and Urban Development (HUD), the Department of Transportation (DOT), and the Environmental Protection Agency (EPA) launched a joint initiative under the name Partnership for Sustainable Communities. Its goal: "to help communities improve access to affordable housing and transportation while protecting the environment." Between 2009 and 2012, the partnership granted over $3.5 billion to regional and local initiatives that aimed to "develop safe, efficient and reliable transportation," "expand housing choices that increase mobility," "encourage transit oriented mixed use development," and invest in safe, healthy, and walkable neighborhoods. These projects have included TODs such as Denver's La Alma/Lincoln Park Development and the Twin Cities' Central Corridor Light Rail project and BRT projects like Cleveland's Euclid Line. Although the Partnership for Sustainable Communities was defunded in 2012—largely through Republican prompting—there is little indication that the movement for sustainable communities will wane. As one sustainability advocate noted following the defunding of the partnership, the "smart growth ethic" has already permeated the work of many "of the agencies involved" and will remain an important part of the projects they choose to fund. Whether we look to documents like East Bay's *Designing with Transit* or to federal initiatives like the Partnership for Sustainable Communities, there is a real sense that TOD, BRT, and Complete Streets are not only here to stay, but that they have escaped the fate of so many other more ephemeral buzzwords. See "Partnership for Sustainable Communities: Three Years of Helping Communities Achieve Their Visions for Growth and Prosperity" (Washington, D.C.: U.S. Environmental Protection Agency), 12; Tanya Snyder, "Why Congress Can't Kill the Partnership for Sustainable Communities," *DCStreetsBlog*, July 19, 2012, http:// dc.streetsblog.org/2012/07/19/why-congress-cant-kill-the-partnership-for-sustainable -communities/.

36. Laplante and McCann, "Complete Streets," 26.

37. Laplante and McCann note that survival rates in automobile collisions correlate strongly with automobile speed. They cite a study showing that a pedestrian hit by a

car traveling 20 mph has an 85 percent survivability rate. The likelihood of survivability drops to 15 percent in the same collision with a car traveling at 40 mph. See Laplante and McCann, "Complete Streets," 26.

38. Ibid.

39. Senior planner, interview by the author, October 13, 2010.

40. "MacArthur Bike Lanes Approved," *San Francisco Chronicle*, December 14, 2000, A32.

41. Senior planner, interview by the author, October 13, 2010.

42. Meyer, Kain, and Wohl, *Urban Transportation Problem*, 102.

43. Denis Cuff and Doug Oakley, "Berkeley Opposes Bus Only Lanes for Transit Project," *Contra Costa Times*, May 7, 2010.

44. Instead of dedicated lanes, Roy and others argued for employing "curbside BRT" and the use of queue-jumping lanes. Curbside BRT restricts the use of right lanes to buses and right-turning cars only. See Joyce Roy, "AC Transit Ignores Concerns of Public," My Town, *Oakland Tribune*, March 1, 2012. See also Joyce Roy, "Residents Must Prevent Low Income Neighborhoods from Being Run Over," editorial, *Oakland Tribune*, July 16, 2012. Despite offering some time savings for transit vehicles, a study like *Designing with Transit* and much of the literature on Complete Streets actually condemn this very practice for safety reasons. Of course, for BRT boosters like AC Transit's lead planner Jim Cunradi, without dedicated lanes BRT cannot do what it is intended to do. The logic of BRT is straightforward: "the more bus only lanes along the route the faster the buses will be able to travel." See Dennis Cuff and Doug Oakley, "Berkeley Opposes Bus Only Lanes for Transit Project," *Contra Costa Times*, May 7, 2010. For BRT to be effective, and to reach the speeds that make it an attractive option, dedicated lanes and passenger loading platforms are necessary, and they also insulate buses from slow traffic. As East Bay transit activist Steve Geller has argued: "The reason for spending all the money and effort on the Bus Rapid Transit project is to make buses faster to attract the people. . . . If free fares or hybrid buses would do the job, fine, but we keep hearing that people won't ride the buses because they are too slow." See Steve Geller, "Environmental Hypocrites," *San Francisco Chronicle*, July 12, 2008, B4.

45. Ibid.

46. See Landau, *Designing with Transit*, 5-22; AC Transit, "AC Transit East Bay Bus Rapid Transit Project in Alameda County: Environmental Impact Report," January 2012, 2–4. Report available at http://www.actransit.org/wp-content/uploads/Volume_I_Part_02_-_Summary.pdf.

47. Chris Mullen, interview by the author, November 10, 2010.

48. Senior planner, interview by the author, October 10, 2010.

49. Landau, *Designing with Transit*, 5-12; "City of Oakland Bicycle Master Plan" (Oakland, Calif.: City of Oakland, 2007). To comply with the federal Americans with Disability Act (ADA) and the Architectural Barriers Act, newly constructed sidewalks that serve the general public must be accessible to people with disabilities. Under the ADA, accessible sidewalks are defined as at least 4 feet in width. Oakland and Berkeley have gone beyond this 4-foot minimum. Oakland requires 5 feet of clearance and Berkeley requires 6 feet of clearance—enough for two wheelchairs width to width. Where street furniture encroaches on that clear path, whether it is bench or a bus stop, then even more space is necessary. Eileen Ng, who works for United Seniors of

Oakland and Alameda County, noted the difficulty in explaining to seniors—who love shelters when it's raining—that sometimes merely a need for a shelter is not sufficient. Where the sidewalk may be too narrow or where a shelter might encroach on wheelchairs' clear path, installing a shelter will be impossible. Due to transit ramp technology, agencies like AC Transit also require a boarding area of 8 feet wide by 5 feet long; this can also make installing a shelter impossible. See Landau, *Designing with Transit*; senior planner, interview by the author, October 13, 2013; Eileen Ng, interview by the author, October 20, 2012.

50. Senior planner, interview by the author, October 10, 2010.

51. Joyce Roy, "AC Transit Ignores Concerns of Public," My Town, *Oakland Tribune*, March 1, 2012.

52. Reconnecting America is the managing partner of the Center for Transit-Oriented Development. According to its website, Reconnecting America and the Center for Transit-Oriented Development are "the only national non-profits funded by Congress to promote best practices in transit-oriented development." See Reconnecting America, "What We Do," http://www.reconnectingamerica.org/what-we-do/. For the quotation, see "Encouraging Transit Oriented Development: Case Studies That Work" (Washington, D.C.: Reconnecting America, 2009), 1, https://www.epa.gov/sites/production/files/2014-05/documents/phoenix-sgia-case-studies.pdf.

53. Ibid., 6.

54. Pollack, Bluestone, and Billingham, *Maintaining Diversity*; "Encouraging Transit Oriented Development"; Chapple, *Mapping Susceptibility to Gentrification*.

55. Snyder, "Why Congress Can't Kill."

56. Pollack, Bluestone, and Billingham, *Maintaining Diversity*, 4.

57. In her classic work, *The Death and Life of Great American Cities*, Jane Jacobs contrasted the policies of automobile attrition with the more common reality of what she called urban "erosion"—the process by which automobiles demand ever more space and accommodation. Attrition, on the other hand, encompassed policies that "would steadily decrease the number of persons using private automobiles in a city"—decreasing both "the need for cars" and "decreasing [their] convenience." Such policies, Jacobs argued, were probably "the only realistic means by which better public transportation can be stimulated." See Jacobs, *Death and Life*, 364.

58. Henderson, *Street Fight*, 4.

59. Ibid., 20.

60. Ibid., 24.

61. Ibid., 197.

62. Ibid.

63. Ibid., 201.

64. Ibid., 200.

65. Ibid.

66. Ibid., 199.

67. Ibid., 197.

68. Ibid., 201.

69. Lawson, interview by the author.

Conclusion. From Civil Rights to a Right to the City

1. Michael Cabanatuan, "AC Bus Cut Hits Sunday—More in December," *San Francisco Chronicle*, October 30, 2010, C1. See also "General Managers Memo to the Board: Consider the Adoption of Resolution 10–045 Approving the December 2010 Service Reduction Plan, Pending Receipt of a Final Title VI Disparate Impacts Study" (GM-memo 09-217j, Oakland, Calif., September 22, 2010).

2. See Mike Rosenberg, "Running on Empty—Bay Area Transit in Trouble," *San Jose Mercury*, January 10, 2010, 1A; "Transportation Development Act Guidelines" (Placer County Transportation Planning Agency Report, Placer County, Calif., August 2011).

3. See Robert Gammon, "The Buses from Hell," *East Bay Express*, January 23, 2008, http://www.eastbayexpress.com/oakland/the-buses-from-hell/Content?oid=1088265.

4. AC Transit board member, interview by the author, November 12, 2010.

5. In 2008 and 2009, 53 percent of AC Transit's ridership was defined as "very low income"—or as earning below 50 percent of the Oakland Freemont HUD median income ($86,100 per year). See "2008/2009 On Board Rider Survey: Prepared for Alameda-Contra Costa Transit Division of Long Range Planning by the Public Research Institute, San Francisco State University" (Public Research Institute, San Francisco, October 2010), 12.

6. Steve Gerstle, interview by the author, October 13, 2010.

7. See Bullard, "Addressing Urban Transportation Equity," 1; Sanchez and Brenman, "Transportation and Civil Rights"; Golub, Marcantonio, and Sanchez, "Race, Space, and Struggles," 700.

8. Waldron, *Liberal Rights*, 24; Berlin, *Four Essays on Liberty*.

9. France, *Red Lily*, 95.

10. Lefebvre, *Writings on Cities*, 178. For a richer discussion of Lefebvre's life, see Merrifield's *Henri Lefebvre*.

11. Tony McNeill, "Les Trente Glorieuses: 1945–1975," *Comminqué*, 1998, http://eserve.org.uk/tmc/contem/trente1.htm.

12. Harvey, "Right to the City."

13. Ibid.; also see Harvey's early work on the entrepreneurial city: "From Managerialism to Entrepreneurialism."

14. Mitchell, *Right to the City*.

15. Whitt, *Urban Elites and Mass Transportation*.

16. Joe Fitzgerald Rodriguez, "The San Francisco Rent Explosion: Median Rent for Two Bedroom Apartment Tops $4K," *San Francisco Bay Guardian Online*, August 13, 2014, https://48hills.org/sfbgarchive/2014/08/13/san-francisco-rent-explosion-median-rent-two-bedroom-apartment-tops-4k.

17. Jim Edwards, "Map Shows Evictions in San Francisco Are Often Near 'Google Bus' Stops," *Business Insider Blog*, April 10, 2014, http://www.businessinsider.com/san-francisco-google-bus-stop-evictions-2014-4.

18. Alexei Oreskovic, "Protestors Block Apple, Google Buses in San Francisco Area," Reuters, December 20, 2013, http://www.reuters.com/article/us-techbus-protest-sanfrancisco-idUSBRE9BJ1BC20131221.

19. Ibid.

20. Rebecca Solnit, "Diary," *London Review of Books* 35, no. 3 (2014): 34–35, http://www.lrb.co.uk/v35/n03/rebecca-solnit/diary.

21. Lindsey Imai, interview by the author, October 19, 2010.

22. See Bullard, "Addressing Urban Transportation Equity." Also, for discussion of "service minimums," see Golub and Martens, "Using Principles of Justice."

BIBLIOGRAPHY

Interviews and Focus Groups

Steve Geller. Interview. October 5, 2010.

Fran Hastlestiener. Interview. October 10, 2010.

Joyce Roy. Interview. October 11, 2010.

Steven Gerstle. Interview. October 13 2010.

Senior Planner at AC Transit. Interview. October 13, 2010.

Lindsay Imai. Interview. October 19 2010.

Eileen Ng. Interview. October 20, 2010.

East Bay Center for the Blind. Focus Group. November 9, 2010.

Chris Mullen. Interview. November 10, 2010.

AC Transit board member. Interview. November 12, 2010.

Anthony Rodgers. Interview. November 19, 2010.

John Katz. Interview. November 29. 2010.

David Lyons. Interview. December 1, 2010.

Kristan Lawson. Interview. December 7, 2010.

Claudia Hudson. Interview. December 8, 2010.

Tony Withington. Interview. December 8 2010.

Published Print Sources and Dissertations

Adler, Seymour. "The Political Economy of Transit in the San Francisco Bay Area, 1945–1963." PhD diss., University of California, Berkeley, 1980.

Attoh, Kafui. "Public Transportation and the Idiocy of Urban Life." *Urban Studies* 54, no. 1 (2017): 196–213.

Attoh, Kafui. "Rights in Transit: Public Transportation and the Right to the City in California's East Bay." PhD diss., Syracuse University, Syracuse, 2013.

Attoh, Kafui. "What *Kind* of Right Is the Right to the City?" *Progress in Human Geography* 35, no. 5 (2011): 669–85.

Bentham, Jeremy. "Anarchical Fallacies." In *Nonsense on Stilts*, edited by Jeremy Waldron. New York: Routledge, 2015.

Berlin, Isaiah. *Four Essays on Liberty*. Oxford, UK: Oxford University Press, 1969.

Blomley, Nick. "Mobility, Empowerment, and the Rights Revolution." *Political Geography* 13 (1994): 407–22.

Bullard, Robert. "Addressing Urban Transportation Equity in the United States." *Fordham Urban Law Journal* 31, no. 5 (2003): 1183–209.

Bullard, Robert. "The Anatomy of Transportation Racism." In Bullard, Johnson, and Torres, *Highway Robbery*, 15–33.

Bullard, Robert, Glenn Johnson, and Angel Torres, eds. *Highway Robbery: Transportation Racism and New Routes to Equity*. Cambridge, Mass.: South End Press, 2004.

Burgess, Ernest, and Robert Park. *The City: Suggestions for Investigation of Human Behavior in the Urban Environment*. Chicago: University of Chicago Press, 1984.

Burke, Edmund. *Reflections on the Revolution in France*. London: J. M. Dent and Sons, 1955.

Castells, Manuel. *The Urban Question: A Marxist Approach*. Cambridge, Mass.: MIT Press, 1979.

Chapple, Karen. "Mapping Susceptibility to Gentrification: The Early Warning Toolkit." Berkeley: Center for Community Innovation, Institute of Urban and Regional Development, University of California, Berkeley, 2009.

Chaskin, Robert, and Mark Joseph. "Positive Gentrification, Social Control and the 'Right to the City' in Mixed Income Communities: Uses and Expectations of Space and Place." *International Journal of Urban and Regional Research* 37, no. 2 (2003): 480–502.

Chomitz, Kenneth, and Charles Lave. "Forecasting the Financial Effects of Work Rule Changes." *Transportation Quarterly* 37, no. 3 (1983): 453–73.

Cohen, Stuart, and Amber Elizabeth Crabbe. *Cutting Transit Eliminating the Economy: Quantifying the Economic and Social Effects of Governor Schwarzenegger's Transit Cuts on the Bay Area*. Oakland, Calif.: Transportation and Land Use Coalition, 2004.

Cohen, Stuart, and Jeff Hobson. "Transportation Choices in the San Francisco Bay Area." In Bullard, Johnson, and Torres, *Highway Robbery*, 99–121.

Coxson, Harold. "Impact of Proposition 13 on Labor Relations in the Public Sector: A Private Sector View." *State and Local Government Review* 11, no. 3 (1979): 89–92.

Davis, Mike. "Planet of Slums." *New Left Review* 26 (2004): 5–34.

Demoro, Harre. *The Key Route: Transbay Commuting by Train and Ferry*. Vol. 1. Glendale, Calif.: Interurban Press, 1985.

Draper, Hal. *The Adventures of the Communist Manifesto*. Alameda, Calif.: Center for Socialist History, 2004.

Dworkin, Ronald. *Taking Rights Seriously*. Cambridge, Mass.: Harvard University Press, 1977.

Engels, Friedrich. *The Condition of the Working Class in England*. London: George Allen and Unwin, 1936.

Fainstein, Susan. *The Just City*. Ithaca, N.Y.: Cornell University Press, 2010.

Fernandes, Edesio. "Constructing the 'Right to the City' in Brazil." *Social & Legal Studies* 16, no. 2 (2007): 201–19.

Fischer, Robert, Yuseph Katiya, Christopher Reid, and Eric Shragge. "'We Are Radical': The Right to the City Alliance and the Future of Community Organizing. *Journal of Sociology & Social Welfare* 40, no. 1 (2013): 157–82.

France, Anatole. *The Red Lily*. Charleston, S.C.: Bibliolife, 2008.

Freeman, Joshua B. *In Transit: The Transport Workers Union in New York City, 1933–1966*. New York: Oxford University Press, 1989.

Fried, Charles. *Right and Wrong*. Cambridge, Mass.: Harvard University Press, 1978.

Frieden, Lex. "Independent Living: The Movement and Its Programs." *American Rehabilitation* 3, no. 6 (1978): 6–9.

Glendon, Mary. *Rights Talk: The Impoverishment of Political Discourse.* New York: Free Press, 1993.

Golub, Aaron, Richard Marcantonio, and Thomas Sanchez. "Race, Space, and Struggles for Mobility: Transportation Impacts on African Americans in Oakland and the East Bay." *Urban Geography* 34, no. 5 (2013): 699–728.

Golub, Aaron, and Karel Martens. "Using Principles of Justice to Assess the Modal Equity of Regional Transportation Policies." *Journal of Transport Geography* 41 (2014): 10–20.

Gough, Jamie. "A Brief History of the Right to the City." *Capital and Class* 38, no. 2 (2014): 417–21.

Greenberg, Miriam, and Penny Lewis, eds. *The City Is the Factory: New Solidarities and Spatial Strategies in an Urban Age.* Ithaca, N.Y.: Cornell University Press, 2017.

Harvey, David. "From Managerialism to Entrepreneurialism: The Transformation in Urban Governance in Late Capitalism." *Geografiska Annaler Series B, Human Geography* 71, no. 1 (1989): 3–17.

Harvey, David. *Rebel Cities: From the Right to the City to the Urban Revolution.* New York: Verso, 2012.

Harvey, David. "The Right to the City." *New Left Review* 53 (2008): 23–40.

Henderson, Jason. *Street Fight: The Struggle over Urban Mobility in San Francisco.* Amherst: University of Massachusetts Press, 2013.

Hirsh, A. *The French Left: A History and Overview.* Montreal: Black Rose Books, 1982.

Hodge, David. "Fiscal Equity in Urban Mass Transit Systems: A Geographic Analysis." *Annals of the American Association of Geographers* 78, no. 2 (1988): 288–306.

Issel, William. "Land Values, Human Values, and the Preservation of the City's Treasured Appearance: Environmentalism, Politics and the San Francisco Freeway Revolt." *Pacific Historical Review* 68, no. 4 (1999): 611–46.

Jacobs, Jane. *The Death and Life of the Great American City.* New York: Vintage Press, 1961.

Johnson, Mary, and Barrett Shaw, eds. *To Ride the Public's Buses: The Fight That Built a Movement.* Louisville, Ky.: Avocado Press, 2001.

Jones, Peter. *Rights.* New York: St. Martin's Press, 1994.

Kain, John, and John Meyer. "Transportation and Poverty." *Public Interest* 18 (1970): 75–87.

Karner, Alex, and Deb Niemeier. "Civil Rights Guidance and Equity Analysis Methods for Regional Transportation Plans: A Critical Review of Literature and Practice." *Journal of Transport Geography* 33 (2013): 126–34.

Kelley, Blair. *Right to Ride: Streetcar Boycotts and African American Citizenship in the Era of* Plessy v. Ferguson. Chapel Hill: University of North Carolina Press, 2010.

Laplante, John, and Barbara McCann. "Complete Streets: We Can Get There from Here." *Institute of Transportation Engineers* 78, no. 5 (2008): 24–28.

Lefebvre, Henri. *Writings on Cities.* Edited and translated by Eleonore Kofman and Elizabeth Lebas. Oxford, UK: Blackwell, 1996.

LeRoy, Greg. *Organizing Transit Riders: A How-to Manual.* Washington, D.C.: Good Jobs First, 2011.

Lewis, Tom. *Divided Highways: Building the Interstate Highways, Transforming American Life*. Harmondsworth, UK: Penguin Books, 1997.

Litman, Todd. *Evaluating Transportation Equity: Guidance for Incorporating Distributional Impacts in Transportation Planning*. Victoria, B.C.: Victoria Transport Policy Institute, 2016.

Litman, Todd, and Marc Brenman. *A New Social Equity Agenda for Sustainable Transportation*. Victoria, B.C.: Victoria Transport Policy Institute, 2012.

Lutz, Catherine, and Anna Fernandez. *Carjacked: The Culture of the Automobile and Its Effects on Our Lives*. New York: St. Martin's Press, 2010.

Mann, Eric. "Los Angeles Bus Riders Union." In Bullard, Johnson, and Torres, *Highway Robbery*, 33–49.

Mann, Eric. *A New Vision for Urban Transportation*. Los Angeles: Strategy Center, 1996.

Mann, Eric, Ramsey Kikanza, Barbara Lott-Holland, and Geoff Ray. "An Environmental Justice Strategy for Urban Transportation." *Race, Poverty and the Environment* 12, no. 1 (2006): 6–9.

Marcantonio, Richard, and Angelica Jongco. "From the Back of the Bus to the End of the Line: The Discriminatory Funding of Public Transit in California." *Human Rights* 34, no. 3 (2007): 10.

Marcuse, Peter. "From Critical Urban Theory to the Right to the City." *City* 13, no. 2–3 (2009): 185–97.

Marx, Karl. *Capital: A Critique of Political Economy*, Vol. 1. New York: International, 1967.

Marx, Karl. *On the Jewish Question*. New York: McGraw Hill, 1964.

Marx, Karl, and Friedrich Engels. *The Communist Manifesto*. New York: Signet Classics, 1998.

Mayer, Gerald. *Union Membership Trends in the United States*. Washington, D.C.: Congressional Research Service, 2004.

Mayer, Guillermo, and Richard Marcantonio. "Bay Area—Separate and Unequal." *Race, Poverty and the Environment* 12, no. 1 (2005): 20–23.

Mayer, Margit. "The 'Right to the City' in the Context of Shifting Mottos of Urban Social Movements." *City* 13, no. 2–3 (2009): 362–74.

McCann, Eugene. "Urban Citizenship, Public Participation and a Critical Geography of Architecture." In *Rights to the City*, edited by Doris Wastl-Walter, Lynn Staeheli, and Lorraine Dowler. International Geographical Union, Home of Geography Publications Series, vol. 3. Rome: Societa Geographica Italiana, 2005.

Merewitz, Leonard. "Public Transportation: Wish Fulfillment and Reality in the San Francisco Bay Area." *American Economic Review* 62, no. 1/2 (1972): 78–86.

Merrifield, Andy. *Henri Lefebvre: A Critical Introduction*. New York: Routledge, 2006.

Meyer, John, John Kain, and Martin Wohl. *The Urban Transportation Problem*. Cambridge, Mass.: Harvard University Press, 1965.

Mitchell, Don. *The Right to the City: Social Justice and the Fight for Public Space*. New York: Guilford Press, 2003.

Mohl, Raymond. "Stop the Road: Freeway Revolts in American Cities." *Journal of Urban History* 30, no. 5 (2004): 674–706.

National Bus Rapid Transit Institute. *Bus Rapid Transit: Elements, Performance, Benefits.* Washington, D.C.: U.S. Department of Transportation, Federal Transportation Administration, 2013.

Nellis, Kenneth. "California Governmental Tort Liability and the Collateral Source Rule." *Santa Clara Law Review* 9, no. 1 (1969): 227–43.

Nozick, Robert. *Anarchy, State, Utopia.* Oxford, UK: Blackwell, 1974.

Pelka, Fred. *ABC-CLIO Companion to the Disability Rights Movement.* Santa Barbara, Calif.: ABC-CLIO, 1997.

Pollack, Stephanie, Barry Bluestone, and Chase Billingham. *Maintaining Diversity in America's Transit-Rich Neighborhoods: Tools for Equitable Neighborhood Change.* Boston: Dukakis Center for Urban and Regional Policy, Northeastern University, 2010.

Price, Roger. *A Concise History of France.* Cambridge UK: Cambridge University Press, 1993.

Prosser, William. *Handbook of the Law of Torts.* St. Paul, Minn.: West, 1941.

Pucher, John. "Who Benefits from Transit Subsidies? Recent Evidence from Six Metropolitan Areas." *Transportation Research* 17, no. 1 (1983): 39–50.

Purcell, Mark. "Citizenship and the Right to the Global City: Reimagining the Capitalist World Order." *International Journal of Urban and Regional Research* 27, no. 3 (2003): 564–90.

Rawls, John. *A Theory of Justice.* Cambridge, Mass.: Harvard University Press, 1971.

Rhomberg, Chris. *No There There: Race, Class and Political Community in Oakland.* Berkeley: University of California Press, 2004.

Rodriguez, Joseph. "Rapid Transit and Community Power: West Oakland Residents Confront BART." *Antipode* 31, no. 2 (1999): 212–28.

Ross, Kristin. *Fast Cars, Clean Bodies: Decolonization and the Reordering of French Culture.* Cambridge, Mass.: MIT Press, 1995.

Sanchez, Thomas, and Marc Brenman. "Transportation and Civil Rights." *Poverty and Race* 19, no. 4 (2010): 1–20.

Sanchez, Thomas, Marc Brenman, Jacinta Ma, and Rich Stolz. *The Right to Transportation: Moving to Equity.* Chicago: American Planning Association, 2007.

Sanchez, Thomas, Rich Stolz, and Jacinta Ma. *Moving to Equity: Addressing Inequitable Effects of Transportation Policies on Minorities.* Cambridge, Mass.: Civil Rights Project at Harvard University, 2003.

Sandt, Claire. "Schools' Duty to Protect Students." *ABA Juvenile and Child Welfare Law Reporter* 12, no. 10 (1993): 156–59.

Sawers, Larry. "The Political Economy of Urban Transportation: An Interpretive Essay." In *Marxism and the Metropolis: New Perspectives in Urban Political Economy,* edited by William K. Tabb and Larry Sawers, 223–54. Oxford UK: Oxford University Press, 1984.

Scargill, Ian. *Urban France.* New York: St. Martin's Press, 1983.

Schrag, Zachary. *The Great Society Subway: The History of the Washington Metro.* Baltimore: Johns Hopkins University Press, 2006.

Seidman, Joel. *American Labor from Defense to Reconversion.* Chicago: University of Chicago Press, 1953.

Self, Robert. *American Babylon: Race and the Struggle for Postwar Oakland*. Princeton, N.J.: Princeton University Press, 2003.

Shue, Henry. *Basic Rights: Subsistence, Affluence, and U.S. Foreign Policy*. Princeton, N.J.: Princeton University Press, 1989.

Siegel, Kevin. "Discrimination in the Funding of Mass Transit Systems." *West-Northwest* 4 (1997): 107–26.

Sinha, Anita, and Alexa Kasdan. "Inserting Community Perspective Research into Public Housing Policy Discourse: The Right to the City Alliance's 'We Call These Projects Home.'" *Cities* 35 (2013): 327–34.

Smith, David. *Geography and Social Justice*. London: Wiley Blackwell, 1994.

Smith, Neil. Foreword to *The Urban Revolution*, by Henri Lefebvre, vii–xxiii. Minneapolis: University of Minnesota Press, 2003.

Smythe, Dallas. "An Economic History of the Local and Inter-urban Transportation in the East Bay Cities, with Particular Reference to the Properties Developed by F. M. Smith." PhD diss., University of California, Berkeley, 1937.

Stokes, Bill. "Bay Area Rapid Transit: A Transportation Planning Breakthrough." *Public Administration Review* 33, no. 3 (1973): 206–14.

Thomas, Larry, and James McDaniel. "State Limitations on Tort Liability on Public Transit Operations." *Legal Research Digest* 12, no. 3 (1994): 3–14. (Transit Cooperative Research Program report)

Tocqueville, Alex de. *Democracy in America*. New York: Signet Classics, 2001.

Tuppen, John. *The Development of French New Towns: An Assessment of Progress*. *Urban Studies* 20, no. 1 (1983): 11–30.

Tushnet, Mark. "A Critique of Rights: An Essay on Rights," *Texas Law Review* 63 (1984): 1363–404.

United Nations Human Settlement Programme. *The Challenges of Slums: Global Report on Human Settlements*. London: Routledge, 2003.

United States Department of Labor. *A Brief History of the Labor Movement*. Washington, D.C.: GPO, 1970.

Urban Habitat. *MTC, Where Are Our Buses? Challenging the Bay Area's Separate and Unequal Transit System*. San Francisco: Creative Commons, 2006.

Waldron, Jeremy. *Liberal Rights: Collected Papers 1981–1991*. Cambridge, UK: Cambridge University Press, 1993.

Webber, Melvin. "The BART Experience—What Have We Learned?" *Public Interest* 45 (Fall 1976): 79–108.

Whitt, J. Allen. *Urban Elites and Mass Transportation: The Dialectics of Power*. Princeton, N.J.: Princeton University Press, 1982.

Williams, Patricia. *Alchemy of Race and Rights*. Cambridge, Mass.: Harvard University Press, 1991.

Wolman, Phillip. "The Oakland General Strike of 1946." *Southern California Historical Review* 57, no. 2 (1975): 147–79.

INDEX

Page numbers in italics refer to illustrations.

Job Access and Reverse Commute (JARC), 119n46
Johnson, Lyndon, 134n13
Johnson, Mary, 112n29
judicial review. *See* court cases
"just city," 115n67
justice, 11, 122n5. *See also* environmental justice; social justice; transportation justice movement

Kahn's and Hastings department stores, 67–68
Kain, John, 94, 134n13
Kaiser Hospital, 24
Kansas City, Mo., 123n27
Karner, Alex, 36, 40
Katz, John, 44, 49, 53, 118n36, 124n35
Kelley, Willis, 62, 76
Kessler, Elana, 75
Key Route (San Francisco–Oakland–San Jose Railroad), 17, 62–63, 65, 128n22. *See also* Key System
Key System, 17–18, 64, 128n22, 129n43; contract negotiations, 131n68; fare hikes, 69; strike of 1953, 66–71, 76; as tool of real estate speculation, 17, 107; track removal, 131n79. *See also* AC Transit
Klehs, Johan, 118n37

La Alma / Lincoln Park Development (Denver), 136n35
labor solidarity, 66, 70. *See also* ATU Local 192; strikes; transit workers
Landau, Nathan, 87
land-use policies, 87, 89–101
Laplante, John, 91, 93–94, 136n37
Laporte, Elizabeth, 32, 34
Lave, Charles, 133n106
Lawson, Kristan, 82, 84–87, 100–101, 104
lawsuits, 5; antitrust, 131n79; against Key System, 69. *See also* court cases
Lee, Barbara, 32
Lee, Bill Lann, 22, 32
Lefebvre, Henri, 3, 11–14, 19–20, 42, 57–59, 106–8
liability, 23–29, 39
liberal notion of civil rights, 3, 14, 19; as different from right to the city, 14, 109–10
Lindsey, Martha, 84
Litman, Todd, 9–11, 42, 52–53
loitering, 46, 123n27
Lopez, Carmen and Carla, 27

Lopez v. Southern California Rapid Transit District (SCRTD), 23, 27–29
Los Angeles Bus Rapid Transit (BRT), 92
Los Angeles Bus Riders Union (BRU), 31–32, 44, 54–55, 113n32
Los Angeles Metropolitan Transportation Authority (MTA), 31–32, 54, 113n32
low-income riders, 16, 46, 115n77, 139n5; democratic process and, 14–15, 20, 56, 101, 106; political influence of, 102–3; transit dependency, 30 (*see also* transit-dependent riders); transit strikes and, 81; transportation justice and, 59
Lyons, David, 73, 78, 79, 109

Ma, Jacinta, 9
Mahon, President (National Carmen's Union), 62–63
Maintaining Diversity in America's Transit Rich Neighborhoods, 97
majority, tyranny of, 14–15
Mann, Eric, 54
Manolius, Kimon, 35, 121n56
Mapping Susceptibility to Gentrification, 97
Marcantonio, Richard, 36
Marcuse, Peter, 14
marginalized people, democratic process and, 14–15, 20, 56, 101, 106. *See also* low-income riders; minority riders; racial discrimination
Markely, H. B., 70
Martinez, Virginia, 117n26
Marx, Karl, 5–6, 12, 41, 42, 57–58, 106; *Communist Manifesto* (with Engels), 58; critique of rights, 6
Marxism, 12–13
mass transit: development of, 18; highway funds redirected to, 45, 50, 53. *See also* public transportation; *and specific transit systems*
McCann, Barbara, 90–91, 93–94, 136n37
McClain, Jeremy, 24
McMillan, Therese, 119n41, 120n50
Measure B, 49
Merrifield, Andrew, 114n58
Metal Trades Council, 66
Metro-North, 31
metropolitan planning organizations (MPOs), 10, 119n47. *See also* MTC
Mexico City, 14
Meyer, John, 94, 134n13
Miami, 92

CPSIA information can be obtained
at www.ICGtesting.com
Printed in the USA
LVHW041804270219
608947LV00002B/157